The Religion Guarantees

Recent Titles in
Reference Guides to the United States Constitution
Jack Stark, Series Editor

The Right to the Assistance of Counsel
James J. Tomkovicz

Prohibited Government Acts
Jack Stark

State Sovereign Immunity
Melvyn R. Durchslag

Constitutional Remedies
Michael Wells and Thomas A. Eaton

Privileges and Immunities
David Skillen Bogen

Searches, Seizures, and Warrants
Robert M. Bloom

The Supremacy Clause
Christopher R. Drahozal

Procedural Due Process
Rhonda Wasserman

Double Jeopardy
David S. Rudstein

Freedom of the Press
Lyrissa Barnett Lidsky and R. George Wright

The Taxing Power
Erik M. Jensen

Freedom of Speech
Keith Werhan

The Religion Guarantees

A Reference Guide to the United States Constitution

Peter K. Rofes

REFERENCE GUIDES TO THE
UNITED STATES CONSTITUTION, NUMBER 13
Jack Stark, *Series Editor*

PRAEGER

Westport, Connecticut
London

Library of Congress Cataloging-in-Publication Data

Rofes, Peter K., 1956–
The religion guarantees : a reference guide to the United States Constitution / Peter K. Rofes.
p. cm.—(Reference guides to the United States Constitution, ISSN 1539–8986; no. 13)
Includes bibliographical references and index.
ISBN 0–313–31371–7 (alk. paper)
1. Freedom of religion—United States—Popular works. I. Title. II. Series.
KF4783.Z9R64 2005
342.7308'52—dc22 2004022508

British Library Cataloguing in Publication Data is available.

Library of Congress Catalog Card Number: 2004022508
ISBN: 0–313–31371–7
ISSN: 1539–8986

First published in 2005

Praeger Publishers, 88 Post Road West, Westport, CT 06881
An imprint of Greenwood Publishing Group, Inc.
www.praeger.com

Printed in the United States of America

The paper used in this book complies with the Permanent Paper Standard issued by the National Information Standards Organization (Z39.48–1984).

10 9 8 7 6 5 4 3 2

To my father
and his grandson

Contents

Series Foreword

Jack Stark

One can conceive of the United States Constitution in many ways. For example, noting the reverence in which it has been held, one can think of it as equivalent to a sacred text. Unfortunately, most of its devotees have had less knowledge and even less understanding of the document than they have had reverence for it. Sometimes it is treated as primarily a political document and on that basis has been subjected to analysis, such as Charles Beard's *An Economic Interpretation of the Constitution of the United States*. One can plausibly argue that the Constitution seems most astounding when it is seen in the light of the intellectual effort that has been associated with it. Three brief but highly intense bursts of intellectual energy produced, and established as organic law, most of the Constitution as it now exists. Two of these efforts, sustained over a long period of time, have enabled us better to understand that document.

The first burst of energy occurred at the Constitutional Convention. Although some of the delegates' business, such as the struggle between populous and nonpopulous states about their representation in Congress, was political, much of it was about fundamental issues of political theory. A few of the delegates had or later achieved international eminence for their intellects. Among them were Benjamin Franklin, Alexander Hamilton, and James Madison. Others, although less well known, had first-rate minds. That group includes George Mason and George Wythe. Many of the delegates contributed intelligently. Although the Convention's records are less than satisfactory, they indicate clearly enough that the delegates worked mightily to constitute not merely a polity but a rational polity—one that would rise to the standards envisioned by the delegates' intellectual ancestors. Their product, though brief, is amazing. William Gladstone called it "the most wonderful work ever struck off."

Despite the delegates' eminence and the Constitution's excellence as seen from our place in history, its ratification was far from certain. That state of affairs necessitated the second burst of intellectual energy associated with that document: the debate over ratification. Soon after the Convention adjourned, articles and speeches—some supporting the Constitution and some attacking it—began to proliferate. A national debate commenced, not only about the document itself, but also about the nature of the polity that ought to exist in this country. Both sides included many writers and speakers who were verbally adroit and steeped in the relevant political and philosophical literature. The result was an accumulation of material that is remarkable for both its quantity and its quality. At its apex is *The Federalist Papers*, a production of Alexander Hamilton, James Madison, and John Jay that deserves a place among the great books of Western culture.

Another burst, not as impressive as the first two but highly respectable, occurred when the Bill of Rights was proposed. Some delegates to the Constitutional Convention had vigorously asserted that such guarantees should be included in the original document. George Mason, the principal drafter of the Virginia Declaration of Rights, so held, and he walked out of the Convention when he failed to achieve his purpose. Even those who had argued that the rights in question were implicit recognized the value of adding protection of them to the Constitution. The debate was thus focused on the rights that were to be explicitly granted, not on whether any rights *ought* to be explicitly granted. Again many writers and speakers entered the fray, and again the debate was solidly grounded in theory and was conducted on a high intellectual level.

Thus, within a few years a statement of organic law and a vital coda to it had been produced. However, the meaning and effect of many of that document's provisions were far from certain; the debates on ratification of the Constitution and the Bill of Rights had demonstrated that. In addition, the document existed in a vacuum, because statutes and actions had not been assessed by its standards. The attempt to resolve these problems began after Chief Justice John Marshall, in Marbury v. Madison, asserted the right of the U.S. Supreme Court to interpret and apply the Constitution. Judicial interpretation and application of the Constitution, beginning with the first constitutional case and persisting until the most recent, is one of the sustained exertions of intellectual energy associated with the Constitution. The framers would be surprised by some of the results of those activities. References in the document to "due process," which seems to refer only to procedures, have been held also to have a substantive dimension. A right to privacy has been found lurking among the penumbras of various parts of the text. A requirement that states grant the same "privileges and immunities" to citizens of other states that they granted to their own citizens, which seemed to guarantee important rights, was held not to be particularly important. The corpus of judicial interpretations of the Constitution is now as voluminous as that document is terse.

As the judicial interpretations multiplied, another layer—interpretations of interpretations—appeared, and also multiplied. This layer, the other sustained intellectual effort associated with the Constitution, consists of articles, most of them published in law reviews, and books on the Constitution. This material varies in quality and significance. Some of these works of scholarship result from meticulous examination and incisive thought. Others repeat earlier work, or apply a fine-tooth comb to matters that are too minute even for such a comb. Somewhere in that welter of tertiary material is the answer to almost every question that one could ask about constitutional law. The problem is finding the answer that one wants. The difficulty of locating useful guidance is exacerbated by the bifurcation of most constitutional scholarship into two kinds. In "Two Styles of Social Science Research," C. Wright Mills delineates macroscopic and molecular research. The former deals with huge issues, the latter with tiny issues. Virtually all of the scholarship on the Constitution is of one of those two types. Little of it is macroscopic, but that category does include some first-rate syntheses such as Jack Rakove's *Original Meanings.* Most constitutional scholarship is molecular and, again, some fine work is included in that category.

In his essay, Mills bemoans the inability of social scientists to combine the two kinds of research that he describes to create a third category that will be more generally useful. This series of books is an attempt to do for constitutional law the intellectual work that Mills proposed for social science. The author of each book has dealt carefully and at reasonable length with a topic that lies in the middle range of generality. Upon completion, this series will consist of thirty-seven books, each on a constitutional law topic. Some of the books, such as the book on freedom of the press, explicate one portion of the Constitution's text. Others, such as the volume on federalism, treat a topic that has several anchors in the Constitution. The books on constitutional history and constitutional interpretation range over the entire document, but each does so from one perspective. Except for a very few of the books, for which special circumstances dictate minor changes in format, each book includes the same components: a brief history of the topic, a lengthy and sophisticated analysis of the current state of the law on that topic, a bibliographical essay that organizes and evaluates scholarly material in order to facilitate further research, a table of cases, and an index. The books are intellectually rigorous—in fact, authorities have written them—but, due to their clarity and to brief definitions of terms that are unfamiliar to laypersons, each is comprehensible and useful to a wide audience, one that ranges from other experts on the book's subject to intelligent nonlawyers.

In short, this series provides an extremely valuable service to the legal community and to others who are interested in constitutional law, as every citizen should be. Each book is a map of part of the U.S. Constitution. Together they map all of that document's territory that is worth mapping. When this series is complete, each book will be a third kind of scholarly work that combines the macroscopic and the molecular. Together they will explicate all of the important constitutional topics. Anyone who wants assistance in understanding either a topic in constitutional law or the Constitution as a whole can easily find it in these books.

Acknowledgments

The talents, diligence, and commitment of others have contributed in substantial ways to this volume. Jack Stark—who, after a colloquium sponsored by the University of Wisconsin Law Review, invited me to participate in this ambitious series—supplied the intellectual vision that enabled the series to be conceived. Seven terrific students from Marquette University Law School—Douglas Raines, Amireh Zeyghami, Janilyn Knorr, Natalia Sokolova, Hillary Kowalski, Kristofor Hanson, and Kathleen Lindgren—provided skillful, conscientious, and cheerful assistance throughout the project, assistance that ranged from research to drafting to editing to proofing. To observe that their efforts have enhanced the quality of this volume is to engage in serious understatement. Librarians and staff of the Marquette Law Library extended considerable help, both to me and to my research assistants. The folks at Greenwood/Praeger have made the process of transforming the manuscript into a book one of genuine collaboration.

Marquette University Law School has been my professional home for nearly two decades now. Throughout my time at Marquette, I have been blessed to work in a community that has supported my work in all the ways that matter. Three distinctive aspects of that support are of not insubstantial relevance to this volume. One is that my interest in, and curiosity regarding, the constitutional law of religious freedom—strong since childhood—have been nourished by working in a law school community whose members have affirmatively encouraged scholarly pursuits devoted to religious matters. A second, related apsect concerns the fact that this volume directly grows out of my experiences leading a seminar devoted to First Amendment law that I have had the joy to teach to 2Ls and 3Ls since my early years at Marquette. Finally, my former dean, the late Howard Eisenberg, supported the early stages of the project with a summer research stipend, and my current dean, Joseph Kearney, provided much-needed incentive during the concluding stages by appointing me Associate Dean for Academic Affairs and thereby ensuring that the time for procrastination had come and gone.

Peter K. Rofes

1

The Origins of the Religion Guarantees

This volume devotes itself principally to the current status of the Constitution's twin protections for religious freedom. It seeks to convey to readers an understanding of free exercise and anti-establishment principles as these constitutional principles operate today—on contemporary Americans, living in contemporary America, coping with contemporary American problems.

To a considerable extent, of course, this understanding arrives on our doorstep courtesy of those robed characters who serve, and have served, on the nation's highest court. Not surprisingly, therefore, much of this volume will be devoted to examining cases—especially cases decided by the Supreme Court of the United States—and ideas about religious freedom expressed in those cases. This examination will enable us to discern much about the contours of religious liberty at work in America today.

Before turning to that task, however, we pause briefly to examine the historical origins of our constitutional protections for religious freedom. More precisely, we pause briefly to examine how and why it came to pass that the words contemporary American judges squabble over in our own time found their way into our constitutional text, and thus into cases that seek to give meaning to that text.

This historical terrain has been ploughed well and thoroughly by generations of scholars. The expertise these scholars have brought to bear on the history, religion, politics, and culture of the colonial era far surpasses whatever isolated insights the author might have to offer. Nevertheless, we begin with a glimpse backward to remind ourselves that the constitutional principles from which we seek guidance today emerged out of the real and tangible experiences of those who occupied our nation more than two centuries ago.

INTRODUCTION

Colonists brought with them to the New World both an established tradition of religious intolerance and a fervent desire to escape that intolerance. These competing impulses would tug at colonists from well before the initial musings of what would later become the First Amendment's religious freedoms to well after these freedoms had found their place in the Constitution.

The struggle to separate religion from government in colonial America by and large represented an unprecedented effort. The effort engendered intensive debate and, over time, surprising success. Colonial proponents of religious freedom garnered much of their success as a result of the confluence of three distinct phenomena at work in their time: discriminatory treatment doled out to those individuals who did not belong to the particular established religions; taxation to support those established religions; and the link between established religions and English control. The discussion set forth below seeks to capture the climate that prompted the move toward the First Amendment's protections for religious freedom, the debate concerning those protections as it evolved from the First Constitutional Convention through the First Congress, and, finally, the post-enactment response to the Constitution among the colonists.

COLONIAL ROOTS OF RELIGIOUS LIBERTY: DISENTANGLING CROSS AND CROWN

Michael Ariens and Robert Destro—in their fine work, *Religious Liberty in a Pluralistic Society* (1996)—have observed that the particular ingredients in the mix of church and state varied substantially from colony to colony, that the distinctive experience and conditions of each particular colony combined to produce a distinctive set of relationships among government, religion, and inhabitants. For that reason, as Ariens and Destro observe, a geographic tour through the colonies offers a glimpse into each distinctive mix.

New England

Massachusetts

Pilgrims and Puritans—two dissenting groups from the Church of England—founded the Massachusetts colony. Pilgrims disapproved of the resemblance the established Church of England bore to the Roman Catholic Church. They met with persecution in England after their formal separation from the Church of England,[1] prompting them to flee—initially to the Netherlands and then, after King James I of England awarded them a charter in 1620 to settle in what we now know as Virginia,[2] to the colonies. Landing instead at Plymouth Rock—as Ariens and Destro note, well north of their intended destination—the Pilgrims eventually settled in colonial Massachusetts.[3] Despite their status as the first English inhabitants of the colony, the Pilgrims exerted only modest influence in Massachusetts, a fact stemming from both their limited number and the lack of a charter for the area.[4]

The more influential Puritans arrived a decade later, in 1630, with a royal charter from King Charles I to form the Massachusetts Bay Colony.[5] They neither fled persecution nor formally separated from England's established church. Instead, as Ariens and Destro observe, Puritans sought a place "to create a new, perfect union of church and state."[6] They endeavored to form independent churches free from "Papish hierarchy."[7] In America, each such church represented a "congregation unto itself," a fact that prompted the Puritans to become known as Congregationalists.[8] The Puritan rules of governance sprang directly from the faith's tenets: "Public worship (and rest) on Sundays was required, swearing was a serious criminal offense and the Ten Commandments formed the basic laws of the society."[9]

The Puritan pursuit of religious freedom, however, extended only so far as *their own* beliefs and conduct, resulting in some extreme forms of less favorable treatment doled out to members of competing religious sects. In the mid-1630s, for instance, as Ariens and Destro report, Puritans banished two dissenters from the colony.[10] By statute in 1644, as Thomas Curry reminds, Puritans expelled Baptists who had attempted to settle in Massachusetts.[11] Likewise, from 1658 to 1661, four Quakers who had returned to the colony after expulsion met with an untimely fate: They were hanged in the Boston Common.[12]

This less favorable treatment, as Michael McConnell explains, also took the form of taxation. Puritans imposed compulsory taxes to support local Congregational ministers and churches.[13] The English Act of Toleration of 1689 required the monarchy to grant official religious toleration *in England* to non-Anglicans.[14] Prior to this, the Puritans had lost their colonial charter, prompting the English monarchy to grant a second charter that included the proviso that the colony grant religious toleration to all Protestants. In 1692, therefore, the General Court of Massachusetts proclaimed that there would be no establishment of the Congregational church by name, only that each town support an "able, learned and orthodox" minister voted into power by the town and supported by taxes levied on *all* taxpayers.[15] This ruling—although inviting the theoretical possibility that a minister of any sect could be voted into power—effectively compelled religious dissenters (with rare exceptions) to financially support Congregationalist ministers.[16]

Due in part to the paucity of dissenters, Congregationalism effectively became the established church of the Massachusetts colony. This reflected an ironic twist of power, given that Anglicans—members of the established Church of England—represented part of the dissenting Massachusetts minority.[17] In short, unlike the circumstances prevailing in many other colonies, the de facto established religion of Massachusetts did not reflect English control.

In 1780, four years after the colonies declared their independence, Massachusetts adopted its constitution.[18] Articles II and III captured the relationship between church and state. Article II provided in part that "no subject shall be hurt, molested, or restrained, in his person, liberty, or estate, for worshipping GOD in the manner and season most agreeable to the dictates of his own conscience . . . ."[19] In short, as Jacob Meyer has explained, Article II sought to establish a culture of religious liberty. Article III, by contrast, preserved the power of the legislature to authorize a tax to support public worship.[20]

Above and beyond these particulars germane to activities unfolding within the Massachusetts colony, the Massachusetts experience would produce an individual destined to become an influential figure in the debates surrounding the religious guarantees: Baptist minister Isaac Backus. In 1773, Backus penned a pamphlet that complained of discriminatory treatment suffered by Baptists in the colony.[21] He later would petition the First Continental Congress to respond to concerns arising out of the mandate that nonmembers of the established church nevertheless would be subject to taxation to support that established church.[22]

Connecticut

Connecticut's evolution of church-state relations resembled that of Massachusetts, except that Congregationalism found itself even more firmly rooted in Connecticut. Discriminatory treatment imposed on members of dissenting sects emerged principally through taxation and the inconveniences resulting from actions undertaken to avoid taxation. The colony's town option system—similar to that of Massachusetts—required that everyone pay taxes, regardless of whether the town had a settled minister. As Leonard Levy puts it, "[n]o one was exempt."[23]

Two important legislative acts took effect in 1708. The first, the Dissenters from the Established Order statute, guaranteed "full liberty of worship" in the colony while at the same time continuing to require tax assessments to support the existing Congregational churches.[24] The second, the Saybrook Platform, governed the Congregational churches themselves. This enactment declared that every church united in the platform would be acknowledged "as established by law."[25] In 1784, as Levy notes, the colony "abandoned" the Saybrook Platform and enacted a Toleration Act that redounded to the benefit of those who adhered to other faiths.[26] Connecticut nevertheless enabled such dissenters to avoid paying taxes to support Congregational churches only upon producing documents that certified the dissenters indeed supported a different church.[27] The colony likewise required those individuals who supported no faith at all to contribute toward the established congregation in their town.[28] Opponents protested *both* the inconvenience and expense associated with obtaining the necessary certificates *and* the intrusion into matters of religious belief.[29]

Baptists played a significant role in the struggle against Connecticut's establishment of Congregationalism. Just as Massachusetts had Isaac Backus, Connecticut had its own outspoken Baptist minister, John Leland. As Ariens and Destro note, Leland lived in New London for a mere two months in 1791 before settling in western Massachusetts; he nevertheless exercised substantial influence on Connecticut's history of religious liberty.[30] Leland opposed Connecticut's certificate system, advocating in a 1791 sermon "that even non-Christians had rights of conscience which must be respected: the right to support non-Christian religions or to give no support whatever to religion."[31] Shortly thereafter, the Connecticut legislature repealed the certificate system in favor of one allowing dissenters to write their own certificates attesting to membership in a dissenting religious society.[32]

New Hampshire

The New Hampshire experience, similar to that of Massachusetts and Connecticut because of its Congregationalist establishment, nonetheless reflected what Ariens and Destro characterize as greater leniency toward dissenters.[33] This leniency, as they report, stemmed in part from the dearth of dissenters within the colony; sparsely populated New Hampshire had little to fear given the very limited numbers of dissenters.[34] Accordingly, the colony's 1784 constitution reflected a more tolerant approach to religious liberty, permitting citizens to refrain from taking part in the militia or being compelled to swear oaths when taking office, freedoms, as Ariens and Destro remind, especially meaningful to the colony's Quaker sect.[35]

Members of minority faiths nonetheless did suffer various forms of discriminatory treatment, principally by way of taxation and the absence of representation in government. Like the Massachusetts system, the New Hampshire Congregationalist establishment rested on, and drew funding from, local support, triggering objections from nonmembers forced to pay taxes.[36] The state constitution also mandated that all state legislative representatives "shall be of the protestant religion, and shall cease to represent such town, parish, or place immediately on ceasing to be qualified as aforesaid."[37]

Rhode Island

Rhode Island's encouragement of religious liberty poses a stark contrast to the approach pursued by other New England colonies. Roger Williams—a Puritan minister from Massachusetts banished from that colony for speaking against the Puritan elect—founded Rhode Island.[38] Williams secured a royal patent to the colony and, as Ariens and Destro report, used this power to "enjoin[] the state from interfering in any way with a person's right of religious conscience."[39] The 1663 charter reinforced this idea of religious liberty for all, as it stated:

> [T]hat noe person within the sayd colonye, at any tyme hereafter, shall bee any wise molested, punished, disquieted, or called in question, for any differences in opinione in matters of religion, and doe not actually disturb the civil peace of our sayd colony; but that all and everye person and persons may, from tyme to tyme, and at all tymes hereafter, freelye and fullye have and enjoye his and theire owne judgments and consciences, in matters of religious concernments.[40]

Now, to be clear, the charter contained language referring to religious freedom for *all*. But it happened to be the various forms of Protestant Christianity that the colony practiced and encouraged.[41] Rhode Island never imposed a tax to support religion.[42]

Williams's influence on the development of religious liberty has been a source of debate. Nevertheless, as Ariens and Destro report, Williams generally earns credit for originating the much-invoked "wall of separation" metaphor,[43] referring to a "hedge or wall of separation between the Garden of the Church and the Wilderness of the world."[44]

The Middle Colonies

Pennsylvania

William Penn, the colony's namesake, received a colonial charter in 1681.[45] By the next year, as Ariens and Destro report, Penn had "extended the right of conscience and civil liberties to any person who believed in one God"—an act that effectively extended religious liberty beyond Christian Protestants to include both Jews and Roman Catholics.[46] Moreover, the colony's political landscape featured no established church and provided no support to either churches or ministers.[47]

The Pennsylvania experience appeared to reflect substantial tolerance of dissenting sects. Nevertheless, discriminatory treatment did exist in the form of religious oaths for office, oaths that effectively barred members of certain sects from securing political power. Pennsylvania's constitution of 1776, while guaranteeing religious freedom to all, did require officeholders "to acknowledge a belief in God and in both the Old and New Testaments."[48] This provision served to bar Jewish inhabitants from holding office, prompting some to complain that the provision deprived them of "the most eminent rights of freemen."[49] By 1790, the subsequent Pennsylvania Constitution extended the right to hold office to all who believed in God and in "a future state of rewards and punishments," thereby, as Thomas Curry notes, allowing Jews to hold political office.[50]

Delaware

Delaware's colonial history resembled that of Pennsylvania. This fact should come as no surprise, given that Delaware originally formed part of Pennsylvania and remained under the executive authority of Pennsylvania throughout the colonial period, despite being granted what Ariens and Destro dub "some . . . autonomy" in 1702.[51]

Delaware's 1776 constitution granted wide-ranging rights of individual conscience—including the right to worship God—and forbade the preference of one religious sect over another.[52] Like its Pennsylvania counterpart, however, that constitution also limited access to political office based on religious belief. In particular, as Ariens and Destro report, the Delaware Constitution extended civil rights and political positions to Trinitarian Christians only.[53] Delaware's revised 1792 constitution eliminated this religious test for office.[54]

New York

New York, settled by the Dutch in 1624, came under English control approximately five decades later.[55] The Church of England manifested its presence as part of the English administration of the colony. But its establishment, Ariens and Destro assert, was limited to four counties in and around New York City,[56] a fact due primarily to the diversity of Europeans present in the colony.[57]

With the beginning of the Revolution, the Anglican establishment lost both power and control in New York as a result of its association with the English monarchy.[58] Thomas Curry explains that New York's 1777 constitution expressly disestablished the Church of England, providing that any laws "as may be construed to establish or maintain any particular denomination of Christians or their ministers . . . are abrogated and rejected."[59] That constitution also provided for "[f]ree exercise and enjoyment of religious profession and worship, without discrimination or preference"[60]—a provision analogous to those contained in other state constitutions.

But New York went one unusual step further. It required all foreigners settling in New York to "abjure and renounce all allegiance and subjection to all and every foreign Kin, Prince, Potentate and State, in all matters ecclesiastical as well as civil."[61] Curry opines that the final clause in this provision, proffered by John Jay, sought to discourage Catholics from settling in New York.[62] That objective became even clearer in 1788 when the legislature, deploying similar language, enacted a test oath for officeholders that effectively excluded Catholics from office for the remainder of the eighteenth century.[63] Such developments contributed to the notion that, at the time, *religious liberty for all* meant religious liberty for all *Protestants*.

New Jersey

The New Jersey colonial experience echoed that of New York, with the Dutch settling the territory before being supplanted by the English.[64] Until the turn of the eighteenth century the Quakers ensured religious liberty for all.[65] In 1702, New Jersey became a royal colony and, until 1738, shared a governor with New York.[66] Throughout this period religious freedom found form in the absence of required attendance for religious worship, the lack of taxes to support an established ministry, and laws ensuring that no religious sect would be preferred over another.[67] New Jersey's 1776 constitution contained provisions that reinforced prevailing practices, proclaiming that "[t]here shall be no establishment of any religious sect in the Province in preference to another."[68]

Like the other middle colonies, however, discriminatory treatment relating to eligibility for public office marred these notions of religious liberty. New Jersey permitted only members of the Protestant faith to hold public office.[69]

Maryland

In 1634, with the assistance of a royal charter, the first and second Lords Baltimore (the Calverts) founded Maryland.[70] Maryland was to be something of an experiment in religious toleration. The Calverts had converted from Anglican to Roman Catholicism; the colony was to be comprised of Catholics and Protestants living together with neither enjoying an elevated status from the state.[71]

As Ariens and Destro observe, due both to "religious upheavals" in England and widespread hostility to Catholicism, the Calvert ideal did not succeed.[72] In 1691 King William annulled the Calvert charter; and by 1702 the English government had established the Church of England within the colony.[73] The 1776 Maryland Constitution guaranteed that "all persons professing the Christian religion, are equally entitled to protection in their religious liberty."[74] This new constitution allowed the government to levy a tax to support the Christian religion,[75] though the legislature declined to do so. In 1795, Maryland amended its constitution to require each officeholder to "subscribe a declaration of his belief in the Christian religion."[76]

The Southern Colonies

The Church of England constituted the established church in each of the southern colonies. It greatly intertwined itself with local government. Each of these colonies divided itself into political subdivisions known as parishes.[77] As Chester Antieau, Arthur Downey, and Edward Roberts explain, parishes not only could tax local citizens for support of the established church; they represented the "principal organs" of local government.[78] In fact, each legislative district was required to have an established church in order to be represented in the colonial legislature.[79] Vestrymen "conducted the affairs of the parish and chose the minister"; vestrymen themselves were selected "by members of the parish who, by exclusionary . . . tests and oaths, could only be practicing Anglicans."[80]

The Carolinas

North Carolina, first chartered as a colony in 1663, established the Church of England in 1711.[81] Four years later the Vestry Act of 1715 declared that church the only one eligible to receive public support.[82] By the parish system, non-Anglicans in the colony found themselves on the receiving end of discriminatory treatment in the form of taxation and preclusion from political office.[83]

The state's 1776 constitution included a "Declaration of Rights" that guaranteed individuals "the natural and unalienable right to worship Almighty God according to the dictates of their own conscience."[84] It also ended the Anglican establishment—observing that there would not be "an establishment of any one religious church or denomination in this State, in preference to any other"—and forbade taxing a person for the support of a church in which he did not worship.[85] Nevertheless, the requirement that only Protestants were eligible to hold public office endured.[86]

South Carolina, part of the original land grant of 1663, became a separate colony in 1735.[87] It, too, established the Church of England; the vestry system likewise permeated local government.[88] By contrast to the colonies whose emerging constitutions disestablished the previously dominant faith after the Revolution, however, the 1778 South Carolina Constitution, as Ariens and Destro remind, declared "[t]he Christian Protestant religion . . . the established religion of the state."[89] Religious oaths continued to be required for public office.[90] Notwithstanding the presence of this establishment, the 1778 constitution did *not* provide for public support of the established religion through taxation.[91]

In 1790, a new South Carolina constitution eliminated both the religious test requirement for public office and the establishment of Protestantism, in turn granting "free exercise and enjoyment of religious profession and worship of faith, without discrimination or preference."[92]

Georgia

In 1732, as Ariens and Destro report, Georgia became the last of the original thirteen colonies chartered.[93] Originally formed by what Curry dubs "a group of philanthropists and speculators" hoping to rehabilitate Britain's debtors and unemployed workers, those who settled in Georgia "envisaged a special position for the Church of England in the colony."[94] It reorganized as a royal province in 1754.[95] From 1758 to 1777 the Church of England reigned as the established religion.[96] Nevertheless, due to a lack of ministers, churches, organization, and resources, the Anglican establishment proved weak.[97]

The Georgia constitution of 1777 guaranteed free exercise of religion to all. But the document continued to limit access to public office to Protestants only. In addition, the legislature in 1785 enacted a law taxing individuals to support ministers of their respective religions.[98] Later, the 1798 constitution removed any reference to the duty of financial support for religion;[99] by this time, moreover, Georgia no longer mandated religious oaths for public office.[100] The religious freedom clause of the 1798 constitution provided that "[n]o one religious society shall ever be established in this State, in preference to another; nor shall any person be denied the enjoyment of any civil right merely on account of his religious principles."[101]

Virginia

The Virginia experience provides the richest source of material for the debate surrounding the evolution of colonial religious liberty. The range of intellectual luminaries who called Virginia home—among them Patrick Henry, George Mason, Thomas Jefferson, and James Madison—helps explain why the state dominates much of the published debate. As Ariens and Destro note, Jefferson and Madison, above and beyond serving as the new nation's third and fourth presidents, each held public office in Virginia.[102] These men took to the national stage the influence and experience they earned from dealing with issues of religious liberty within their own state.

Virginia established the Church of England in 1609, two years after the settlement of Jamestown.[103] As Michael McConnell explains, "governing authorities and the local gentry" used the church as a means by which to establish control and maintain social order.[104] The power of the establishment extended well into the justice system, with ecclesiastic courts deployed to punish religious dissent and "dispense summary criminal justice without a trial by jury."[105] Chester Antieau and his co-authors point out that the church's control also allowed it to assume such important functions as "setting tax rates for the support of the minister, making presentments to the court for violations of the laws against drunkenness, swearing, and fornication . . . and [maintaining] the public records of births, deaths and marriages."[106]

As Antieau and coauthors explain, the power of the established church engendered resentment from nonmembers, particularly from Baptists and Presbyterians—a "[b]itterness . . . increased by the fact that the government had never yielded the slightest to their pleas."[107] Baptists began to populate Virginia in the 1760s. They sought more than toleration under England's Act of Toleration of 1689,[108] demanding freedom to practice their religion and refusing to obtain the licenses necessary to preach their beliefs.[109] Incarceration and violence ensued.[110] Madison himself, though not yet in a position to remedy the intolerance, concluded that "[l]iberty of [c]onscience," not just toleration, was necessary.[111]

Virginia adopted the Declaration of Rights of its 1776 constitution on June 12, 1776.[112] The Declaration, as Ariens and Destro report, included a free exercise provision that exempted dissenters from having to pay taxes to support the Anglican establishment.[113] That provision—altered from the original draft of George Mason—[114] read as follows:

> That Religion, or the duty which we owe to our Creator, and the manner of discharging it can be directed only by reason and conviction, not by force or violence, and therefore all men are equally entitled to the free exercise of religion, according to the dictates of conscience; and that it is the mutual duty of all to practice Christian forbearance, love and charity towards each other.[115]

Mason's original draft had provided that "all men should enjoy the fullest toleration in the exercise of religion, according to the dictates of conscience."[116] Madison proposed the change because, he contended, Mason's draft treated free exercise as "an act of legislative grace" and not an individual right.[117] Virginia nevertheless continued to maintain an established church, and the constitution also provided public officials with the discretion to license the meetinghouses of religious dissenters.[118]

Virginia's Declaration—widely distributed throughout the colonies[119]—influenced other states' consideration of their respective legislation regarding free exercise. The laws of many of these other states—among them Delaware, Georgia, New York, Pennsylvania, and South Carolina—featured religious liberty guarantees containing the phrase "free exercise."[120]

In October 1776, Virginia's Presbyterians protested paying taxes to support the established religion by publishing the "Memorial of Presbytery of Hanover, Virginia."[121] As Antieau, Downey, and Roberts suggest, the "Memorial" grounded its opposition to taxes supporting religion in both the diversity of religious sects and the natural rights of the citizen.[122] Virginia's legislature quickly responded to the Presbyterian protest by enacting a statute—effective January 1, 1777 [123]—that suspended the obligation of dissenters to pay taxes levied for support of the established church.[124] This act read:

> Resolved, That so much of the petitions of the several dissenters from the church established by law within this Commonwealth, as desired an exemption from all taxes and contributions whatever towards supporting the said church and the ministers thereof, or towards the support of their respective religious societies in any other way than themselves shall voluntarily agree is reasonable.[125]

In 1776, Virginia ultimately repealed the colonial laws that levied taxes to support the establishment.[126] Nevertheless, it was not until 1779 that members of the established religion were released from the tax requirement.[127]

Also in 1779, as Leonard Levy recounts, two conflicting bills circulated in the legislature.[128] One—Jefferson's "Bill for Religious Freedom"—opposed civil jurisdiction over religion,[129] a position consistent with Jefferson's opposition to any form of state-established church.[130] The other, by stark contrast, proposed both a general tax assessment and the establishment of Christianity as the state religion of Virginia, including articles of faith to which any church was required to subscribe in order to become incorporated.[131] This latter bill, if enacted, would have levied taxes on every taxpayer—including those who did not belong to any established church—for support of a church of the taxpayer's choice, with funds being distributed to all churches incorporated in the county.[132] In short, the threat of multiple establishments coexisted with the possibility of complete autonomy for any religion.

Following the Revolution, Virginia's Episcopal Church found itself in serious financial difficulty as a result of the repeal of its support from tithes.[133] In response, Patrick Henry submitted a bill to the legislature entitled "A Bill Establishing a Provision for Teachers of the Christian Religion."[134] The proposal—also dubbed the "Assessment Bill"—would have provided for a "modest" tax in support of a church and minister of choice,[135] established Christianity as the official religion of Virginia, and even provided parameters for what would have constituted a Christian church.[136] Funds collected from nonreligious taxpayers would go into the county seminaries.[137]

Madison replied, anonymously attacking Henry's Assessment Bill in the "Memorial and Remonstrance against Religious Assessments."[138] Not surprisingly, Madison attacked the bill as discriminatory, given that the proposal sought to elevate Christianity to the status of the preferred religion.[139] In doing so, Madison employed the language of both Virginia's 1776 Declaration of Rights and the Presbyterian Memorial: "[R]eligion, or the duty which we owe to our Creator, and the manner of discharging it, can be directed only by reason and conviction, not by force or violence."[140]

This anonymous reply, Adams and Emmerich observe, engendered public outrage sufficient to cause Henry's bill to die in committee, without a vote[141]—a result facilitated by the fact that its sponsor had been removed from the debate upon his election as Governor of Virginia in 1784.[142] Instead of Henry's Assessment Act, the Virginia legislature enacted Jefferson's "A Bill for Establishing Religious Freedom,"[143] which had been drafted nearly a decade earlier.[144] The effect of the law was to separate completely religion and government in Virginia for the first time.[145]

DEBATES 1787–1789: THE EMERGENCE AND RATIFICATION OF THE RELIGION CLAUSES

The Constitutional Convention of 1787

In the summer of 1787, fifty-five delegates from twelve states met in Philadelphia for the purpose of amending the Articles of Confederation. What unfolded, instead, amounted to a bit more than mere amending. As Adams and Emmerich put it, these men proceeded to "draft a new form of government."[146] And, although the delegates rejected the proposal for a bill of rights originating with Virginia delegate George Mason,[147] the proposed Constitution did contain some references to religious liberty.[148]

On August 20, Charles Pinckney of South Carolina submitted a proposal concerning whether a religious test or oath should be administered as a qualification for federal officeholders. In particular, Pinckney moved that "no religious test or qualification shall ever be annexed to any oath of office under the authority of the U.S."[149] The convention referred the proposal without debate to the Committee of Detail. Ten days later, when that committee reported to the convention, it made no mention of the proposal.[150] Pinckney again moved for the proposal's consideration, prompting the chairman of the committee, Roger Sherman of Connecticut, to respond by observing that such a provision was "unnecessary, the prevailing liberality being a sufficient security against such tests."[151] As Leonard Levy reports, debate ensued, with two delegates offering their support for Pinckney's proposal.[152]

The convention ultimately agreed to marry the ban on religious tests to the portion of the Constitution requiring members of Congress and other officeholders to be "bound by Oath or Affirmation" to support the document.[153] Shortly thereafter, the convention unanimously agreed to the following language: "But no religious test shall ever be required as a qualification to any office or public trust under the authority of the United States."[154] The Committee of Style rephrased the language by eliminating the words "the authority of."[155] As a result, Article VI, section 3 of the proposed Constitution included the following language: "no religious test shall ever be required as a qualification to any office or public trust under the United States."[156]

This ban on religious tests, to be sure, did not equate to a ban on established religion. It nevertheless represented a significant step toward eliminating the concern over the discriminatory treatment that theretofore had been doled out to nonmembers of established religions. As Curry observes, the proposed ban "deprive[ed] the new government of one of the most potent weapons of religious discrimination"—access to political office.[157]

The delegates discussed the idea of a bill of rights late in the convention but rejected the notion.[158] Many in attendance deemed such an approach unnecessary, while others harbored the more mundane concern that sufficient time needed to address the issue was unavailable.[159] Curry reports, for instance, that Isaac Backus harbored the sentiment that the proposed Constitution already provided adequate protection for religious liberty.[160] Curry likewise reminds that Alexander Hamilton remained concerned that a bill of rights enumerating exceptions to federal power might provide a way for the new centralized government to claim more power than that already enumerated.[161] Accordingly, the convention passed along the proposed Constitution to the states for ratification without either a bill of rights or a specific guarantee of religious liberty.

State Ratification Conventions and Proposals

Some of the distinguished talents responsible for piecing together the Constitution expressed confidence that Congress lacked the ability to interfere with religion because the national government possessed only limited, carefully circumscribed powers. Accordingly, they contended, Congress possessed the authority to exercise only such limited, circumscribed powers.[162] Despite these assurances, many who attended the state ratifying conventions believed that the new nation needed additional protection against the federal government.[163] It quickly became clear that the absence of a bill of rights represented the single most important objection to the proposed Constitution.[164]

As Levy reports, six of the original thirteen states (Massachusetts, New Hampshire, New York, North Carolina, Rhode Island, and Virginia) recommended amendments, among them amendments that would fortify individual liberties.[165] Of the six, only Massachusetts failed to include a specific request for an amendment protecting religious liberty—an omission perhaps rooted in the fact that Massachusetts featured an established religion at the time of the ratification. To overcome these objections, Levy reports, many Federalist leaders—Madison included—vowed to pursue a bill of rights as soon as the new government began to operate.[166]

Ratification debates in Virginia centered on concerns regarding the protection of religious liberties. In the course of these debates, Edmund Randolph—who, as Ariens and Destro note, initially had refused to sign the Constitution as a delegate—announced his change in sentiment, stating that, now, "he no longer feared religious freedom was in danger."[167] Randolph, Levy tells us, pointed to the Constitution's prohibition against religious tests for federal officeholders as evidence that such officeholders "are not bound to support one mode of worship, or adhere to one particular sect."[168] He went on to contend that the diversity of religious sects present in the United States would "prevent the establishment of any one sect, in prejudice to the rest, and forever oppose all attempts to infringe religious liberty."[169] Randolph's newfound confidence represented a strikingly different attitude from that manifested by Patrick Henry, who contended that the proposed Constitution effectively placed religious freedom in jeopardy.[170] Henry's suggested amendments to the proposed Constitution included a declaration of rights with a provision reading that "no particular religious sect or society ought to be favored or established, by law, in preference to others."[171] Similar to circumstances unfolding elsewhere, Philip Kurland explains, Virginia's Federalists accepted these amendments as the political price to be paid to Anti-Federalists in order to obtain ratification.[172]

As for New York, reports germane to proposed amendments—including one concerning religious liberty—are sparse, largely because the historical record suggests that this aspect of the state's constitutional debate was not preserved.[173] We nevertheless do know that John Lansing, an Anti-Federalist opposed to ratification, proposed a bill of rights intended to be sent back with the ratified Constitution. That proposal, adopted by the New York convention, provided, insofar as religious liberty was concerned, "[t]hat the People have an equal, natural and unalienable right, freely and peaceably to Exercise their Religion according to the dictates of Conscience, and that no Religious Sect or Society ought to be favoured or established by Law in preference of others."[174] This language, as Levy observes, echoed that deployed in New York's 1777 constitution, language that had disestablished the Church of England without doing so by name.[175]

Records of any debates or speeches that unfolded at the New Hampshire ratification debates do not survive.[176] But New Hampshire did include among its recommendations for ratification a proposed amendment providing that "Congress shall make no laws touching Religion, or to infringe the rights of Conscience."[177]

North Carolina initially refused to ratify the Constitution.[178] The record of its debate reveals that this initial rejection, though unaccompanied by any formal request for additional protections for religious liberty, emerged out of a concern that the new national government could impose a national religion.[179] Later, after Congress added the Bill of Rights, North Carolina threw its support behind the Constitution with an amendment analogous to that of Virginia and New York, expressing the view that "a declaration of rights . . . securing from encroachments the great principles of civil and religious liberty . . . ought to be laid before Congress."[180]

The Rhode Island convention did not meet until after the Constitution had been ratified.[181] The convention nevertheless recommended an amendment addressing religious liberty that resembled those of Virginia, New York, and North Carolina.[182] Given the timing of the Rhode Island recommendation, however, the proposal, as Levy observes, represented "a superfluous flourish that had no effect on the framing of the First Amendment."[183]

Maryland ratified the Constitution without amendments. Many had been offered, Levy advises, including one declaring "that there be no national religion established by law; but that all persons be equally entitled to protection in their religious liberty."[184] These offerings—which, according to Levy, aimed to protect the institutions of state government from the newly created national government[185]—failed, he reports, not because the Federalist majority disagreed with them but, instead, because that majority wished to manifest a display of "confidence" for the new government by "unconditionally" ratifying the Constitution.[186]

Records from the ratification debates of Delaware, New Jersey, and Georgia reveal that all three states ratified the proposed Constitution without conditions or amendment proposals.[187]

What Levy dubs a "fragmentary record" exists for Connecticut, which likewise ratified the Constitution without any amendment proposals.[188] The record that does remain from Connecticut reveals, as Levy reports, reliance on the notion that Congress lacked the power to legislate in connection with religious matters and that the ban against a religious oath requirement for public office evinced adequate enough proof of this lack of authority.[189]

South Carolina passed along recommendations for amendments but none pertained to a bill of rights.[190]

The Pennsylvania convention ratified the Constitution unconditionally—but, Levy reminds, only after rejecting a variety of amendments proposed by the Anti-Federalist minority.[191] The defeated proposals—including one protecting "rights of conscience"—made no express reference to religious liberty.[192]

In sum, the work of the state ratification conventions reflected a diversity of proposed ways to achieve widely shared objectives. States whose convention members largely believed that the Constitution had succeeded in limiting national power generally failed to discern much justification for amending the Constitution, let alone adding an amendment relating to religious liberty. Other state conventions, however, concluded that amendments to the Constitution—including an amendment concerning religious liberty—were imperative in order to curb the power of the new national government. The range and power of particular sentiments within each state's convention played a significant role in determining whether a particular state would propose an amendment germane to religious liberty. In addition, many of the states, as discussed earlier, continued to house in their legislative books laws concerning religion, a fact likely to have reinforced the belief that the new national government would not be endowed with substantial authority in the realm of religion. Quite simply, the state ratifying conventions reflected the range of views harbored by members of the founding generation concerning *both* religious liberty *and* the new national government's power to enact laws germane to religion.

The First Congress

The First Congress met in New York in 1789.[193] It confronted the twin tasks of starting a new government and grappling with demands for further protections from that new and growing federal government.[194] One such demand, as Adams and Emmerich explain, was the push for a bill of rights.[195]

James Madison served as a member of the First Congress, appointed to the Select Committee on Constitutional Amendments, whose responsibility was to put forward a bill of rights for the House of Representatives to consider.[196] Madison's appointment to the committee posed something of a paradox, as Curry notes, given Madison's view that such an undertaking was superfluous because, as Madison himself had observed, "enumerating particular exceptions to the grant of power . . . [might] disparage those rights which were not placed in that enumeration."[197] Nevertheless, in light of both the demands of the ratifying conventions in Virginia and other states and a desire to fulfill a campaign promise,[198] Curry notes, Madison informed his colleagues that he "considered himself 'bound in honor and in duty' " to propose and advocate for such amendments.[199]

Accordingly, on May 4, Madison announced to his colleagues in the House of Representatives his intention to propose amendments to the Constitution.[200] The source of these proposals lay in amendments that state ratifying conventions had submitted to the First Congress.[201] On June 7, Madison introduced to the House the first of his proposals, a proposal that stated as follows:

> The Civil Rights of none shall be abridged on account of religious belief or worship, nor shall any national religion be established, nor shall the full and equal rights of conscience be in any manner, nor on any pretext infringed.
>
> No state shall violate the equal rights of conscience or the freedom of the press, or the trial by jury in criminal cases.[202]

Michael Malbin observes that the wording of the proposal suggests that Madison sought to prohibit both states and the new national federal government "from infringing upon rights of conscience" but, by contrast, endeavored to prevent only the national government from establishing a religion.[203] Adams and Emmerich opine that some of Madison's contemporaries believed that the language relating to a national religion would prove insufficient protection from Congress because the national legislature nevertheless could seek to interfere with state establishments under the Necessary and Proper clause.[204]

Madison's proposal made its way for discussion to the Committee of the Whole House.[205] A month and a half later, the Committee of the Whole House passed it along to the newly formed Select Committee, of which Madison was a member.[206] One member from each of the eleven states represented in Congress served on the Select Committee; because North Carolina and Rhode Island had not yet ratified the Constitution, they lacked representation.

In July, the Select Committee submitted the results of its deliberations to the House.[207] The new version of Madison's handiwork provided that "no religion shall be established by law, nor shall the equal rights of conscience be infringed."[208] The Select Committee had eliminated the phrase "the Civil Rights of none shall be abridged on account of religious belief or worship," and also had deleted the word "national."[209]

The floor debate beginning on August 15 included speeches by eight of the fifty-one representatives.[210] The bulk of these speeches focused on the language of anti-establishment rather than the "rights of conscience" clause, the latter of which ultimately evolved into the "free exercise" guarantee.[211]

Some commentators, musing about this preoccupation with what would become the anti-establishment guarantee, attribute the development to the following mix of factors. At this juncture only two states—Rhode Island and Virginia—"had adopted complete legal guarantees for freedom of religion";[212] the others continued to feature restrictions on religious worship, such as restricting the holding of public office to Protestants or exempting clergy from holding office.[213] These circumstances, the argument proceeds, suggest "an unstated consensus" among the states that the emerging free exercise guarantee "reflect[ed] in large measure the meaning of their own guarantees of religious freedom."[214]

Peter Sylvester of New York spoke first, requesting a change in the language of the anti-establishment provision. Sylvester purported to root his request in the concern that, as written, the guarantee could be construed to "abolish religion altogether."[215] Massachusetts Anti-Federalist Elbridge Gerry proposed that the amendment be reworded to "no religious doctrine shall be established by law,"[216] language that, as Malbin opines, could have lent itself to a construction permitting some aid to religion.[217] Connecticut federalist Roger Sherman argued against the necessity of a bill of rights.[218]

Madison spoke after Sylvester and Gerry, indicating that the proposed language, according to Malbin, signified that "Congress should not establish *a* religion, and enforce the legal observation of it by law, nor compel men to worship God in any manner contrary to their conscience."[219] Madison likewise defended his proposal by reminding that many states had insisted upon amendments that would guarantee religious freedom so as to prevent Congress from establishing a national religion or invoking the Necessary and Proper guarantee in an effort to infringe upon religious freedom.[220] In sum, as Malbin concludes, Madison harbored the view that express guarantees devoted to religious freedom, though unnecessary to prevent the national government from intruding upon such freedom, nonetheless represented a necessary concession to the Anti-federalists.[221]

Connecticut's Benjamin Huntington then articulated some apprehension concerning possible tension between the purpose of the language and the language itself.[222] Huntington professed to agree with all that Madison had expressed, nevertheless noting concern that, down the road, the language might be construed in a manner hostile to religion.[223] John Semonche reports that Huntington harbored concern about the prospects that a federal court would resist enforcing a state obligation to pay a minister or contribute to the cost of building a church because such an action might be construed as inconsistent with the proposed anti-establishment guarantee.[224] Madison replied by submitting a motion—later withdrawn—to again include the word "national" before "religion." This motion sought to clarify the meaning of the amendment by "point[ing] the amendment directly to the object it was intended to prevent,"[225] and in doing so endeavor to quell the fears harbored by the likes of Sylvester and Huntington.[226]

New Hampshire's Samuel Livermore then moved to alter the proposed language to conform to a recommendation from his state providing that "[C]ongress shall make no law *touching* religion, or infringing on the rights of conscience."[227] As Semonche reports, this represented the first time that the initial five words of what ultimately would become the finished product entered the debate.[228] No further discussion occurred until August 20, when Fisher Ames[229] from Massachusetts moved his brethren to enact the following: "Congress shall make no law establishing religion, or prohibiting the free exercise thereof, nor shall the rights of conscience be infringed."[230] The Ames proposal emerged because Massachusetts continued to maintain an established religion and, accordingly, remained apprehensive about interference from the national government invited by Livermore's proposal.[231] The House enacted Ames's version, sending it to the Senate for consideration on August 24.[232]

September 3 marked the Senate's first serious consideration of the House proposal.[233] Discussion began with a motion to replace the words "religion, or prohibiting the free exercise thereof" with "one religious sect or society in preference to others."[234] This proposal, seeking to clarify the meaning of the anti-establishment guarantee, eliminated the language pertaining to free exercise.[235] Eventually the Senate accepted the change.[236] Also on September 3 the Senate rejected a motion to strike entirely the amendment pertaining to liberty of conscience and subsequently rejected two more versions similar to the one that passed.[237] These two versions stated, respectively:

> Congress shall not make any law infringing the rights of conscience, or establishing any religious sect or society.[238]
>
> Congress shall make no law establishing any particular denomination of religion in preference to another, or prohibiting the free exercise thereof, nor shall the rights of conscience be infringed.[239]

The use of "sect or society" in the first version echoed the language submitted in proposed amendments by the ratifying conventions of Virginia, New York, and North Carolina.

In the end, the Senate accepted most of the Ames version, striking only the wording "nor shall equal rights of conscience be infringed," and sending the version quoted below back to the House[240] on September 9, 1789:[241]

Congress shall make no law establishing articles of faith or a mode of Worship, or prohibiting the free exercise of religion.[242]

The House rejected the Senate's final version and all of its changes and subsequently asked the Senate to form a conference committee[243] with members from both the House and the Senate.[244] The committee included Madison from Virginia, Roger Sherman from Connecticut, House Select Committee Chair John Vining from Delaware, Senator Oliver Ellsworth from Connecticut, Senator Charles Carroll from Maryland, and Senator William Paterson from New Jersey.[245] This group ultimately constructed the wording of the First Amendment.[246] Records of the committee's deliberations do not exist.[247] Thus, as Adams and Emmerich observe, "authorship of the amendment and precise intent of the committee remain uncertain."[248]

Semonche notes that the ultimate result of the joint conference was to expand the wording that the Senate had originally opposed,[249] the difference being that Congress was now prohibited from passing laws "respecting an establishment of religion" instead of passing laws that would establish a religion.[250] The final version ultimately ratified by the states read as follows:

Congress shall make no law respecting an establishment of religion, or prohibiting the free exercise thereof.

The House accepted this version on September 24, 1789; the Senate did the same a day later.[251]

POSTENACTMENT REACTION

The First Congress labored hard to ensure that religious liberty would be protected at the national level. Many states, however, did not choose to conform to the example. The historical record makes clear that, in the eyes of many, religious liberty in early America remained a matter subject largely to the whims of state legislatures. For that reason, members of minority faiths continued to receive discriminatory treatment from government well into (and beyond) the nineteenth century.

The Massachusetts establishment lasted longer than that of any other state, finally giving way in 1833 to an amendment to the state constitution that provided equal protection of the laws to "all religious sects and denominations," rather than to "every denomination of [C]hristians."[252] Connecticut did not abandon its general tax assessment for religion until adopting its new constitution in 1818,[253] and even then the state guaranteed civil rights only to "each and every society or denomination of Christians."[254] Not until 1844 did New Jersey lift its prohibition against non-Protestant officeholders, doing so through a constitutional guarantee that forbade religious tests for public office.[255] Maryland waited until 1810 to repeal its tax for the support of religion,[256] and not until well into the twentieth century, after a Supreme Court decision holding the practice unconstitutional, did the state's requirement that individuals holding public office declare a belief in God fade from the scene.[257] And not until 1835 did North Carolina amend its constitution to extend the ability to hold public office beyond Protestants, and then only to individuals believing in the "truth of the '*Christian*' religion." This limitation endured until 1868.[258]

CONCLUSION

The words protecting religious freedom now enshrined in the First Amendment emerged out of the desire of colonists to maximize the prospects that the new nation did not repeat the errors of the mother country. The ideal of religious liberty—an ideal contemporary Americans very much take for granted—did not become a practical reality for the inhabitants of colonial and revolutionary America. Many of these individuals, to be sure, had left England in order to enjoy greater religious freedom. But the historical record makes abundantly clear that, in virtually all of the colonies, religious freedom did not extend to those whose beliefs and practices diverged from those of members of the established faiths, or even to dissenters within established faiths.

Each of the different colonies experienced its own distinctive mix of religion and government. Yet, to a considerable extent, three elements remained common irrespective of the particular colony: discriminatory treatment inflicted on individuals not affiliated with the established religions; taxes levied to support the established religions; and England's continued control of the established religions. The confluence of these three elements precipitated the move toward incorporating protections for religious freedom into the foundational document of the new nation.

Debate concerning the relationship between religion and the new government unfolded in the Constitutional Convention, in the state ratification conventions, and in the First Congress.

The Constitutional Convention provided the first grand forum for discussion. The Federalists prevailed, and the Constitution went out to the states for ratification absent any bill of rights that would include protections for religious liberty. But the proposed Constitution did contain a prohibition on religious tests for officeholders, an important step in the development of religious freedom.

A range of different state ratification conventions pointed to the very absence of a bill of rights as among the proposed Constitution's most glaring deficiencies. That sentiment, as discussed above, was by no means unanimous. Indeed, the approach a particular state convention took to the necessity of a bill of rights with protections for religious liberty depended to a considerable extent on the convention's view as to whether the proposed Constitution already contained adequate restrictions on the power of the new national government. Those state conventions fraught with apprehensions about the potentially expansive power of the new national government offered amendments designed to curb that power, including amendments pertaining to religious freedom. Those states sufficiently mollified so as not to share those apprehensions ratified without offering amendments.

The First Congress faced the challenge of responding to the call for increased protections from the new national government. James Madison, a reluctant convert to the cause, spearheaded a movement that transformed amendments submitted by the state conventions into the Bill of Rights. Indeed, Madison submitted to the House of Representatives the initial proposed amendment, one that would have had the dual impact of forbidding states as well as the national government to infringe on rights of conscience as well as forbidding the national government to establish a religion. Eventually, a conference committee of House and Senate members produced the version of religious freedom now enshrined in the First Amendment.

The First Congress endeavored to ensure that the new national government refrain from interfering with the rights of its citizens, including rights of religious freedom. Many state governments nevertheless continued to disadvantage their inhabitants on the basis of religion after the adoption of the Constitution, through a range of mechanisms that included established religions, eligibility requirements for officeholders, and taxes to support religion.

NOTES

1. Michael S. Ariens & Robert A. Destro, *Religious Liberty in a Pluralistic Society* 46 (1996).
2. *Id.*
3. *Id.*
4. *Id.*
5. *Id.*
6. *Id.*
7. *Id.* at 47.
8. *Id.*
9. *Id.*
10. *Id.*
11. Thomas J. Curry, *The First Freedoms* 13 (1986).
12. *Id.* at 22.
13. Michael McConnell, *The Origins and Historical Understanding of the Free Exercise of Religion*, 103 Harv. L. Rev. 1409, 1422 (1990).
14. Ariens & Destro, *supra* note 1, at 47.
15. Leonard Levy, *The Establishment Clause* 17 (1994).
16. *Id.* at 17–19.
17. Ariens & Destro, *supra* note 1, at 48.
18. *Id.* at 49.
19. *Id.*
20. *Id.* (citing Jacob C. Meyer, *Church and State in Massachusetts from 1740 to 1883* 113 (1930)).
21. *Id.* at 48.
22. *Id.*

23. Levy, *supra* note 15, at 22–23.
24. *Id.*
25. *Id.*
26. *Id.* at 46.
27. *Id.*
28. *Id.*
29. *Id.*
30. Ariens & Destro, *supra* note 1, at 51.
31. *Id.* at 52.
32. Levy, *supra* note 15, at 46–47.
33. Ariens & Destro, *supra* note 1, at 53.
34. *Id.*
35. *Id.*
36. *Id.*
37. *Id.*
38. *Id.* at 54.
39. *Id.*
40. *Id.*
41. *Id.* at 55.
42. *Id.*
43. *Id.*
44. Roger Williams, *Mr. Cottons Letter Lately Printed, Examined and Answered, 1644*, reprinted in John E. Semonche, *Religion and Constitutional Government in the United States* 6 (1985) (citing *I The Complete Writings of Roger Williams* 108 (1963)).
45. Ariens & Destro, *supra* note 1, at 56–57.
46. *Id.* at 57.
47. Curry, *supra* note 11, at 160.
48. *Id.*
49. *Id.* at 161.
50. *Id.*
51. Ariens & Destro, *supra* note 1, at 57.
52. *Id.*
53. *Id.*
54. *Id.*
55. *Id.*
56. *Id.*
57. *Id.*
58. *Id.*
59. Curry, *supra* note 11, at 161.
60. Ariens & Destro, *supra* note 1, at 57.
61. *Id.*
62. Curry, *supra* note 11, at 161–62.
63. *Id.* at 162.
64. Ariens & Destro, *supra* note 1, at 58.
65. *Id.*
66. *Id.*
67. Curry, *supra* note 11, at 159.

68. Ariens & Destro, *supra* note 1, at 58.
69. *Id.*
70. Curry, *supra* note 11, at 31–32.
71. *Id.*
72. Ariens & Destro, *supra* note 1, at 58.
73. *Id.*
74. *Id.*
75. *Id.* at 59.
76. *Id.*
77. Chester James Antieau, Arthur T. Downey, & Edward C. Roberts, *Freedom from Federal Establishment* 4 (1964).
78. *Id.*
79. *Id.*
80. *Id.*
81. Ariens & Destro, *supra* note 1, at 59.
82. Antieau et al., *supra* note 77, at 4.
83. *Id.*
84. Ariens & Destro, *supra* note 1, at 59.
85. *Id.*
86. *Id.*
87. *Id.* at 60.
88. Antieau et al., *supra* note 77, at 4.
89. Ariens & Destro, *supra* note 1, at 60.
90. *Id.*
91. Antieau et al., *supra* note 77, at 36.
92. Ariens & Destro, *supra* note 1, at 60.
93. *Id.*
94. Curry, *supra* note 11, at 152.
95. *Id.*
96. Ariens & Destro, *supra* note 1, at 60.
97. Curry, *supra* note 11, at 152.
98. Ariens & Destro, *supra* note 1, at 60.
99. *Id.*
100. *Id.*
101. *Id.*
102. *Id.* at 61.
103. *Id.*
104. McConnell, *supra* note 13, at 1409, 1423.
105. Antieau et al., *supra* note 77, at 3.
106. *Id.* at 13–14.
107. *Id.* at 32.
108. Robert S. Alley, *The Supreme Court on Church and State* 9 (1988).
109. *Id.*
110. *Id.*
111. *Id.*
112. Ariens & Destro, *supra* note 1, at 62.
113. *Id.*

114. *Id.*

115. *Id.*

116. Michael Malbin, *Religion and Politics: The Intentions of the Authors of the First Amendment* 21 (1978).

117. McConnell, *supra* note 13, at 1409, 1423.

118. Ariens & Destro, *supra* note 1, at 62.

119. *Report to Attorney General: Religious Liberty under the Free Exercise Clause* 5 (1986).

120. *Id.* at 4.

121. Antieau et al., *supra* note 77, at 32.

122. *Id.*

123. *Id.*

124. Levy, *supra* note 15, at 60.

125. Antieau et al., *supra* note 77, at 32–33.

126. Semonche, *supra* note 44, at 10.

127. Arlin M. Adams & Charles J. Emmerich, *A Nation Dedicated to Religious Liberty* 11 (1991).

128. Levy, *supra* note 15, at 61.

129. *Id.*

130. McConnell, *supra* note 13, at 1409, 1450–51.

131. Levy, *supra* note 15, at 61.

132. *Id.*

133. Semonche, *supra* note 44, at 10.

134. Adams & Emmerich, *supra* note 127.

135. *Id.*

136. Semonche, *supra* note 44, at 10.

137. Adams & Emmerich, *supra* note 127, at 11.

138. Robert L. Cord, *Separation of Church and State* 20 (1982).

139. *Id.*

140. James Madison, *Memorial and Remonstrance against Religious Assessments*, 1786, *reprinted in The Complete Bill of Rights* 46–47 (Neil H. Cogan, ed., 1997).

141. Adams & Emmerich, *supra* note 127, at 12.

142. Cord, *supra* note 138, at 20.

143. Ariens & Destro, *supra* note 1, at 69.

144. Antieau et al., *supra* note 77, at 33.

145. Semonche, *supra* note 44, at 12.

146. Adams & Emmerich, *supra* note 127, at 13.

147. Curry, *supra* note 11, at 194.

148. Ariens & Destro, *supra* note 1, at 74.

149. Levy, *supra* note 15, at 80.

150. *Id.*

151. *Id.*

152. *Id.*

153. Ariens & Destro, *supra* note 1, at 74.

154. *Id.*

155. *Id.*

156. Levy, *supra* note 15, at 80.

157. Curry, *supra* note 11, at 194.
158. Semonche, *supra* note 44, at 13.
159. *Id.*
160. Curry, *supra* note 11, at 194.
161. *Id.*
162. Levy, *supra* note 15, at 82–83.
163. Curry, *supra* note 11, at 194.
164. Levy, *supra* note 15, at 84.
165. *Id.*
166. *Id.*
167. Ariens & Destro, *supra* note 1, at 75.
168. Levy, *supra* note 15, at 89.
169. *Id.*
170. *Id.*
171. *Id.*
172. Philip B. Kurland, *The Origins of the Religion Clauses of the Constitution*, 27 Wm. & Mary L. Rev. 839, 850 (1985–86).
173. Levy, *supra* note 15, at 90–91.
174. *Reprinted in The Complete Bill of Rights, supra* note 140, at 12.
175. Levy, *supra* note 15, at 91.
176. *Id.* at 89.
177. *Id.*
178. Antieau et al., *supra* note 77, at 111–12.
179. *Id.*
180. Levy, *supra* note 15, at 91 and Ariens & Destro, *supra* note 1, at 77.
181. Levy, *supra* note 15, at 92.
182. *Id.*
183. *Id.*
184. *Id.* at 88.
185. *Id.*
186. *Id.*
187. *Id.* at 86.
188. *Id.*
189. *Id.*
190. *Id.* at 88.
191. *Id.* at 87.
192. *Id.*
193. Adams & Emmerich, *supra* note 127, at 16.
194. *Id.* at 16–17.
195. *Id.* at 17.
196. Alley, *supra* note 108, at 12.
197. Curry, *supra* note 11, at 199.
198. Ariens & Destro, *supra* note 1, at 78.
199. Curry, *supra* note 11, at 199.
200. *Id.* at 198.
201. Malbin, *supra* note 116, at 4.
202. *I Annals of Congress*, 434 (1834), *reprinted in* Malbin, *supra* note 116, at 4.

203. *Id.*

204. Adams & Emmerich, *supra* note 127, at 46.

205. Malbin, *supra* note 116, at 4.

206. *Id.*

207. Ariens & Destro, *supra* note 1, at 79.

208. *Id.*

209. Malbin, *supra* note 116, at 5.

210. Douglas Laycock, *Nonpreferential Aid to Religion: A False Claim about Original Intent*, 27 Wm. & Mary L. Rev. 875, 888 (1985–86).

211. Malbin, *supra* note 116, at 6.

212. *Report to the Attorney General, supra* note 119, at 1.

213. *Id.*

214. *Id.* at 4.

215. Malbin, *supra* note 116, at 6–7; Adams & Emmerich, *supra* note 127, at 17.

216. *I Annals of Congress* 730 (1834), *reprinted in* Malbin, *supra* note 116, at 7.

217. *Id.*

218. *Id.* at 8.

219. *Id.*

220. Adams & Emmerich, *supra* note 127, at 17.

221. Malbin, *supra* note 116, at 9.

222. *Id.*

223. Semonche, *supra* note 44, at 15.

224. *Id.*

225. *The Complete Bill of Rights, supra* note 140, at 2.

226. Malbin, *supra* note 116, at 8.

227. *Id.* at 9 (emphasis added).

228. Semonche, *supra* note 44, at 16.

229. Adams & Emmerich, *supra* note 127, at 18.

230. Laycock, *supra* note 210, at 879.

231. Semonche, *supra* note 44, at 16.

232. *The Complete Bill of Rights, supra* note 140, at 3; Adams & Emmerich, *supra* note 127, at 18.

233. Malbin, *supra* note 116, at 12.

234. Laycock, *supra* note 230, at 877, 879–880.

235. Malbin, *supra* note 116, at 12.

236. *Id.*

237. *Id.*

238. *Id.*

239. *Id.* at 12–13.

240. *Id.* at 13.

241. Adams & Emmerich, *supra* note 127, at 18.

242. *Annals of Congress* 779 (1834), *reprinted in* Malbin, *supra* note 116, at 13.

243. *Id.*

244. Adams & Emmerich, *supra* note 127, at 18.

245. *Id.* at 18–19.

246. *Id.* at 19.

247. *Id.* at 18.

248. *Id.* at 19.
249. Semonche, *supra* note 44, at 16.
250. *Id.*
251. Malbin, *supra* note 116, at 14.
252. Ariens & Destro, *supra* note 1, at 51.
253. *Id.* at 52.
254. *Id.*
255. *Id.* at 58.
256. *Id.* at 59.
257. *Id.*
258. *Id.*

2

The Anti-establishment Guarantee

"Congress shall make no law respecting an establishment of religion . . ."

INTRODUCTION

Today, at the dawn of the twenty-first century, the First Amendment's anti-establishment principle serves as the source of both national strength and national controversy. Every day Americans of an ever-increasing variety of religious beliefs sustain and cultivate their faiths confident that neither Congress nor any state legislature will declare a particular religion or set of religious practices obligatory for all. Such confidence bespeaks a nation strong in its commitment to religious freedom.

Yet, at the same time, strewn across the contemporary American landscape is a chorus of unharmonious voices passionately contesting the appropriate relationship between religion and government. Some of these voices seek to move the institutions of religion and government closer. Others strive to keep them apart—far apart. Still others stake out the cultural and political territory between these competing poles.

These distinctively American voices share little in common other than the language through which they articulate their views. That language, more often than not, is the language of the First Amendment's anti-establishment principle. Does an invocation or benediction delivered by a clergy member at a public school graduation ceremony constitute an "establishment" of religion?[1] Does a depiction of the baby Jesus with parents Mary and Joseph erected on public property in celebration of the Christmas holiday constitute an "establishment" of religion?[2] What about an educational choice program that allows families to send their children to religiously affiliated elementary and secondary schools at government expense?[3] These questions, and a boundless array of questions analogous to these, frame our national conversation of the anti-establishment principle.

Two features of the constitutional terrain serve especially to complicate analysis of the current status of the anti-establishment principle.

One is that, for nearly three decades now, the nation's highest court has been profoundly and increasingly divided over some fundamental issues concerning the principle. To be sure, every justice appears to accept the proposition that the anti-establishment guarantee forbids the creation of an official, government-sponsored religion. Beyond the consensus on this indisputable proposition, however, much remains up for grabs among the justices regarding the precise contours of the anti-establishment principle. Is the principle essentially one of nonpreferentialism, the notion that government may undertake actions that favor religion over nonreligion so long as it refrains from elevating one particular religious sect over another? Or, instead, does the principle require government to maintain a measure of detached neutrality between the forces of religion and those of nonreligion? Is the evil against which the principle is aimed governmental endorsement or disapproval of religion? Or, instead, is the principle centrally concerned with ensuring that government refrain from coercing support of, or participation in, religion? To repeat, one conspicuous feature of modern anti-establishment jurisprudence continues to be the absence of consensus among the justices on many of these most fundamental questions.

The other such feature, paradoxically, is that the same Court that has mustered clarity and consensus on so few anti-establishment guideposts has been unusually active in the anti-establishment arena. Term after term the Court contributes generously to the burgeoning volume of anti-establishment case law, rarely allowing much time to elapse between the delivery of significant statements construing the principle.

The mix of these two contemporary realities—little consensus, substantial activity—has produced a decisional brew of many decisions exhibiting many differing perspectives. Not surprisingly, therefore, modest changes in the Court's membership can produce dramatic changes in the jurisprudence of the anti-establishment guarantee.

In general, disputes implicating the anti-establishment principle appear on the constitutional stage wrapped in two different sets of analytical clothes.[4] One set features religion in one form or another slipping *into* the institutions of American government, with the institution often (but not always) being the American public school. The other set features the institutions of American government reaching *out to* assist religious institutions, with the assistance often (but again, not always) consisting of financial benefits. To be sure, this pair of categories by no means exhausts the range of issues arising out of the anti-establishment guarantee. But a good deal of order can be imposed on what may otherwise be deemed decisional chaos by conceptualizing the law in such a manner.

Beginning with the 1971 case of Lemon v. Kurtzman,[5] the Court often (but not always) has employed a much discussed three-part test to assist it in determining whether a particular governmental action amounts to a violation of the anti-establishment principle. The *Lemon* Court—endeavoring to synthesize both the historical materials surrounding the creation of the anti-establishment guarantee and the evolving precedent construing the guarantee up to that time—announced that, to withstand judicial scrutiny, a government action challenged as clashing with anti-establishment principles:

> [f]irst, . . . must have a secular legislative purpose; second, its principal or primary effect must be one that neither advances nor inhibits religion; finally, the [action] must not foster 'an excessive entanglement with religion.'[6]

This standard set forth in *Lemon*—at least the standard as initially articulated and applied—makes clear that, in the Court's view, the anti-establishment principle mandates judicial inquiry into *the purposes* of the challenged governmental action, *the effects* of the governmental action, and *the relationship* that the governmental action forges between the institutions of government and religion. A law that runs afoul of any single one of the three prongs of *Lemon*—because the law lacks a secular purpose, or because its principal effect is to advance religion, or because it will require excessive entanglement between the institutions of government and religion—represents an unconstitutional government action, one that amounts to an impermissible establishment of religion.

As we will see, the application of the *Lemon* test to the wide variety of circumstances implicated by the anti-establishment guarantee—not unlike the application of many tests purportedly rooted in the language, purpose, and spirit of a particular constitutional provision—remains very much subject to the whims and outlooks of the particular judges undertaking the application. Judges committed to the proposition that the Constitution requires religion and government to place significant distance between them tend to construe *Lemon* to require such an outcome. By contrast, judges who find nothing in the Constitution to require religion to be purged from public places or treated as an archenemy of government tend both to lament the *Lemon* standards and to construe them to be more forgiving of interactions between institutions of government and those of religion. In addition, the test itself has undergone some evolution, most notably the recent effort to tuck analysis of the third-prong "entanglement" issue into the analysis of the second-prong "effect" issue rather then to grapple with entanglement as a separate and distinct constitutional challenge.

Most judicially crafted tests designed to give practical meaning to constitutional imperatives garner criticism. Indeed, this proposition rings true irrespective of whether the particular test at issue concerns unreasonable searches and seizure and the Fourth Amendment, affirmative action and the equal protection guarantee, the regulation of abortion against the backdrop of due process protections, the extent of national legislative authority under the commerce power, or the panoply of other judicial efforts to articulate principles intended to guide and circumscribe both the adjudication of constitutional cases and the conduct of government that can give rise to such cases. Yet, even considered alongside the judicial standards crafted out of efforts to be faithful to the constitutional sources implicated in these other disputed areas, the *Lemon* test has ignited an unusually wide range of hostility from a wide range of sources, including sitting members of the very Court responsible for creating and applying it. Such an outpouring continues to fuel the periodic speculation that the test soon will be put out to pasture. Nevertheless, no majority opinion of the Court has expressly rejected the three-pronged tool. Nor has a majority of the justices ever agreed upon the measure of assessment that would replace the *Lemon* test. To be sure, every now and then the Court ignores *Lemon*, self-consciously refraining from applying it to a limited number of anti-establishment challenges. And, yes, the justices—both collectively and in their individual capacities—have worked some modest changes in the test, imposing some jurisprudential spin to the different prongs. For the most part, however, the test announced in *Lemon* persists in meandering through the contemporary jurisprudence of anti-establishment, a testament less to its inherent soundness than to the inability of its critics to muster agreement on a suitable replacement around which to coalesce.

Will the *Lemon* test remain the touchstone for anti-establishment analysis as we move through the twenty-first century? Will the test, instead, be set aside, supplanted by a new and different measuring stick? And, if some new and different constitutional standard for assessing anti-establishment challenges indeed emerges, will that standard be *more* or *less* tolerant of governmental action that advances religion? Even those among us who possess rare and distinctive psychic powers would find these questions difficult.

ONE SIDE OF THE ANTI-ESTABLISHMENT COIN: RELIGION IN GOVERNMENT

As noted above, a feature common to many cases adjudicated under the anti-establishment principle is that religion, in some form or another, has been invited into the institutions of government. Often that institution of government happens to be the public school. Sometimes, however, the institution turns out to be the legislative chamber or merely property owned or operated by government. This chapter begins by exploring the evolution and current status of this dimension of anti-establishment law.

Religion in Public Education (I): School Prayer

Beginning at the height of the Cold War and continuing up through today, the nation's highest court repeatedly has confronted efforts to infuse aspects of religion into public school classrooms and ceremonies. One set of efforts has concerned the impulse to introduce prayer of some form into elementary and secondary public schools. The Court consistently has deployed the anti-establishment guarantee to rebuff these efforts, though each time it has done so at least one justice—and, increasingly in our own time, a group more numerous than one—has expressed strong displeasure with the Court's understanding and exposition of both anti-establishment principles and the application of those principles to the particular context of school prayer.

Government-composed Prayer

The Court's initial encounter with the school prayer issue would set the justices on a course from which they would not materially stray for four decades. (Engel v. Vitale, 1962).[7] That course would manifest profound skepticism about the constitutional legitimacy of efforts to invite prayer into the American public school.

This initial encounter emerged out of New York. New York's Board of Regents, the statewide governing body responsible for public education, drafted the following prayer and encouraged local school districts in turn to have students recite it in the classroom: *"Almighty God, we acknowledge our dependence upon Thee, and we beg Thy blessings upon us, our parents, our teachers and our Country."*[8] One local school board directed that the prayer be recited daily, excusing from participation children whose parents objected. Shortly thereafter, a group of parents whose children attended school within the district challenged *both* the state law authorizing school districts to deploy the prayer *and* the district's decision to accept the invitation.

The Supreme Court invalidated the practice, finding it "wholly inconsistent with" the anti-establishment principle.[9] In so doing the Court's majority, speaking through Justice Hugo Black, observed that whatever else the anti-establishment guarantee meant it "must at least mean that in this country it is no part of the business of government to compose official prayers for any group of the American people to recite as a part of a religious program carried on by government."[10] In short, in the eyes of the justices the fact that government officials undertook to compose a prayer for the state's public school students represented the most glaring constitutional flaw of the New York practice.

The Court's majority devoted a substantial portion of its opinion seeking to explain and justify, through the lens of American history, the insuperable anti-establishment problem with government-composed prayer. According to the majority, the very conduct engaged in by New York officials in the case accounted for one reason that prompted the colonists to leave England several centuries earlier and settle in America. For, as Justice Black observed, Parliament's approval of The Book of Common Prayer in the middle of the sixteenth century had played a significant role in inducing Puritans who unsuccessfully had sought changes in the Book eventually to make their way to America.

Out of this historical synthesis the *Engel* majority extracted the following constitutional lesson:

> The First Amendment was added to the Constitution to stand as a guarantee that neither the power nor the prestige of the Federal Government would be used to control, support or influence the kinds of prayer the American people can say—that the people's religions

> must not be subjected to the pressures of government for change each time a new political administration is elected to office. Under the Amendment's prohibition against governmental establishment of religion . . . government in this country, be it state or federal, is without power to prescribe by law any particular form of prayer which is to be used as an official prayer in carrying on any program of governmentally sponsored religious activity.[11]

First and most fundamentally, therefore, *Engel* contributes to anti-establishment law the proposition that government-composed or government-prescribed prayers pose serious and substantial constitutional problems. But the case contributes more than merely that constitutional nugget.

In the course of its discussion the majority paused to consider—and reject—two arguments put forth by the school district to justify the constitutionality of the practice under scrutiny. The first of these arguments concerned the fact that the particular prayer at issue was essentially "nondenominational" and thus did not discriminate *among* religions. The second emphasized the fundamentally noncoercive nature of the New York practice, given the fact that pupils whose families wished to have them excused from the state-imposed recitation could be excused from participation. The Court's rejection of these arguments, and its explanations for doing so, contribute measurably to current understandings of the meaning of the anti-establishment guarantee. In addition, this pair of arguments, though attracting little sympathy from the justices who decided *Engel*, would come to earn more serious consideration over the next generation, as a new generation of justices would continue the struggle over how best to effectuate the core concerns of the anti-establishment principle.

As to the first point, the contention that the "nondenominational" nature of the prayer should militate in favor of its permissibility, the *Engel* majority readily conceded that the New York prayer did not constitute an establishment of a particular religious sect. Indeed, Justice Black candidly acknowledged that the prayer at issue "seem[ed] relatively insignificant"[12] when compared to governmental encroachments on religious freedom going back a few centuries. Nevertheless, the majority, quoting James Madison, indicated that today's seemingly insignificant and nondenominational incursion, left unchecked, could well evolve into tomorrow's unequivocal establishment.[13]

The majority likewise rejected the notion that an individual student's ability to stand silently while others recited or to leave the room altogether mitigated the anti-establishment problem by sapping the circumstances of any governmental coercion. The Court rejected this argument in two quite different ways. First, Justice Black maintained that in order for the concerns on which the anti-establishment guarantee rests to kick in no "direct governmental compulsion" need be afoot, no proof need be adduced that individual nonbelievers altered their conduct as a result of government inducement.[14] In short, the Court made clear that a violation of the anti-establishment guarantee did not depend upon evidence of government coercion. At the same time, however, the majority paused to note the "indirect coercive pressure"[15] suffusing the New York practice. Justice Black observed that "[w]hen the power, prestige and financial support of government is placed behind a particular religious belief, the indirect coercive pressure upon religious minorities to conform to the prevailing officially approved religion is plain."[16]

We noted earlier that each Supreme Court case devoted to issues of school prayer has featured at least one member of the Court expressing dismay at the conclusion and implications of the Court's resistance to the practice. *Engel* represents the first of these phenomena. Justice Potter Stewart, planting a jurisprudential seed that would blossom more fully over the course of a generation, mused about what an unfortunate turn of events his colleagues had wrought by their action in *Engel*. An observation toward the beginning of the dissent captures nicely the core of Justice Stewart's discomfort:

> I cannot see how an "official religion" is established by letting those who want to say a prayer say it. On the contrary, I think that to deny the wish of these schoolchildren to join in reciting this prayer is to deny them the opportunity of sharing in the spiritual heritage of our Nation.[17]

The Stewart dissent took particular issue with *both* the majority's historical effort to analogize the New York Board of Regents Prayer to the English Book of Common Prayer *and* its disregard for what to Justice Stewart represented a longstanding national heritage of presidents, Congresses, and courts to interweave religious practices, values, and references into the institutions of American government.[18] Within a few decades, the perspective reflected in the Stewart dissent gradually would assume a more prominent role, both in the anti-establishment case law and throughout American politics and culture more generally. As of yet, however, that perspective continues to find itself on the losing end of Supreme Court decisions assessing the constitutionality of school prayer.

Bible Reading

As noted above, *Engel* represented the first of several High Court looks at the constitutional issues implicated by prayer in the public schools. The case likewise reflected the first of a series of high court conclusions revealing that, at least in the justices' view, a proper understanding of anti-establishment principles forecloses such practices.

A year after *Engel*, the Court confronted a Pennsylvania law that required ten or more verses from "the Holy Bible" be read at the beginning of each public school day, followed by the recitation of the Lord's Prayer (School District of Abington Township v. Schempp, 1963).[19] Siblings Roger and Donna Schempp attended Abington Senior High School, where each morning during homeroom a group of students would recite over the school's intercom system Holy Bible verses selected by the reciting students. Following that reading, students throughout the building, including those reciting over the intercom, would repeat the Lord's Prayer. Pursuant to the law, participation in the exercises remained voluntary.

The Schempp family, members of the Unitarian faith, challenged the law as an infringement on anti-establishment principles. As had been the case in *Engel*, the nation's highest court agreed that the challenged practice indeed clashed with such principles.

Speaking through Justice Tom Clark, the Court's majority concluded that the Pennsylvania practice clashed with "the wholesome 'neutrality' "[20] mandated by the anti-establishment principle. Among the constitutionally problematic features of the Pennsylvania practice, according to the majority, was that (1) government officials mandated readings from religious texts, (2) with the participation of teachers employed by government, (3) as part of what the majority insisted were the curricular activities of (4) students required by law to attend school.[21] In short, for the justices, the anti-establishment concerns implicated in *Schempp* went considerably beyond those at issue in *Engel*.

As had been the case a year earlier, the Court maintained that the anti-establishment problems created by the Pennsylvania law simply could not be vitiated by the choice retained by each family to absent its children from the exercise.[22] In addition, the majority paid short shrift to the contention—one that would be voiced with increasing frequency and vigor over the next few decades—that, unless exercises such as those provided by the Pennsylvania legislature were permitted to occur in public schools, a "religion of secularism" essentially would be established.[23] To this contention the justices mustered a reply that likely struck those who pressed (and continue to press) the concern as not especially responsive: While nothing in our opinion ought be construed as forbidding government to mandate the *educational* study of the Bible for "its literary and historic qualities," the Court noted, the "religious exercises" provided for by the Pennsylvania legislature represent a far cry from those otherwise permissible curricular experiences.[24]

In the course of seeking to explain this distinction and elaborate on its view of the proper approach to anti-establishment challenges more generally, the *Schempp* majority deployed words that would prove profoundly significant for subsequent development of the law. The Court observed that a central tenet of the anti-establishment guarantee was to ensure that neither *the purpose* nor *the primary effect* of a governmental enactment be to advance or inhibit religion:

> The test may be stated as follows: what are the purpose and primary effect of the enactment? If either is the advancement or inhibition of religion then the enactment exceeds the scope of legislative power as circumscribed by the Constitution. That is to say that to withstand the strictures of the Establishment Clause there must be a secular legislative purpose and a primary effect that neither advances nor inhibits religion.[25]

This language, and in particular the talk of "purpose" and "effect," would serve as the lynchpin of the landmark anti-establishment "test" that would be enunciated in *Lemon* in 1971.

The Pennsylvania school practices reviewed in *Schempp*, straightforward though they may have been, nevertheless provided an opportunity for lengthy and thoughtful conversation among the justices concerning the scope and limitations of the Constitution's protections for religious liberty.

Justice William Brennan, agreeing fully with the majority's invalidation of the Pennsylvania practices at issue, penned a lengthy concurrence in which he explored both the historical developments that produced the First Amendment and the Court's subsequent interpretation of that portion of the Constitution.[26] In the course of the concurrence Justice Brennan paused to confront, and reject, three substantial contentions put forth by those seeking to defend the Pennsylvania practice at issue in *Schempp*, contentions that continue to play a significant role on the anti-establishment stage.

The first of these focused on the charge that the practices at issue in the case served such a transparently secular purpose that whatever religious attributes attending them should be overlooked. To this Justice Brennan countered with a two-part reply. First, to the extent that the secular benefits educational administrators sought to achieve by the recitation of prayer (for instance, fostering harmony and tolerance among students, fortifying the authority of teachers, and engendering self-restraint among students) depended upon the students sharing a religious experience through religious materials, Justice Brennan opined that the anti-establishment guarantee foreclosed such benefits. Correspondingly, to the extent that such benefits resulted from a fact other than the religious nature of the experience and materials, Justice Brennan observed that educational administrators should be able to produce such benefits without deploying the stuff of religion.

The second challenge concerned the important argument that the Pennsylvania practices ought to be understood as unobjectionable because they reflected support for no *particular* religious sect over any other. To this, the nonpreferentialist argument, Justice Brennan again replied with two insights. The first was that, on the facts of *Schempp*, the contention rang a bit hollow. According to Justice Brennan, given the fact that the religious materials used at Abington High School to some considerable extent depended on the students who chose the materials, those religious sects with the most members in the student population would be preferred to those of more sparsely populated denominations. The second aspect of the Brennan reply went more directly to the heart of the nonpreferentialist claim. According to Justice Brennan, the notion of required prayer poses a constitutional problem because it offends *both* those nonbelievers to whom any version of the Bible is objectionable *and* those devout believers for whom prayer is intended to be an intensely private experience.

The third contention marshaled by the supporters of the Pennsylvania practice centered on the contention that the opt-out provision of the law mitigated any anti-establishment concern that otherwise could have existed. According to Justice Brennan, however, the fact that Pennsylvania authorities afforded students the opportunity to excuse themselves from a religiously grounded recitation was beside the point once it had been found that the recitation indeed was religiously grounded.

Justice Stewart, the sole dissenter in *Engel*, reprised that role in *Schempp*.[27] The dissent put forth a host of reasons to justify its conclusion that the majority's invalidation of the Pennsylvania practice could not withstand scrutiny. One such reason related to the fact that, according to the dissent, the majority's disposition of the case—invalidating religious exercises in the public school—placed religion "at an artificial and state-created disadvantage" and promoted "a religion of secularism,"[28] thereby clashing conspicuously with the notion of government "neutrality" toward matters religious. A second had to do with the dissent's contention that the sorts of dangers that typically attend government support of religion could not be found in the case, in part because the Bible readings unfolded without comments from teachers that otherwise might constitute instruction.[29] A third objection centered on the observation that the opt-out provision rendered it difficult to discern any genuine coercion at work on any student who harbored a desire to refrain from participating in the exercise.[30] As in *Engel*, however, the Stewart dissent in *Schempp* represented a lone voice, one singing a strikingly different tune from that sung by the other members of the judicial chorus.

Moments of Silence

The constitutional aspects of prayer in America's public schools range well beyond the issues of the recitation of government-composed verbiage that acknowledges God's existence and mandatory Bible reading. Two decades after the justices deployed the weapon of the anti-establishment guarantee to invalidate such practices, the high court returned to confront a more contemporary incarnation of the school prayer issue. This time around, the context concerned an unusual twist on what recently has come to be called the "moment of silence" issue.

Some background will prove useful in order to grasp precisely what the justices have and have not declared with regard to the moment-of-silence issue. That background concerns three laws enacted by Alabama in a four-year stretch from 1978 to 1982.

The first of the three provided as follows:

> At the commencement of the first class each day in the first through the sixth grade in all public schools, the teacher in charge of the room in which such class is held shall announce that a period of silence, not to exceed one minute in duration, shall be observed for meditation, and during any such period silence shall be maintained and no activities engaged in.[31]

In short, this first Alabama enactment mandated a straightforward moment of silence that would begin the public school day for children in first through sixth grades.

The second Alabama enactment served to amend the first. This second law provided as follows:

> At the commencement of the first class each day in the first through sixth grade in all public schools, the teacher in charge of the room in which such class is held shall announce that a period of silence not to exceed one minute in duration shall be observed for meditation or voluntary prayer, and during any such period no other activities shall be engaged in.[32]

This second law, by inserting the language of "or voluntary prayer" into the portion of the law that characterized the state's justification for the moment of silence, the way in which it wished students to observe the silence, explicitly noted that for the duration of the silence students could opt to spend the time engaging in (silent, of course) prayer as well as meditation.

The last of Alabama's enactments provided as follows:

> From henceforth, any teacher or professor in any public educational institution within the state of Alabama, recognizing that the Lord God is one, at the beginning of any homeroom or any class, may pray, may lead willing students in prayer, or may lead the willing students in the following prayer to God:
>
> > "Almighty God, You alone are our God. We acknowledge You as the Creator and Supreme Judge of the world. May Your justice, Your truth, and Your peace abound this day in the hearts of our countrymen, in the counsels of our government, in the sanctity of our homes and in the classrooms of our schools in the name of our Lord. Amen."[33]

This third enactment, of course, went considerably beyond the pair that preceded it. It explicitly acknowledged the existence of God. It explicitly acknowledged a particular kind of God. It explicitly authorized public school teachers to engage in prayer—aloud as well as silently—with their students. It explicitly passed along a particular government-sponsored prayer in which teachers could choose to lead their students.

Ishmael Jaffree challenged the public school practices invited by these laws on behalf of his three minor children, one a kindergarten student and the other two second graders. Prior to the case arriving at the Supreme Court, two preliminary developments unfolded that would sharpen the contributions the case would make to the constitutional law of school prayer. First, Jaffree "abandoned" his challenge to the first enactment—the straightforward moment-of-silence law—in the face of the trial court's conclusion that such a law posed no problem with anti-establishment principles. Second, an initial round of litigation established that the third enactment clashed with core anti-establishment principles, essentially because the legislature rooted the law in the impermissible purpose of seeking to advance religion. Accordingly, the Court took on and proceeded to invalidate the second enactment, the amended law that had added the words "or voluntary prayer" to the initial enactment (Wallace v. Jaffree, 1985).[34]

The Court's treatment of this Alabama moment of silehce "for meditation or voluntary prayer" enactment continued the justices' tradition of holding unconstitutional a variety of government-sponsored efforts to introduce prayer into the public schools. That treatment, however, drew heavily on the strikingly unusual history of the Alabama law.

An important part of that history, according to the majority opinion of Justice Stevens, included the candid representation of the law's principal sponsor that the statutory enterprise that culminated in the "for meditation or voluntary prayer" enactment indeed constituted an "effort to return voluntary prayer" to Alabama's public schools.[35] This representation, coupled with the Court's observation that in endeavoring to defend the constitutionality of the enactment lawyers for Alabama put forth no evidence at all that could lead the justices to find *any* secular purpose undergirding the law, made the case an easy one for the majority—at least with *Lemon* as its guide. It concluded that "[t]he wholly religious character of [the law] is plainly evident from its text"[36] and thus reasoned that it need not pursue the constitutional analysis beyond the first of *Lemon*'s three prongs. In short, the absence of any genuinely secular purpose for amending the first law to add the words "or voluntary prayer" spelled doom for the enactment. Justice Stevens, in reaching this conclusion, noted that while students of course retained the right to engage in voluntary silent prayer at appropriate times throughout the school day—a right the Alabama legislature had made clear in its previous enactment concerning "meditation"—the explicit reference to "voluntary prayer" in the subsequent law revealed that Alabama "intended to characterize prayer as a favored practice."[37] This intention, the Court observed, clashed with the "complete neutrality" government must maintain toward religion.[38]

The case produced three dissents, each one speaking exclusively for its author. Chief Justice Warren Burger, echoing a political and cultural voice that would grow louder in the ensuing decades, expressed the view that the invalidation of a moment-of-silence statute that expressly invited prayer "manifests not neutrality but hostility toward religion."[39] Justice Byron White sought to expose the hypocrisy of his colleagues who voted to invalidate the Alabama law, contending that, under their logic, an otherwise constitutional moment-of-silence law that failed to mention prayer as a permissible way of passing the time magically would be transformed into an anti-establishment problem were a student to inquire of a teacher whether the student could pray during the moment, and the teacher reply in the affirmative.[40]

It nevertheless fell to Justice William Rehnquist to contribute the most provocative and wide-ranging of the trio of dissents. The Rehnquist dissent, devoted principally to reviewing the history out of which the religion clauses emerged, boldly contended that the Court's anti-establishment jurisprudence had been off target from its inception.[41] In particular, Justice Rehnquist contended that the "wall of separation" metaphor that had crept into the case law devoted to the religion clauses, and the *Lemon* test that subsequently emerged out of that metaphor, served to steer the Court's jurisprudence substantially off its proper course. To Justice Rehnquist, the purposes of the anti-establishment guarantee could not be more modest or straightforward: to forbid government to establish a religion or to discriminate among religious sects. According to Justice Rehnquist, however, the guarantee assuredly does *not* require government to assume a neutral role between the institutions of religion and irreligion. Nor does it, Justice Rehnquist maintained, foreclose government from using religious institutions or practices to achieve legitimate secular ends. For those latter reasons, Justice Rehnquist concluded, the anti-establishment guarantee in no way prevents Alabama from advising its students that they are free to engage in prayer during a morning moment of silence. Justice Rehnquist strenuously urged his colleagues to abandon the *Lemon* test and return to what he contended represented a more accurate and circumscribed understanding of the anti-establishment guarantee.

Wallace represents the sole Supreme Court case dealing with the merits of an anti-establishment challenge to laws with moment-of-silence features. For that reason, it remains important to refrain from reading too much into the Court's disposition of the Alabama dispute. The particular law invalidated in *Wallace* exhibited a distinctively unusual constitutional flaw, at least in the eyes of the justices who found that it clashed with anti-establishment principles: No purpose other than to advance the cause of religion could account for why the legislature self-consciously added the words "or voluntary prayer" to an already existing moment-of-silence law. Accordingly, it would be unwise, and almost surely erroneous, to make the leap from *Wallace* to the conclusion that straightforward moment-of-silence laws either offend the anti-establishment guarantee or would be found by the current Court to do so. Quite the contrary. Indeed, a majority of the justices who participated in *Wallace* itself—including two who voted to invalidate the law at issue there—made clear that a straightforward moment-of-silence law, such as the first of the three Alabama laws discussed above, would withstand anti-establishment scrutiny. Without question a majority of the current justices, and in all likelihood a substantial majority, shares that view.

Prayer at Graduation Ceremonies

Government-composed prayer, recitations from the Bible and the Lord's Prayer, an unusual juxtaposition of moment-of-silence laws—such had been the triggers that occasioned the Supreme Court's interaction with matters of school prayer, at least until the 1990s. Seven years after *Wallace* a sharply divided Court reinforced and refined the lessons of these earlier school prayer decisions in a Rhode Island case devoted to prayer at graduation ceremonies (Lee v. Weisman, 1992).[42]

The Court encountered a policy of the Providence school district that authorized public school principals to invite members of the clergy to participate in graduation ceremonies. Pursuant to the practice, in June of 1989, the principal of Nathan Bishop Middle School invited a local rabbi to deliver the invocation and benediction at the school's graduation exercises, providing the rabbi a pamphlet recommending that such prayers be inclusive and sensitive.

At the graduation exercises, the rabbi proceeded to usher in the ceremony with the following invocation:

> God of the Free, Hope of the Brave:
>
> For the legacy of America where diversity is celebrated and the rights of minorities are protected, we thank You. May these young men and women grow up to enrich it.
>
> For the liberty of America, we thank You. May these new graduates grow up to guard it.
>
> For the political process of America in which all its citizens may participate, for its court system where all may seek justice we thank You. May those we honor this morning always turn to it in trust.
>
> For the destiny of America we thank You. May the graduates of Nathan Bishop Middle School so live that they might help to share it.
>
> May our aspirations for our country and for these young people, who are our hope for the future, be richly fulfilled.[43]

The rabbi closed the ceremonies with similar sentiments:

> O God, we are grateful to You for having endowed us with the capacity for learning which we have celebrated on this joyous commencement. Happy families give thanks for seeing their children achieve an important milestone. Send Your blessings upon the teachers and administrators who helped prepare them. The graduates now need strength and guidance for the future, help them to understand that we are not complete with academic knowledge alone. We must each strive to fulfill what You require of us all: To do justly, to love mercy, to walk humbly. We give thanks to You, Lord, for keeping us alive, sustaining us and allowing us to reach this special, happy occasion.[44]

To many readers and listeners, the rabbi's words no doubt come across as relatively tame and inclusive stuff. Four days prior to the ceremonies, however, Daniel Weisman, the father of a fourteen-year-old female middle school student, instituted an action seeking to prevent the upcoming event from including an invocation or benediction. The trial court denied the request, citing inadequate time to consider it. For that reason, the ceremonies unfolded as planned. Shortly thereafter, however, Weisman sought a permanent injunction that would bar the school district from inviting clergy to deliver invocations or benedictions at future graduations. The Supreme Court, dividing five to four, agreed with Weisman, invalidating the practice as inconsistent with the anti-establishment guarantee.

The majority opinion of Justice Anthony Kennedy pointed to the combination of two facts that, for the majority of justices, compelled the conclusion that the Rhode Island practice clashed with constitutional norms.

One such fact was that attendance at graduation exercises, though not compulsory in any formal sense, nonetheless was among one of the most significant rites of passage for any youngster, sufficiently significant that attendance, according to the majority, was essentially "obligatory."[45] In other words, the overriding importance of public school graduation ceremonies contained one key piece to the anti-establishment puzzle. The second had to do with the fact that a practice the majority characterized as "state-sponsored" religious activity occurred at the graduation exercises.[46] The confluence of these two facts—state-sponsored religious exercises at an event so important as to be deemed essentially obligatory—prompted the majority to conclude that the practice essentially coerced unwilling attendees into participating (even by remaining silent) in a religious practice.

The case likewise prompted both those who joined the reasoning expressed by the majority and those who opposed such reasoning to elaborate at length on their views of the meaning of the anti-establishment guarantee. In particular, Justice David Souter (who agreed with the majority's disposition of the case) and Justice Antonin Scalia (who did not) took the opportunity to share their thoughts about the proper meaning to be ascribed to the constitutional language and history.

Justice Souter, joined by Justices Stevens and O'Connor, used the occasion to underscore his disagreement with the nonpreferentialist view of the First Amendment, the view that had been espoused most powerfully by Justice Rehnquist in *Wallace*. The Souter concurrence endeavored to justify the continued rejection of the nonpreferentialist position on two grounds: precedent and history. In connection with the former, Justice Souter observed as follows:

> [W]e have consistently held the Clause applicable no less to governmental acts favoring religion generally than to acts favoring one religion over another. . . . Such is the settled law. Here, as elsewhere, we should stick to it absent some compelling reason to discard it.[47]

But Justice Souter's defense of the Court's long-standing rejection of nonpreferentialism went beyond the mere fact that the Court consistently had rejected the argument. Venturing back to colonial days, Justice Souter directly challenged the historical account of the religion clauses Justice Rehnquist had offered in *Wallace*. At the conclusion of this historical review Justice Souter summed up his findings as follows:

> What we thus know of the Framers' experience underscores the [view] that confining the Establishment Clause to a prohibition on preferential aid "requires a premise that the Framers were extraordinarily bad drafters—that they believed one thing but adopted language that said something substantially different, and that they did so after repeatedly at-

tending to the choice of language." . . . We must presume, since there is no conclusive evidence to the contrary, that the Framers embraced the significance of their textual judgment. Thus, on balance, history neither contradicts nor warrants reconsideration of the settled principle that the Establishment Clause forbids support for religion in general no less than support for one religion or some.[48]

In short, according to Justice Souter, *both* the concerns that initially produced the anti-establishment guarantee *and* the case law construing that guarantee reveal that government action (such as the invocation and benediction at issue in *Lee*) can clash with anti-establishment principles even when that action (again, such as the invocation and benediction at issue) does not manifest a preference for one religious sect over another.

By contrast, Justice Scalia, joined by three colleagues, employed a vigorous dissent to make a range of strikingly different points, of which the following two stand out. First and foremost, Scalia lambasted his colleagues in the majority for a decision that "lays waste" to the long-standing American tradition of "nonsectarian prayer to God at public celebrations generally."[49] The invocations and benedictions the majority sought to declare off-limits from now onward, Justice Scalia observed, happen to be the very sorts of invocations and benedictions that have been uttered at American public ceremonies, including public school graduation ceremonies, for nearly two centuries. Second, Justice Scalia scoffed at the majority's insistence that any modicum of coercion suffuses the circumstances of prayer at graduation ceremonies. The only conduct even arguably "coerced" by the invocation and benediction, Justice Scalia contended, was that nonbelieving students may have been induced to stand and maintain a respectful silence—hardly the sort of "coercion" amounting to a constitutional problem. Justice Scalia's unhappiness with both the decision of his colleagues and what he believed to be the analytic shortcomings of that decision led him to pass along the following invitation toward the conclusion of the dissent:

Given the odd basis for the Court's decision, invocations and benedictions will be able to be given at public school graduations next June, as they have for the past century and a half, so long as school authorities make clear that anyone who abstains from screaming in protest does not necessarily participate in the prayers. All that is seemingly needed is an announcement, or perhaps a written insertion at the beginning of the graduation program, to the effect that, while all are asked to rise for the invocation and benediction, none is compelled to join in them, nor will be assumed, by rising, to have done so. That obvious fact recited, the graduates and their parents may proceed to thank God, as Americans have always done, for the blessings He has generously bestowed on them and their country.[50]

As the dust from this important case settled, therefore, three developments stood out. First, the Court continued its long-standing practice of invoking anti-establishment principles to resist allowing prayer to play a role in public school events and activities. Second, the chorus of dissent expressing dismay with such a development had grown in volume and intensity, creating a deep chasm separating the groups. Third, the *Lemon* test—supposedly the touchstone for all anti-establishment analysis—played essentially no role in the majority's analysis, engendering doubt as to both the enduring value of that test and the role it would continue to play in matters relating to school prayer.

Prayer at Public School Football Games

The Court undertook its most recent treatment of the school prayer issue in connection with a New Mexico case featuring student-led prayer at high school football games. In invalidating the school district's policy, the Court's majority borrowed a good deal from its prior analysis of graduation ceremonies in the Rhode Island case (Santa Fe Independent School District v. Doe, 2000).[51]

The precise practice at issue had emerged from a complicated history within the Santa Fe school district. Prior to 1995, the Santa Fe High School student who occupied the elective office of student council chaplain had delivered a prayer over the school's public address system prior to each varsity football game. Litigation challenging that practice prompted the district to change its policy. In essence, the revised policy authorized the high school student body to determine by vote whether to feature invocations prior to football games and, if so, to choose a student to deliver such invocations. A divided Court held the revised policy unconstitutional.

The majority, speaking through Justice Stevens, grounded its conclusion that such a practice clashed with anti-establishment concerns in a range of justifications.

First, the majority rejected the district's contention that the arguably student-initiated invocations constituted *private* speech rather than *government* speech and that, as a result, the anti-establishment principle should not be construed to prohibit the practice.[52] The majority sought to justify and explain its rejection of this argument by pointing to a variety of aspects of the Santa Fe experience.

One was that these student-led invocations, despite the seemingly private act of individual initiative, just so happened to be "authorized by a government policy and take place on government property at government-sponsored school-related events."[53]

A second was that the school allowed only a single student, selected by the majority, to deliver the invocations.[54] This aspect of the policy led the majority to conclude that student candidates representing minority religions were unlikely to prevail and that, for this reason, only the religious perspective of the dominant majority would be voiced in the invocations.

A third factor undergirding the majority's rejection of the argument was its conclusion that the school district had failed to adequately divorce itself from the religious content of the invocations.[55] In short, the majority distilled from the history and operation of the Santa Fe policy the notion that the school district's actions came substantially closer to "endorsing" the religious aspects of the invocations than to maintaining "neutrality" with regard to them. The majority pointed to a cluster of facts to account for its conclusion that the district was anything but "neutral" with regard to the invocations, among them that (1) the school board itself formulated the practice in the first place; (2) the stated policy provided that one of the purposes of the invocations was to "solemnize" the event; and (3) the invocation was delivered at a school-sponsored function over a public address system that remained subject to the control of school officials.[56]

A second important aspect of the majority's explanation concerned its treatment of the purported differences between two sorts of public school activities: graduation exercises and football games. The majority rejected the district's request that the Court carve out a distinction of constitutional magnitude between public school football games and public school graduation exercises, with the purported distinction grounded in the asserted difference in the "voluntariness" of the two activities.[57] In rejecting this distinction, the majority made clear that "the delivery of a pregame prayer has the improper effect of coercing those present to participate in an act of religious worship"—echoing the central message of *Lee* to the effect that prayer at graduation exercises suffered from analogous "coercive" tendencies.

As noted earlier, no important Supreme Court case devoted to the issue of school prayer has emerged without a dissent. Santa Fe v. Doe proved no exception to the rule. Accusing his colleagues of producing an opinion whose tone "bristles with hostility to all things religious in public life,"[58] Chief Justice Rehnquist, joined by two colleagues, assumed the dissenting role in this most recent of school prayer decisions. The dissent's critique of the majority's handiwork in the case focused on two aspects of the majority opinion.

A central portion of the Rehnquist dissent criticized the majority's unwillingness to acknowledge the plausible secular purpose for the district's policy. According to the dissent, the explanation the district provided to account for the policy—"to solemnize the event, to promote good sportsmanship and student safety, and to establish the appropriate environment for the competition"[59]—more than satisfied the *Lemon* requirement of a secular purpose.

In addition, the dissent chided the majority for applying the logic of *Lee* in a context in which, according to the chief justice, logic simply did not fit. The dissent put it this way:

> In *Lee*, we concluded that the content of the speech at issue, a graduation prayer given by a rabbi, was "directed and controlled" by a school official. . . . In other words, at issue in *Lee* was *government* speech. Here, by contrast, the potential speech at issue . . . would be a message or invocation selected or created by a student. That is . . . *private* speech.[60]

Despite the valiant efforts of the dissent, the Court refused to deviate from its long-standing anti-establishment objection to prayer in public school or at public school events.

The Pledge of Allegiance

The opening decade of the twenty-first century finds one other aspect of the school prayer issue consuming widespread national attention: the implications of anti-establishment principles for the Pledge of Allegiance and laws and practices relating to the Pledge. Indeed, the explosive debate ignited by efforts to invalidate the Pledge on anti-establishment grounds has become yet another colorful battle in our nation's contemporary culture wars.

The Pledge originally came about in the late nineteenth century as part of an effort to commemorate the 400th anniversary of the discovery of America by Christopher Columbus.[61] Half a century later, in the midst of World War II, Congress codified the Pledge, whose content at that time read: "I pledge allegiance to the flag of the United States of America and to the Republic for which it stands, one Nation indivisible, with liberty and justice for all."[62] Twelve years later, as the Cold War intensified, Congress self-consciously amended the Pledge by adding the words "under God" prior to the word "indivisible."[63] For the last half century, therefore, the Pledge has contained an unmistakable reference to the Almighty.

California law governing education requires public schools to begin each school day with "appropriate patriotic exercises."[64] California law also provides that recitation of the Pledge of Allegiance satisfies the requirement of "appropriate patriotic exercises."[65] Accordingly, the Elk Grove Unified School District, located just outside of Sacramento, promulgated a policy mandating that each elementary school class recite the Pledge once each day. The policy excuses from the recitation students who object to the Pledge on religious grounds.

In 2000, Michael Newdow—a self-professed atheist whose daughter attended public school in Elk Grove—filed suit, alleging that *both* the 1954 congressional law inserting the language of "under God" *and* the Elk Grove policy clashed with anti-establishment principles. The defendants Newdow chose to sue included the United States Congress, the president of the United States, the state of California, the Elk Grove district and its superintendent, and the Sacramento School District and its superintendent.

Among the facts emerging as the case unfolded was that Newdow and Sandra Banning, the mother of his daughter, had never married and that the superficially conventional joint custody arrangement in place to care for their daughter contained a provision granting Banning final say over decisions regarding the daughter's health, welfare, and educational needs in the event that the parents could not forge agreement. In addition, as the course of the litigation unfolded, Banning contended that the daughter on whose behalf Newdow purported to be proceeding was a Christian who believed in God and harbored no objection either to reciting the Pledge or having others recite it in her presence. These developments eventually would assume a role of substantial magnitude as the case unfolded in the nation's highest court four years down the road.

In June 2002, a three-judge panel of the United States Court of Appeals for the Ninth Circuit issued the first of its decisions concerning Michael Newdow's constitutional challenge (Newdow v. United States Congress, 2002 ("*Newdow I*")).[66] That decision concluded that *both* the 1954 federal law *and* the Elk Grove policy clashed with anti-establishment principles, and by three distinct measures. The Ninth Circuit panel concluded that these pieces of law could not withstand scrutiny under *Lemon*, constituted impermissible endorsements of religion in violation of Justice Sandra Day O'Connor's "no endorsement" principle, and likewise engendered the kind of unconstitutional coercion against which Justice Kennedy and the *Lee* majority claimed the anti-establishment principle was principally aimed.

The *Newdow I* panel began by expressing its view that both the 1954 federal law and the school district policy represented an impermissible endorsement of religion:

> [The 1954 federal law] is a profession of religious belief, namely, a belief in monotheism. The recitation that ours is a nation "under God" is not a mere acknowledgment that many Americans believe in a deity. Nor is it merely descriptive of the undeniable historical significance of religion in the founding of the Republic. Rather, the phrase "one nation under God" in the context of the Pledge is normative. To recite the Pledge is . . . to swear allegiance to the values for which the Flag stands: unity, indivisibility, liberty, justice, and—since 1954—monotheism. The text of the official Pledge, codified in federal law, impermissibly takes a position with respect to the purely religious question of the existence and identity of God. . . . Furthermore, the school district's practice of teacher-led recitation of the Pledge aims to inculcate in students a respect for the ideals set forth in the Pledge, and thus amounts to state endorsement of these ideals. Although students cannot be forced to participate in the recitation of the Pledge, the school district is nonetheless conveying a message of state endorsement of a religious belief when it requires public school teachers to recite, and lead the recitation of, the current form of the Pledge.[67]

The panel thus concluded that, as currently codified, the Pledge sends a message to nonbelievers "that they are outsiders, not full members of the political community"[68]—the central mischief against which the "no endorsement" approach endeavors to protect.

The panel likewise held that the Pledge and the school district policy mandating teacher-led recitation of it amount to unconstitutional coercion. As the court put, "to an atheist or a believer in certain non-Judeo-Christian religions, [the recitation of the Pledge] may reasonably appear to be an attempt to enforce a 'religious orthodoxy' of monotheism."[69] These sentiments, the court noted, may prove especially likely to be experienced by students in the elementary school setting, given the age and impressionability of youngsters.[70] The court sought to buttress its conclusion regarding coercion by observing that President Eisenhower himself, during the ceremony in which he signed into law the 1954 Act, expressly noted that "[f]rom this day forward . . . millions of our school children will daily proclaim . . . the dedication of our Nation and our people to the Almighty."[71]

Insofar as the three-part *Lemon* test itself was concerned, the Ninth Circuit panel concluded that the 1954 insertion of the words "under God" lacked a secular purpose and thus could not withstand anti-establishment scrutiny.[72] Those seeking to defend the Pledge and its recitation contended that the Pledge rested on the eminently secular purpose of "solemnizing public occasions, expressing the confidence in the future, and encouraging the recognition of what is worthy of appreciation in society."[73] The court rejected such a contention, chiding defendants for conveniently glossing over the very language of the 1954 Act inserting the words "under God." As the majority put it:

> [t]he [1954] Act's *sole* purpose was to advance religion, in order to differentiate the United States from nations under communist rule. . . . [Congress inserted the new words] to support the existence and moral authority of God, while "deny[ing] . . . atheistic and materialistic concepts."[74]

Such a purpose, the court concluded, clashes fundamentally with *Lemon*'s mandate that government action be rooted in a secular purpose.

In short, *Newdow I* represented a decisive constitutional rejection of both the Pledge and the school district policy mandating its daily recitation—a rejection sufficiently inclusive to take into account the variety of idiosyncratic anti-establishment tests favored by different members and coalitions of the nation's highest court.

Public reaction to *Newdow I* emerged quickly and predictably. Congress and President Bush each condemned the opinion within one day of its release.[75] Eight months later—in all likelihood chastened by the uproar its handiwork had triggered—the Ninth Circuit backtracked a bit from its earlier analysis (Newdow v. United States Congress, 2003 ("*Newdow II*")).[76] The amended opinion in *Newdow II* deleted entirely that portion of its prior decision devoted to the 1954 federal law through which the "under God" language had been added. Instead, *Newdow II* rested its anti-establishment conclusion on the ground that the Elk Grove policy mandating daily recitation of the Pledge in its elementary schools amounted to unconstitutional coercion.

In October 2003, the Supreme Court of the United States announced that it would enter the maelstrom and devote its resources to deciding the case.[77] In connection with its grant of certiorari the justices ordered briefing on two issues: first, whether, given the unusual custody arrangement, plaintiff Michael Newdow had "standing"—a sufficient stake in the outcome of the dispute to justify the Court expending its resources to decide the merits of the matter; and, second, whether the Elk Grove policy clashed with anti-establishment principles.[78] Oral argument took place in March 2004 before an eight-person Court,[79] fueling speculation that the justices could divide four to four and thereby cast a shadow of uncertainty over the constitutional status of Pledge recitations in schools all across the nation. Less than three months later, the justices delivered their decision, and with it a jurisprudential and cultural anticlimax that robbed the case of its anticipated status as a landmark ruling (Elk Grove Unified School District v. Newdow, 2004).[80]

A five-member majority dodged the core anti-establishment issue, instead opting to dispose of the case on the ground that Michael Newdow lacked standing to initiate the action. For that reason, the case makes no *formal* contribution to the ever-burgeoning law devoted to anti-establishment principles. Nevertheless, three justices—Chief Justice William Rehnquist, Justice Sandra Day O'Connor, and Justice Clarence Thomas—took advantage of the opportunity presented by the case both to lambaste their colleagues for ducking the anti-establishment issue and to themselves confront the merits of Michael Newdow's constitutional claim.

The chief justice, in a portion of his concurrence joined by Justice O'Connor, made abundantly clear that, in his view, neither the Pledge of Allegiance nor the California law requiring that the Pledge be recited daily in California schools poses even the slightest anti-establishment problem.[81] According to Chief Justice Rehnquist, the reason for such a conclusion stemmed from his premise that the Pledge and its recitation fundamentally concern patriotism rather than religion:

> I do not believe the phrase "under God" in the Pledge converts it into a "religious exercise" of the sort described in *Lee*. Instead, it is a declaration of belief in allegiance and loyalty to the United States flag and Republic that it represents. The phrase "under God" is in no sense a prayer, nor an endorsement of any religion, but a simple recognition [that] . . . "[f]rom the time of our earliest history our peoples and our institutions have reflected the traditional concept that our Nation was founded on a fundamental belief in God."[82]

In short, because the Pledge represents an exercise of patriotism rather than of religion, Chief Justice Rehnquist reasoned, the preoccupation with coercion that animated the Court in *Lee* in its consideration of prayer at graduation simply does not come into play with the recitation of the Pledge. Put slightly differently, the chief justice appeared to be saying that any coercion at work on elementary school children in connection with the recitation of the Pledge simply failed to implicate anti-establishment principles.

Justice O'Connor likewise went on record expressing the view that Pledge recitation in elementary schools falls short of an anti-establishment problem.[83] Not surprisingly, Justice O'Connor's assessment of the Elk Grove Pledge recitation policy mirrored the approach to anti-establishment challenges she had been advocating for two decades: the "no endorsement" measuring stick.

That measuring stick, Justice O'Connor reminded, means above all else that "government must not make a person's religious beliefs relevant to his or her standing in the political community by conveying a message 'that religion or a particular religious belief is favored or preferred.' "[84] Such a standard does not suggest, Justice O'Connor maintained, that government may *never* "refer to or commemorate religion in public life."[85] Rather, she contended, anti-establishment principles permit government to invoke the references of religion—such as the invocation of God in the Pledge—on a range of occasions, among them those in which such references reflect little more than secular acknowledgments of the role of religion in our history. As Justice O'Connor explained:

> [G]overnment can, in a discrete category of cases, acknowledge or refer to the divine without offending the Constitution. This category of "ceremonial deism" most clearly encompasses such things as the national motto ("In God We Trust"), religious references in traditional patriotic songs as the Star-Spangled Banner, and the words with which the Marshal of this Court opens each of its sessions ("God save the United States and this honorable Court"). These references are not minor trespasses upon the Establishment Clause to which I turn a blind eye. Instead, their history, character, and context prevent them from being constitutional violations at all.[86]

Justice O'Connor proceeded to identify four particular aspects of the Pledge of Allegiance that accounted for her conclusion that the Pledge should be understood to represent an instance of such constitutionally unproblematic ceremonial deism. First, Justice O'Connor explained that the half-century history of the Pledge as currently codified with its "under God" language coupled with the strikingly few constitutional challenges to it combine to lend credence to the argument that reasonable observers simply do not construe the Pledge as a government endorsement of religion.[87] Second, she observed that these same reasonable observers would not and do not confuse recitation of the Pledge with religious worship or prayer, entirely irrespective of the motives animating the congresspeople who in 1954 voted to insert the "under God" language.[88] Third, the absence in the Pledge of any reference to a particular religion, Justice O'Connor noted, fortifies the argument that the Pledge fails to constitute an endorsement.[89] Fourth, Justice O'Connor maintained that the fact that the Pledge's reference to God remains brief, even fleeting—constituting a mere two of the thirty-one words comprising the Pledge—likewise reveals something short of a government-sponsored endorsement of religion at work.[90]

Justice Thomas, the third of the three justices who confronted the constitutional issue ducked by the majority, used Michael Newdow's challenge to the Pledge of Allegiance to demonstrate yet again his distaste for the body of law to which his colleagues believed they owed some fidelity.[91] Justice Thomas readily acknowledged that, as anti-establishment case law stood in 2004, the Pledge of Allegiance remained vulnerable to the conclusion reached by the Ninth Circuit panel.[92] Indeed, Justice Thomas observed, given the Court's conclusion in *Lee* that impermissible coercion attended invocations and benedictions delivered at public school graduation exercises, daily recitation of the Pledge of Allegiance surely could not withstand similar "anti-coercion" analysis. For Justice Thomas, however, these truths demonstrated not the unconstitutionality of the Elk Grove policy but, instead, the fact that something remained terribly amiss with the body of rules promulgated by his brethren to govern the anti-establishment game.

Justice Thomas proceeded to urge his colleagues to wipe clean the slate of anti-establishment precedent and return to an understanding of the guarantee that, for Justice Thomas, captures more accurately the intentions of those who inserted the words into the constitutional text.[93] Quite simply, Justice Thomas contended, the guarantee meant little more than that the *national* government lacked power to establish a national religion and that the *national* government should refrain from interfering with preexisting state establishments.[94] Moreover, Justice Thomas continued, even were we to identify the sorts of "establishments" targeted by the Framers, such prohibited practices necessarily featured "actual legal coercion"—that is to say, "coercion of religious orthodoxy . . . by force of law and threat of penalty."[95] Mandating attendance at a particular church designated by government, punishing dissenters with a range of civil disabilities—these practices capture the kind of coercion against which the Framers directed the anti-establishment guarantee. Such practices, Justice Thomas observed, bear absolutely no resemblance to the coercion claims of contemporary students requested to do little more than maintain a respectful silence while an invocation or benediction gets delivered at graduation ceremonies or the Pledge of Allegiance gets recited at the beginning of the school day.[96]

The Supreme Court's treatment of the Pledge of Allegiance in Michael Newdow's case represented something of a microcosm of contemporary anti-establishment jurisprudence. The picture, to be candid, appeared none too pretty. One justice rendered himself ineligible to participate in the case by making public comments that called into question whether he could be perceived as dispensing justice fairly to Michael Newdow. Five justices seemingly apprehensive about the implications of affirming the Ninth Circuit's invalidation of Elk Grove's Pledge recitation policy took a pass on the constitutional question, opting to cower behind the issue of father Newdow's standing. The three remaining justices both chastised their colleagues and expounded three strikingly different justifications to substantiate their collective conclusion that anti-establishment principles do not bar the Elk Grove policy. In short, just another day at today's anti-establishment beach.

Our examination of the high court's treatment of the school prayer issue reveals two distinct messages, each of which emerges with reasonable clarity despite the paradox that, together, the messages produce.

First and most fundamentally, the anti-establishment guarantee consistently has been deployed as a weapon to root out prayer in, and connected to, the American public school. In short, the Court consistently exercises a watchful and skeptical eye over attempts to introduce prayer into our nation's system of public education.

Second, the justices who sit on the Supreme Court at the dawn of the twenty-first century find themselves deeply divided over the wisdom of this approach, with a chorus of justices urging a serious reconsideration of the prevailing approach. This latter undeniable fact makes it appropriate, perhaps even necessary, to remind ourselves that the decades to come conceivably could produce a Court more sympathetic to the approach to school prayer issues that has been propounded by the dissenters during the four decades in which the high court has grappled with the variety of ways in which the school prayer issue has presented itself.

Religion in Public Education (II): The Curriculum

The Origins of Mankind: Evolution and Creationism

American public schools confront a host of powerful forces when they seek to educate their students about the origins of mankind, especially when the particular school or school district places its institutional authority behind a distinctive answer to the mystery. The Constitution's anti-establishment guarantee represents one of the powerful forces at work in these circumstances. Twice the Supreme Court has ventured into the turbulent waters of creationism and evolution. Each time it has invalidated a state law that, in its view, sought to elevate a religiously sponsored theory of creation over a nonreligious theory.

The first of these ventures prompted the justices to evaluate an Arkansas law enacted during the decade fondly referred to as the roaring twenties (Epperson v. Arkansas, 1968).[97] The Court confronted an Arkansas law enacted in 1928 that forbade the state's public school teachers, including those who taught at public universities, to teach the theory that man evolved from other species of life. Susan Epperson, a tenth-grade biology teacher at an Arkansas high school, found herself in something of a dilemma as the fall of 1965 approached, and with it the new academic year. A textbook recently adopted by her school district included a chapter setting forth "the theory about the origin . . . of man from a lower form of animal."[98] According to Epperson's understanding, the school district expected her to teach from the recently adopted casebook, including teaching the chapter that, under Arkansas law, would expose her to criminal sanctions and dismissal from her job.

Not surprisingly, therefore, Epperson sought relief from the dilemma, instituting an action urging, among other things, that the law in question be invalidated as inconsistent with the anti-establishment guarantee. The high court, sidestepping some interpretive difficulty with the statutory scheme, found it unnecessary to answer the thorny question of whether the law forbade teachers such as Epperson *to explain* the theory of evolution or merely *to advocate the truth of* such theory. Either way, the Court concluded, the law clashed with the anti-establishment principle.

According to the majority opinion of Justice Abe Fortas, the constitutional flaw with the Arkansas law was that it could not be explained by any legitimate purpose apart from the legislative desire to rid Arkansas schools of an idea that happened to clash with a central aspect of religious teachings. As the majority put it, the Arkansas law:

> selects from the body of knowledge a particular segment which it proscribes for the sole reason that it is deemed to conflict with a particular religious doctrine; that is, with a particular interpretation of the Book of Genesis by a particular religious group.[99]

The Court acknowledged that states retain substantial authority to prescribe the appropriate curriculum for its public schools. But it made clear that the anti-establishment principle does not allow such authority to extend to curricular decisions that "require that teaching and learning . . . be tailored to the principles or prohibitions of any religious set or dogma."[100]

Two decades later the Court encountered another state effort to deal with the issue of mankind's origins. Once again, the Court concluded that the manner in which the state had done so proved unfaithful to anti-establishment principles (Edwards v. Aguillard, 1987).[101]

Louisiana had enacted a law, entitled "Balanced Treatment for Creation-Science and Evolution-Science in Public School Instruction," that forbade the teaching of evolution in the public school curriculum unless that instruction was accompanied by the teaching of "creation science." State officials sought to defend the law by contending that it served secular principles of academic freedom, ensuring that the two principal theories of mankind's origins be taught together in order for impressionable students to be better equipped to make decisions for themselves concerning which explanation proved more persuasive. The Court rejected that defense, suggesting it was little more than "a sham,"[102] and invalidated the law.

According to the majority opinion of Justice Brennan, careful scrutiny of the legislative history revealed that the legislature's "preeminent purpose"[103] in crafting and enacting the Balanced Treatment law had little to do with academic freedom. The Court pointed to a range of facts surrounding the passage of the law that led it to this skeptical conclusion. One such fact was that the legislative sponsor of the bill proudly acknowledged that he deplored the theory of evolution, that such sentiments were rooted in his own religious beliefs, and that whatever evidence existed supporting his religious views should be included in the public school curriculum to counter the presence of a theory antithetical to those beliefs.[104] Another fact was that the statutory guidelines promulgated along with the law strongly favored the teaching of creation science—by requiring curriculum guides for instruction in creation science but not for instruction in evolution, providing research services for instruction in creation science but not for instruction in evolution, and forbidding school boards to discriminate against teachers who opted to teach creation science while failing to offer analogous protections for those teachers who, say, refused to teach creation science or chose to teach a non-creation-science theory.[105] All this, coupled with what the Court dubbed "[the] . . .

historic and contemporaneous link between the teachings of certain religious denominations and the teaching of evolution,"[106] prompted the majority to observe that the purpose of the Louisiana law "was clearly to advance the religious viewpoint that a supernatural being created humankind."[107]

But not all the justices found the Louisiana law constitutionally problematic. Justice Scalia, joined by Chief Justice Rehnquist, issued a vigorous dissent. The dissent expressed dismay at the majority's application of *Lemon* to the Louisiana law, especially the majority's treatment of *Lemon*'s purpose prong.

According to the dissent, the majority's contention that Louisiana's Balanced Treatment Act lacked a secular purpose, and for that reason clashed with anti-establishment principles, simply could not withstand scrutiny. Justice Scalia endeavored to expose the flaws in the majority's analysis in part by exploring the legislative process out of which the act emerged. That process, according to the dissent, featured a variety of testimony from a variety of sources, including from the act's proponents. Indeed, the dissent summarized the testimony of the act's proponents as essentially reducing to five propositions:

1. There are two and only two scientific explanations for the beginning of life.
2. The body of scientific evidence supporting creation science is as strong as that supporting evolution.
3. Creation science is educationally valuable.
4. Although creation science is educationally valuable and strictly scientific, it is now being censored from or misrepresented in the public schools.
5. The censorship of creation science has harmful effects.[108]

This legislative history, the dissent observed, made it abundantly clear that the Balanced Treatment Act could not fairly be understood as lacking a secular purpose.

The dissent pointed to other places as well in its effort to undermine the majority's contention that the act must be invalidated for lack of a secular purpose. One such place to which the dissent pointed happened to be the very text of the act itself, a text that, as Justice Scalia reminded, reported that "protecting academic freedom" had been an animating purpose of the law.[109] That articulated purpose, the dissent explained, meant essentially the freedom of students "to decide for themselves how life began, based upon a fair and balanced presentation of the scientific evidence"[110]—in short, the freedom of students from unwanted indoctrination. As the dissent put it:

> We have . . . no adequate basis for disbelieving the secular purpose set forth in the Act itself, or for concluding that it is a sham enacted to conceal the legislators' violation of their oaths of office. I am astonished at the Court's unprecedented readiness to reach such a conclusion, which I can only attribute to an intellectual predisposition . . . that any gov-

ernmentally imposed requirements bearing upon the teaching of evolution must be a manifestation of Christian fundamentalist repression.[111]

Despite the dissent's provocative protestations, the Louisiana law challenged in *Edwards* met the same constitutional fate as that experienced earlier by the Arkansas law at issue in *Epperson*: death by anti-establishment.

The effort to ensure that the attention public schools devote to issues concerning the origins of mankind does not undercut the message that religions within the same community deliver to students outside of the public schools stems from a sentiment easy to understand. Families who belong to particular religious faiths tend not to want to induce confusion in their developing youngsters by exposing the youngsters to inconsistent messages about the origins of mankind. Nevertheless, the periodic efforts to infuse the curriculum of the American public school with an approach to these issues that meshes with the approach of dominant religions within the community has been thwarted by the invocation of the anti-establishment guarantee.

To some religious believers, this development embodies the hostility to all things religious to which the contemporary Court has led the Constitution, the regrettable triumph of secularism over faith. To others, such a result represents nothing more than the reality that the Constitution insists that religiously driven messages be disseminated in venues other than the American public school. These differing cultural perspectives likely will not reconcile anytime soon. For now, however, anti-establishment principles cast shadows of constitutional doubt over efforts to use the institutions of public education to inculcate students with a view of mankind's origins that comports with the view espoused by religious teachings.

Religious Symbolism in the Classroom

Closely related to the sensitive constitutional issues of school prayer and the teaching of the origins of mankind is the issue of posting items of religious significance in the public school classroom. A high court case concerning the posting of the Ten Commandments in Kentucky classrooms reveals the important role played by the anti-establishment guarantee in such circumstances (Stone v. Graham, 1980).[112]

A Kentucky law required that a copy of the Ten Commandments be posted on a wall of every elementary and secondary school classroom. The law also required that the costs of the enterprise be borne by private contributions rather than by government funds. Seeking to blunt the force of a potential constitutional challenge, the law craftily mandated as well that each such posted copy bear the notation that "The secular application of the Ten Commandments is clearly seen in its adoption as the fundamental legal code of Western Civilization and the Common Law of the United States."[113] Kentucky courts found the law entirely unproblematic, rejecting the constitutional challenge grounded in the *Lemon* test.[114] Despite the imaginative legislative effort, the Supreme Court held the law unconstitutional—and did so without even hearing argument on the merits.

The brief, unsigned opinion for the majority rested its decision principally on *Lemon*'s purpose prong. More specifically, in setting aside the conclusions of both the trial court and Kentucky's highest court that the law at issue furthered a legitimate secular purpose, the justices boldly declared that the "[p]osting of religious texts on the wall serves no educational function" and that "[t]he pre-eminent purpose for posting the Ten Commandments on schoolroom walls is plainly religious in nature."[115] The majority's reasoning, reasoning that Justice Rehnquist endeavored to skewer in dissent, appeared to rest on the notion that because (1) the Ten Commandments do not confine themselves to arguably secular matters such as honoring parents and refraining from murder and adultery, and thus (2) also include the expression of religious duties such as worshipping God alone, avoiding idolatry, refraining from using God's name in vain, and observing the Sabbath, then (3) the likely effect of such a posting will be to "induce" students "to read, meditate upon, perhaps to venerate and obey" the commandments, and such a result (4) bespeaks an impermissible governmental purpose under the anti-establishment guarantee.[116]

As suggested above, Justice Rehnquist took his colleagues in the majority to task, principally for running roughshod over the conclusions of two other courts in the majority's eagerness to conclude that no secular purpose could conceivably support a governmental decision to require the posting of the Ten Commandments in public school classrooms. The Rehnquist dissent rested on two seemingly powerful contentions.

The first was that Kentucky's legislators could well have concluded that meaningful educational benefits could accrue to elementary and secondary school students by exposing such students to a document with the huge secular influence of the Ten Commandments.[117] The second was that the anti-establishment principle does not mandate that public institutions be cleansed of all things that may have some religious significance or religious origin.[118] The dissent, which began by noting that the majority could find "no support beyond its own *ipse dixit*,"[119] concluded by dubbing the majority's decision "a cavalier summary reversal."[120]

Justice Stewart, the high court member who had been most troubled by his colleagues' use of the anti-establishment weapon to invalidate school prayer, likewise dissented in *Stone*, curtly observing that the Kentucky courts "applied wholly correct constitutional criteria in reaching their decisions."[121]

The position espoused by Justices Rehnquist and Stewart in their *Stone* dissents—that a proper understanding of the anti-establishment guarantee simply cannot lead to the conclusion that public schools are forbidden to post the Ten Commandments in their classrooms—probably garners more support on the Court today than it did two decades ago when the justices handed down their decision summarily invalidating the Kentucky practice. The majority's conclusion in *Stone* nevertheless remains the law. For now, therefore, the anti-establishment guarantee continues to render it constitutionally problematic for public schools to post the Ten Commandments, particularly in classrooms.

But *Stone* may not be governing anti-establishment law for long. In 2004, the high court announced that it again would confront the Ten Commandments issue. This development affords the Court the opportunity to determine whether both the evolution of the law and personnel changes unfolding over the past two decades—and, in particular, the post-*Stone* appointments of Justices O'Connor, Scalia, Kennedy, and Thomas, four members of the Court likely to adopt the approach to the Ten Commandments issue advocated by the *Stone* dissenters—have rendered obsolete the conclusions articulated in *Stone*. Accordingly, the likelihood remains high that, as this volume proceeds to press, the central message of *Stone* will be undercut by the current group of justices, a group less hospitable to anti-establishment challenges than the group that decided *Stone*. A wonderful irony of this most recent anti-establishment development happens to be that the new case, like *Stone* itself, emerges from Kentucky (McCreary County v. ACLU of Kentucky).[122]

The case arises out of the erection of displays of framed copies of the Ten Commandments in public schools and courthouses in three Kentucky counties.[123] The American Civil Liberties Union and a variety of individuals instituted an action seeking to put a stop to the displays, not surprisingly citing anti-establishment concerns. The counties, endeavoring to snuff out the constitutional challenge, responded to the challenge by proceeding to modify the displays in question—essentially by adorning the walls on which the Ten Commandments hung with a variety of more secular historical and legal documents. The counties hoped that by situating the Ten Commandments in a context dotted with these more secular documents, the Commandments would retain their appearance as moral prescription while diminishing the air of religious edict, thereby mitigating any anti-establishments concerns. Despite these changes, plaintiffs pressed on, contending that public display of the Ten Commandments clashed with anti-establishment principles. The trial court agreed.

As a result, the counties modified the displays yet again. The current version of the courthouse displays now consists of copies of the Ten Commandments along with copies of the Star Spangled Banner, the Declaration of Independence, the Mayflower Compact, the Bill of Rights, the Magna Carta, the National Motto ("In God We Trust"), the Preamble to the Kentucky Constitution, Lady Justice, and a one-page document entitled "The Foundations of American Law and Government Display."[124] The current version of the school displays consists of virtually the identical items, with the exception of the fact that Lady Justice and The Foundations of American Law and Government Display have been replaced with a copy of a Kentucky statute regarding the posting of historical displays and a School Board Resolution asserting in pertinent part that "[w]e believe these . . . documents positively contribute to the educational foundations and moral character of students in our schools."[125] The constitutional status of these most recent displays remains at issue in *McCreary*.

The trial court concluded that these revised displays continued to pose an anti-establishment problem.[126] A three-judge panel of the United States Court of Appeals for the Sixth Circuit agreed.[127] The Sixth Circuit's majority opinion began its analysis by observing that, despite dissatisfaction expressed by a range of justices, *Lemon* remained the law and, for that reason, it was obliged to apply *Lemon* "until the Supreme Court explicitly overrules or abandons it."[128] The majority proceeded to undertake an analysis of the purpose and effects prongs of *Lemon*, the aspects of *Lemon* that had prompted the trial court to conclude that the displays could not withstand anti-establishment scrutiny.

With *Stone* as backdrop, the court of appeals majority concluded that the principal purpose of the displays was religious and that, accordingly, the displays failed *Lemon*'s purpose prong.[129] In reaching this conclusion, the Sixth Circuit majority summarized *Stone* as follows:

> To comply with *Stone* . . . a purported historical display must present the Ten Commandments objectively and integrate them with a secular message. . . . Several factors are relevant . . . : the content of the displays, the physical setting in which the Ten Commandments are displayed and any changes that Defendants have made to the displays since their inception.[130]

In applying these factors to the displays at issue, the Sixth Circuit majority concluded that the displays could not withstand scrutiny under *Lemon*'s purpose inquiry. Central to the court's reasoning was that the displays at issue "provided the viewer with no analytical or historical connection between the Ten Commandments and the other historical documents"[131] and amounted to little more than an effort "to convey the bald assertion that the Ten Commandments formed the foundation of American legal tradition"[132]—a purpose that, according to *Stone*, was insufficiently secular to avoid clashing with anti-establishment principles. The court's conclusions regarding the impermissible purpose of the displays in question flowed out of its explanation of the evolution of the displays from government actions featuring the Ten Commandments alone to displays in their current form that, at least in the court's view, sought to dilute the religious message attendant to the Ten Commandments display to the minimum extent possible by having the Ten Commandments share attention with a range of less constitutionally problematic items. This evolution, the Sixth Circuit maintained, mars the displays with "an unconstitutional taint" and prompts the conclusion that the purpose of the government officials who caused them to be erected was principally religious.[133] In short, in the Sixth Circuit's view each of the three factors it enumerated—content, context, and evolution—revealed a predominantly religious purpose.

The Sixth Circuit found as well that the displays constituted government "endorsement" of religion. It deployed the "endorsement" test of Justice O'Connor instead of the "effects" analysis because, in its view, the endorsement approach represented essentially a "refinement" of *Lemon*'s effects prong.[134] The court found that the reasonable observer viewing the range of symbols featured in the displays would fail to discern an "analytical connection" between the Ten Commandments and the other items displayed and for that reason such an observer would "think religion, not history" in examining such displays.[135] Once again, the court's reasoning was rooted to a considerable extent in the evolution of the particular displays at issue: A reasonable observer, the majority noted, has a grasp of the fact that such evolution "indicates that the displays were originally intended to enshrine the Ten Commandments . . . [and] only upon fear of litigation . . . were modified to include secular material in the hope of rendering the displays constitutional."[136]

A dissenting judge took sharp issue with the majority's analysis and conclusions. The dissent expressed its dismay at the majority's heavy reliance on *Stone*—which it accurately dubbed "a two-page, *per curiam* decision of the Court that preceded both *Lynch* and *Allegheny*, that was decided without the benefit of oral argument or briefs on the merits, and that bears no factual similarity to the case before us."[137] The dissent sided conspicuously with then Justice (now Chief Justice) Rehnquist's dissent in *Stone*, calling the *Stone* decision "a cavalier summary reversal" with no precedent to support it.[138] The dissent also charged the majority with the misapplication and misinterpretation of *Stone*. It noted that *Stone*—a case in which the Ten Commandments stood alone in display—differed in that crucial respect from the instant case. In addition, the dissent opined that the notion that all displays of the Ten Commandments on public property must be integrated into a curriculum of study—a conclusion the majority purported to glean from *Stone*—simply was not to be found in the case.[139] The dissent urged instead that *Lynch* and *Allegheny* represent the cases most closely analogous to the issue under review, and that the pair of post-*Stone* cases does not support the conclusion that the displays in question pose an anti-establishment problems.

With regard to the majority's analysis of *Lemon*'s purpose prong, the dissent expressed the view that there exists no reason to doubt the sincerity of the five secular purposes articulated by defendants for the erection of the modified versions of the displays:

1. to erect a display containing the Ten Commandments that is constitutional;
2. to demonstrate that the Ten Commandments were part of the foundation of American Law and Government;
3. [to include the Ten Commandments] as part of the display for their significance in providing "the moral background of the Declaration of Independence and the foundation of our legal tradition;"
4. to educate the citizens of the county regarding some of the documents that played a significant role in the foundation of our system of law and government; and

5. . . . to create a limited public forum on designated walls within the school district for the purpose of posting historical documents which played a significant role in the development, origins or foundations of American or Kentucky law.[140]

The dissent rejected the majority's suggestion that the historical evolution of the displays somehow "tainted" the constitutional status of the current displays, challenging the premise that "a history of unconstitutional displays can be used as a sword to strike down an otherwise constitutional display."[141]

With regard to *Lemon*'s "effects" prong, the dissent maintained that the ten items featured in the displays must be examined in their totality. Such an examination, the dissent noted, would reveal that (a) nine of the items are secular, (b) none is displayed more prominently than the others, and (c) all ten possess a "unifying theme"—the foundations of American law and government. Accordingly, the dissent concludes that no reasonable observer could come away from the displays believing that government had conveyed a message of religious endorsement.[142]

The high court's 2004 decision to devote time and resources to the anti-establishment implications of public displays of the Ten Commandments suggests that *Stone* could soon be consigned to the scrap heap. To be sure, predictions concerning the nation's highest court remain as much an art as a science. It nevertheless appears reasonably likely that Chief Justice Rehnquist will garner support sufficient to transform his *Stone* dissent into a majority opinion.

Released-Time Programs

Yet another feature of the anti-establishment landscape—more prominent in past generations than it is today—has been the so-called released-time program, a program whose central feature is that the ongoing educational activities of the public school come to a halt in order to facilitate the opportunity for students to receive religious instruction during what otherwise would have been the public school day. Twice the Court has examined the constitutionality of such programs, arriving at strikingly different conclusions in the pair of cases.

A challenge to the released-time practice of an Illinois school district provided the Court its initial opportunity to confront the constitutional implications of such programs (McCollum v. Board of Education, 1948).[143] Once a week for less than one hour teachers employed by religious organizations came into the public schools during the course of the school day to deliver religious instruction to students in grades four through nine whose families had requested that their children receive such instruction. The school district paid nothing for the instruction, either to the instructors or to their religious organizations. But the program did require that the religious school instructors be approved by the school district superintendent. The instructors themselves consisted of Catholic priests, a Jewish rabbi, and two Protestant teachers. Students whose families chose to enroll them in such religious instruction were required to attend the classes, which were conducted in classrooms otherwise used for public school instruction; the religious instruction teachers submitted attendance reports to the office of the public school superintendent. Students whose families opted *not* to enroll them in the religious instruction left the classrooms during this period and moved to a location elsewhere in the building.

The Supreme Court invalidated the program, concluding that such a practice "falls squarely under the ban of the First Amendment."[144] Writing for the majority, Justice Black succinctly characterized the facts to include "the use of tax-supported property for religious instruction and the close cooperation between [public school authorities and religious organizations] in promoting religious education."[145] The Court thus appeared to ground its conclusion that the Illinois program clashed with the anti-establishment principle in two distinctive factors: the use of public school facilities for the inculcation of religious doctrine *and* the assistance public institutions provided religious groups by deploying the mechanism of compulsory public education to the advantage of religion.

Four years later, the Court purported to find a difference of constitutional magnitude between the Illinois program invalidated in *McCollum* and the New York City program under scrutiny (Zorach v. Clauson, 1952).[146] The released-time program at issue in *Zorach* permitted public school students—once again, at the request of parents—to leave the building during the course of the school day in order to travel to what the Court called "religious centers" where the students would participate in religious instruction or devotional exercises.[147] The students from families opting not to participate in the program remained behind in the public school classrooms. As in *McCollum*, the religious institutions submitted attendance reports to public school authorities.

The Court upheld the New York City program, opining that the anti-establishment guarantee had not been breached. Speaking for the six-member majority, Justice William Douglas observed—in words that would engender substantial scrutiny over the next half century—that "[w]e are a religious people whose institutions presuppose a Supreme Being."[148] The majority opinion closed with an effort to reconcile its approval of the New York City program with the Court's invalidation of the Illinois scheme in *McCollum* four years earlier:

> In the *McCollum* case the [public school] classrooms were used for religious instruction and the force of the public school was used to promote that instruction. Here, public schools do no more than accommodate their schedules to a program of outside religious instruction. We follow [*McCollum*]. But we cannot expand it to cover the present released time program unless separation of Church and State means that public institutions can make no adjustments of their schedules to accommodate the religious needs of the people. We cannot read into the Bill of Rights such a philosophy of hostility to religion.[149]

A dissent by Justice Black, the author of *McCollum*, suggested that the Court's retreat from the principles of *McCollum* had been triggered by the fact that some commentators "thought the McCollum decision fundamentally wrong and have pledged continuous warfare against it."[150] Justice Felix Frankfurter, also dissenting, concluded his expression of disagreement with a set of provocative observations:

> The deeply divisive controversy aroused by the attempts to secure public school pupils for sectarian instruction would promptly end if the advocates of such instruction were content to have the school "close its doors or suspend its operations"—that is, dismiss classes in their entirety, without discrimination—instead of seeking to use the public schools as the instrument for securing attendance at denominational classes. The unwillingness of the promoters of this movement to dispense with such use of the public schools betrays a surprising want of confidence in the inherent power of the various faiths to draw children to outside sectarian classes—an attitude that hardly reflects the faith of the greatest religious spirits.[151]

As suggested above, the "released-time" programs examined by the Court in *McCollum* and *Zorach* no longer play a prominent role in the American educational system. For that reason, the treatment such programs would earn against the backdrop of anti-establishment analysis today could be said to represent something of a moot point.

Religion in Public Education (III): Access by Religious Groups to Public School Facilities and Funding

For public schools at all educational levels, one institutional challenge traditionally has been whether, and the extent to which, facilities and funding can be made available to religiously affiliated groups without igniting anti-establishment concerns. Over the past two decades the Court repeatedly has returned to this issue, and has tended to provide a consistent answer.

The Court's initial encounter with the access issue emerged out of a dispute at the University of Missouri at Kansas City (Widmar v. Vincent, 1981).[152] Like that of most schools, UMKC policy reflected a commitment to make available school facilities for meetings of registered student organizations. Cornerstone, an organization of evangelical students belonging to a variety of faiths, conducted its meetings on campus for four years. The meetings typically included prayer, Bible commentary, and discussion of religious views and experiences. In 1977, however, the school informed Cornerstone that no longer would it be allowed to meet in school facilities, largely due to a regulation that forbade the use of school facilities for *religious* worship or teaching. Student members of Cornerstone instituted an action claiming that the decision violated a range of rights guaranteed by the Constitution. The university replied with the argument that anti-establishment principles forbade it to permit religious organizations to use its facilities, because doing so would produce the impermissible effect of advancing religion. The Court disagreed with the university.

The Court acknowledged that religious groups such as Cornerstone would reap a benefit from access to UMKC facilities. But that fact, in the Court's view, did not lead to the conclusion that such access would clash with *Lemon*'s prohibition on government acts whose principal effect is to advance religion. Two factors persuaded the Court that religious-group access to facilities would not pose anti-establishment concerns.

One was that such access would not "confer any imprimatur of state approval on religious sects and practices."[153] The Court noted that providing a meeting room for the students of Cornerstone would no more link the school with the evangelical principles of the organization than making rooms available for students in the Young Socialist Alliance or Students for a Democratic Society has placed the school's support behind the principles of those organizations.

The second factor the Court cited as significant to its conclusion had to do with the fact that more than one hundred student groups existed at UMKC. That fact, the Court indicated, strongly undercut the concern that having one or more of these groups linked to religion would have the impermissible effect of advancing religion. It observed that if indeed the anti-establishment guarantee meant that religious groups could not profit from public benefits extended to a broad class of recipients, then "a church could not be protected by the police or fire departments or have its public sidewalk kept in repair."[154] In short, the Court made clear that an equal access policy that enabled religious organizations to avail themselves of public facilities would not clash with anti-establishment principles.

Congress shortly thereafter placed its support behind such an approach with the passage of the Equal Access Act of 1984. The act essentially extended the principle of *Widmar* to public secondary schools by forbidding such schools that invite access to their facilities during noninstructional time to discriminate against students based on, among other factors, the religious content of the speech likely to unfold at the meeting. A high school located in Omaha, Nebraska, nevertheless denied a request from students to form a Christian club that, like thirty other student organizations, would meet after school. School officials sought to defend the decision by explaining that anti-establishment principles impelled their decision. Once again, the Court rejected such a defense (Board of Education v. Mergens 1990).[155]

Four justices, speaking through Justice O'Connor, applied relatively straightforward *Lemon* analysis. These justices concluded that the Equal Access Act furthered the secular purpose of seeking to ward off discrimination on the basis of religion, thereby satisfying the first *Lemon* inquiry. They also concluded that the act did not have the primary effect of advancing religion, principally because high school students were unlikely to confuse the equal access policy with school sponsorship of religion; the act imposed serious limits on the role faculty could play at meetings of student religious groups, and the wide variety of student organizations at the high school served to counteract any conceivable message of school endorsement of religion. The plurality likewise minimized any concerns of excessive entanglement, noting again that the act forbade *both* faculty from participating in the meetings of any religious student group *and* nonschool personnel from directing or regularly attending the activities of any student group.

The central lesson emerging from the Court's initial treatments of the anti-establishment implications of the equal access issue—the conclusion that anti-establishment principles do not require schools to discriminate against religious groups insofar as access to facilities is concerned—continues to be reaffirmed and expanded. A unanimous Court applied such a principle to reject a New York school district's policy to deny a local evangelical church the ability to use school property at a time classes were not in session (Lamb's Chapel v. Center Moriches Union Free School District 1993).[156]

Twice the church had applied for permission to use school facilities in order to show a film series featuring a noted psychologist and radio commentator, films whose central purpose was to persuade viewers that instilling Christian family values at an early age represented the only way to counterbalance the destructive influence the contemporary American media wreaked on individuals and society. Twice the school district denied the request, explaining that "[t]his film does appear to be church related and therefore your request must be refused."[157] The majority concluded that the district's effort to justify the denials as mandated by the anti-establishment guarantee could not withstand scrutiny, precisely for the reasons set out in the earlier pair of cases: No realistic danger existed that, were the district to grant access to the church, the community would conclude that the district had endorsed religion or any particular religious sect and, in addition, any such benefit access to school facilities would deliver to religion generally or the church in particular would have been "incidental" at best.[158]

A case arising on the campus of the University of Virginia divided the justices but nevertheless fortified the principles set out in these earlier access cases (Rosenberger v. University of Virginia, 1995).[159] A university policy authorized the school to pay outside contractors for the costs incurred in printing a host of student publications. The school refused, however, to pay for the costs incurred in printing a Christian-based newspaper put out by Wide Awake Productions, a student organization committed to promoting campuswide discussion that "fosters an atmosphere of sensitivity to and tolerance of Christian viewpoints."[160] The majority opinion of Justice Kennedy rejected the argument that anti-establishment concerns justified the school's treatment of Wide Awake. In so doing, it emphasized that the "neutrality" of the program at issue obviated any anti-establishment concern:

> The government program here is neutral toward religion. There is no suggestion that the University created it to advance religion or adopted some ingenious device with the pur-

pose of aiding a religious cause. The object of the [University's general policy of paying printing costs incurred by student organizations] is to open a forum for speech and to support various student enterprises, including the publication of newspapers, in recognition of the diversity and creativity of student life. . . . WAP did not seek funding because of its Christian editorial viewpoint; it sought funding as a student journal, which it was. . . . Government neutrality is apparent . . . in a further meaningful respect. The program respects the critical difference "between *government* speech endorsing religion, which the Establishment Clause forbids, and *private* speech endorsing religion, which the Free Speech and Free Exercise Clauses protect."[161]

Justice Souter spoke for four justices in a thoughtful, wide-ranging dissent. The dissent took issue with virtually every aspect of the majority opinion, particularly the majority's suggestion that the so-called neutrality with which the majority characterized the UVA program was a sufficient reason to conclude that no anti-establishment problems attended the funding of a religious publication. The dissent contended that the Court had "never before upheld direct state funding of the sort of proselytizing published in Wide Awake"[162] and, quite the contrary, had "categorically condemned state programs directly aiding religious activity."[163] Summing up, the dissent observed that "[t]he Court is ordering an instrumentality of the State to support religious evangelism with direct funding. This is a flat violation of the Establishment Clause."[164]

The most recent reaffirmation of the general themes of the equal access cases arose out of a New York elementary school's refusal to permit a Christian organization for youngsters aged six through twelve to have access to the facility during after-school hours (Good News Club v. Milford Central School, 2001).[165] Sponsors of the Good News Club requested to use the school's cafeteria for the organization's weekly after-school meeting. The request noted that the proposed use included the club's desire to have "a fun time of singing songs, hearing a Bible lesson and memorizing scripture."[166] The district superintendent denied the request, noting that the district's access policy required the denial of access to individuals or organizations whose use of the facility encompassed "religious purposes," thereby foreclosing the club's prospects for using school space. A few months later the Board of Education adopted a formal resolution rejecting the club's request, citing the religious nature of the proposed use. Shortly thereafter the club instituted legal action, with the trial court issuing an injunction against the school ordering it to refrain from enforcing its policy. For approximately a year thereafter, the club used a room in the high school and a middle school special education room to hold its meetings. But the trial court proceeded to vacate the injunction and hold for the school, bringing about a situation in which the club no longer had access to school facilities.

The school defended the denial of access to the club by maintaining that had it agreed to allow Good News Club to use the school facility it would have violated anti-establishment principles. The high court rejected the contention, as it had in the prior equal access cases, labeling the activities the club sought to engage in "materially indistinguishable"[167] from those upheld in *Lamb's Chapel* and *Widmar*. The majority spun out a host of reasons to explain its conclusion that anti-establishment principles do not justify the denial of access: its view that the neutrality principle would be *advanced* by allowing access to Good News Club and *undermined* by denying such access on the basis that the activity sought to be engaged in on school grounds constituted religious activity; its view that no one in the community would feel coerced to participate in the club's activities merely by virtue of the fact that meetings took place in a public school; and its view that the mere fact that an after-school meeting of a religious organization unfolds on public school property—even public school property on which elementary school students may be lingering—has never been deemed to pose an anti-establishment problem.[168]

The law emerging out of this line of recent cases examining the anti-establishment implications of public schools denying access to their facilities and funding to religious groups sends a relatively clear message. That message reduces to this: Public schools that open up their facilities and pocketbooks to a wide variety of organizations will not be permitted to use anti-establishment principles to justify treating religious groups differently, less advantageously, insofar as access issues are concerned. In other words, to the extent that a public school—be it an elementary school, a secondary school, or a college or university—invites a wide variety of organizations to use its facilities or apply for funding, the school in all likelihood will be unable to deny religious groups the opportunity to share in those benefits.

Religion in Other Institutions of Government (I): Prayer in the Legislature

The high court's treatment of prayer in the legislature diverges considerably from the law at work on public schools. The Court confronted a challenge to Nebraska's long-standing policy of opening each legislative session with a prayer offered by a chaplain paid by the government—a chaplain who, in Nebraska's case, for nearly two decades had been the same Presbyterian minister (Marsh v. Chambers, 1983).[169]

The United States Court of Appeals for the Tenth Circuit, the court whose appellate decision the high court was reviewing, had found that the Nebraska practice violated each of the three prongs of the *Lemon* test.[170] That court had found that the practice lacked a secular purpose; that its primary effect was to advance religious expression; and that the use of government funds for the chaplain's salary and the publication of the collection of prayers fostered an excessive entanglement of government and religion. But a divided Supreme Court reversed, upholding the practice and, surprisingly, refusing even to measure the Nebraska tradition against the usual measuring stick deployed in challenges implicating the anti-establishment guarantee: the *Lemon* test itself.[171]

Writing for the majority, Chief Justice Warren Burger grounded the Court's approval of legislative prayer squarely in the fact that the practice had been a part of the American political landscape for more than two centuries:

> The opening of sessions of legislative and other deliberative public bodies with prayer is deeply embedded in the history and tradition of this country. From colonial times through the founding of the Republic and ever since, the practice of legislative prayer has coexisted with the principles of disestablishment and religious freedom. In the very courtrooms in which the United States District Judge and later three Circuit Judges heard and decided this case, the proceedings opened with an announcement that concluded, "God save the United States and this Honorable Court." The same invocation occurs at all sessions of this Court.[172]

This use of history and tradition represents one avenue the Court pursues when it seeks to uphold against anti-establishment challenge a law or practice that otherwise might seem to prove problematic under *Lemon*'s purpose/effect/entanglement trilogy. The *Marsh* majority did concede that long-standing historical patterns cannot render legitimate a practice that otherwise clashes with the anti-establishment principle. It nevertheless maintained that this "unique" history of legislative prayer suggests that those who crafted the anti-establishment principle "saw no real threat" to that principle from prayer in the legislative chamber.[173] Indeed, the chief justice cited the unsuccessful objections of John Jay and John Rutledge to beginning the initial session of the Continental Congress with prayer, as well as Samuel Adams's response to those objections, as evidence supporting the conclusion that the Founding generation harbored few reservations about such practices. As Chief Justice Burger observed:

> We do not agree that evidence of opposition to a measure weakens the force of the historical argument; indeed, it infuses it with power by demonstrating that the subject was considered carefully and the action not taken thoughtlessly, by force of long tradition and without regard to the problems posed by a pluralist society.[174]

Three justices parted company with the majority, concluding that legislative prayer clashes with core anti-establishment principles.

Justice Brennan, joined by Justice Marshall, issued an extensive dissent, one that sought to make two overarching contributions.[175] The first concerned his colleagues' refusal even to apply applicable anti-establishment principles—that is to say, the *Lemon* standards—to the practice of legislative prayer.[176] The second had to do with the core functions served by the anti-establishment guarantee.[177]

The Brennan dissent began by pausing to chide his colleagues for self-consciously refraining from applying the governing law set out in *Lemon* to the Nebraska practice at issue. In one sense, Justice Brennan observed, that development represented a good thing: Carving out a modest exception to anti-establishment principles for legislative prayer, he noted, works a less disturbing upheaval of the law than would fundamentally "reshaping" those principles. Justice Brennan nevertheless proceeded to contend that a dispassionate assessment of legislative prayer "through the unsentimental eye of our settled doctrine"[178]—that is to say, straightforward application of the *Lemon* test—would lead unquestionably to a contrary decision. The very purpose of legislative prayer, Brennan contended, is "preeminently religious rather than secular."[179] Likewise, he argued, the primary effect of the practice also is to advance religion, to a considerable extent by coercing religious minorities to conform to prevailing religious practices.[180] Justice Brennan also discerned an entanglement problem with the Nebraska practice, maintaining that government hiring and supervision of a chaplain responsible for delivering such prayers and ensuring that the prayers conform to appropriate standards excessively links the institutions of government and religion.[181] In an effort to underscore the point that garden variety *Lemon* analysis would have compelled the Court to invalidate the practice of legislative prayer, Justice Brennan passed along an amusing observation, one more likely than not accurate: "I have no doubt that, if any group of law students were asked to apply the principles of *Lemon* to the question of legislative prayer, they would nearly unanimously find the practice to be unconstitutional."[182]

The dissent then turned to articulate four underlying functions served by the "neutrality" and "separation" dictated, in its view, by the anti-establishment guarantee, functions that, separately and together, reveal the constitutional flaws of government-sponsored legislative prayer. Those four functions, according to Justice Brennan, include (1) to protect the right to conscience—that is to say, to ensure the right of individuals not to be compelled to support religious practices with which the individuals disagree;[183] (2) to prevent government from interfering in the autonomy of religious life—that is to say, to keep government from assuming responsibility for religious decisions or unduly intruding itself in the supervision of religious institutions or officials;[184] (3) to avoid the "trivialization and degradation" of religion—that is to say, to require government to maintain a safe distance from religion so as to avoid perverting religious messages;[185] and (4) to maximize the prospects that religious issues not serve to ignite political divisiveness and encourage partisan appeals to religion.[186] Each of these functions served by anti-establishment principles, the Brennan dissent noted, militates in favor of the conclusion that legislative prayer clashes with the anti-establishment principles of neutrality and separation, and for much the same reasons, Justice Brennan noted, that most aspects of *school* prayer clash with such principles.

Justice John Paul Stevens, too, dissented from the conclusion that the Constitution permitted prayer in legislative chambers. For Justice Stevens, however, the constitutional problem with the practice stemmed from the fact that the religious affiliation of the chaplain in a particular legislature "tend[ed] to reflect the faith of the majority of the lawmakers' constituents."[187] As Justice Stevens put it:

Prayers may be said by a Catholic priest in the Massachusetts Legislature and by a Presbyterian minister in the Nebraska Legislature, but I would not expect to find a Jehovah's Witness or a disciple of Mary Baker Eddy or the Reverend Moon serving as the official chaplain in any state legislature. . . . [I]t seems to me plain that the designation of a member of one religious faith to serve as the sole official chaplain of a state legislature for a period of 16 years constitutes the preference of one faith over another in violation of the Establishment Clause.[188]

The Court's willingness to finesse anti-establishment analysis in such a way as to tolerate prayer in the context of legislative sessions ought not be viewed as either terribly surprising or especially illuminating. Instead, such an approach—along with the outcome the approach produced—can perhaps best be understood as little more than the Court bowing to a long-standing practice from which it saw little if any tangible harm having emerged or likely to emerge. Perhaps as well, the justices sensed that a decision telling state legislators around the nation (and, presumably, congresspeople and the justices themselves as well) that the Constitution forbade them to begin their sessions with a brief prayer would be met with a level of skepticism and bewilderment that could have exposed the Court to ridicule it simply did not wish to invite.

Nevertheless, separate and apart from whatever precisely accounts for the decision of the *Marsh* majority to place the weight of anti-establishment law behind the practice of legislative prayer, it remains the case that this distinctive subcategory of the law has earned distinctive constitutional treatment. In general, prayer that opens sessions of government tends to withstand anti-establishment scrutiny.

Religion in Other Institutions of Government (II): Holiday Displays and Other Symbols of Religious Significance

Over the past two decades, anti-establishment challenges to religious displays erected by government or on government-owned property have produced some of the most important, explosive, and difficult to reconcile constitutional conversations among the justices. The law unfolding in this area has subjected the Court to some harsh criticism, especially for the lines the justices have sought to draw demarcating the permissible from the impermissible.

Christmas Display with a Crèche

A landmark Supreme Court decision arising in a Rhode Island municipality inaugurated this strand of anti-establishment law (Lynch v. Donnelly, 1984).[189] In that case, the justices considered the impact of the anti-establishment guarantee on a Christmas display owned and erected annually by the city of Pawtucket. The display, situated in a park owned by a nonprofit organization and located in the heart of the city's shopping district, included what the Court's majority reported were:

> many of the figures and decorations traditionally associated with Christmas, including, among other things, a Santa Claus house, reindeer pulling Santa's sleigh, candy-striped poles, a Christmas tree, carolers, cutout figures representing such characters as a clown, an elephant, and a teddy bear, hundreds of colored lights, a large banner that reads "SEASONS GREETINGS," and the crèche at issue here.[190]

The final item on the majority's descriptive list—what it referred to as "the crèche at issue here"—consisted of figures of the infant Jesus, Mary and Joseph, angels, shepherds, kings, and animals, each ranging in height from five inches to five feet.

Plaintiffs challenged the inclusion of the crèche in the display as inconsistent with the anti-establishment guarantee. Both the trial court and the United States Court of Appeals for First Circuit agreed, invalidating the display.[191] With Chief Justice Warren Burger speaking for the five-member majority, however, the high court reversed.

The majority's analysis of the constitutionality of the Pawtucket crèche began with page after page of unusual musings about the anti-establishment guarantee. Chief Justice Burger reported, among other things, that the "total separation" of church and state "is not possible" or constitutionally required[192] and that the "wall of separation" metaphor "is not a wholly accurate description of the practical aspects of the relationship that in fact exists between church and state."[193] The chief justice likewise observed that, since the nation's inception, all three branches of the national government have continued to acknowledge the role of religion in American life. As support for this proposition the majority cited a host of examples, from President Washington's Thanksgiving Day proclamation to the national motto "In God We Trust" to the congressional practice of compensating chaplains for the Senate, House, and the military to the language of "One nation under God" in the Pledge of Allegiance to long-standing government support of museums that house artistic masterpieces with religious messages.[194]

These musings about the anti-establishment principle led the majority to conclude that "no fixed, *per se* rule"[195] can be deployed in each and every factual situation to produce the correct constitutional outcome. Instead, Chief Justice Burger reminded that "in each case, the inquiry calls for line drawing"[196] because, in the majority's view, the principle "erects a 'blurred, indistinct, and variable barrier depending on all the circumstances of a particular relationship.' "[197] These observations by the chief justice strongly suggested that conventional anti-establishment analysis would not be forthcoming from the *Lynch* majority—or at least that the analysis to be undertaken would diverge from prior understandings.

The majority did turn, finally, to confront the constitutional status of the Pawtucket display. Not entirely surprisingly given its unusual preliminary observations, the majority concluded that, applying the three-pronged *Lemon* test, the crèche withstood constitutional scrutiny.

Insofar as *Lemon*'s purpose prong was concerned, Chief Justice Burger reasoned that the municipality's desire "to celebrate the Holiday and . . . depict [its] origins" eminently satisfied the requirement of a secular purpose.[198] In so doing the majority explicitly took issue with the trial court's conclusion that the inclusion of the crèche in the display lacked a secular purpose.

The majority's review of the "effect" prong required a lengthier discussion. Essentially the majority maintained that the benefits Pawtucket imposed on "the Christian faith" by including the crèche in the holiday display were no more substantial in magnitude than benefits the Court previously had approved as not clashing with the anti-establishment principle.[199] Analogizing the inclusion of the crèche in a municipal display to prayer in the legislature and Sunday blue laws, the chief justice concluded that the mere fact that the crèche "happens to coincide" with the tenets of some religions does not lead to the conclusion that anti-establishment principles have been breached.[200]

The majority concluded with an examination of entanglement, *Lemon*'s third prong. In the course of that examination, the majority was forced to confront the trial court's conclusion that the political divisiveness along religious lines engendered by the presence of the crèche in the holiday display amounted to unconstitutional entanglement. Not surprisingly, the majority disagreed. According to Chief Justice Burger, the entanglement forbidden by *Lemon* and the anti-establishment guarantee has little to do with whether a particular set of circumstances triggers divisiveness along denominational lines. Rather, the forbidden entanglement between the institutions of government and religion—admittedly, as the majority conceded, "a question of kind and degree"[201]—has more to do with whether a particular set of circumstances impels "ongoing, day-to-day interaction"[202] between these institutions. Because the facts surrounding the holiday display revealed no such interaction, the majority dismissed any concerns rooted in excessive entanglement.[203]

The constitutional challenge to Pawtucket's holiday display produced a concurrence by Justice Sandra Day O'Connor that has proven enormously influential. In that concurrence, Justice O'Connor sketched an approach to the adjudication of anti-establishment cases rooted in the notion that, above all else, the principle aims to outlaw government "endorsement" of religion. Justice O'Connor expressed the crux of her approach as follows:

> The Establishment Clause prohibits government from making adherence to a religion relevant in any way to a person's standing in the political community. Government cases can run afoul of that prohibition in two principal ways. One is excessive entanglement with religious institutions, which may interfere with the independence of those institutions, give the institutions access to government powers not fully shared by nonadherents of the religion, and foster the creation of political constituencies divided along religious lines. . . .
>
> The second and more direct infringement is government endorsement or disapproval of religion. Endorsement sends a message to nonadherents that they are outsiders, not full

members of the political community, and an accompanying message to adherents that they are insiders, favored members of the political community. Disapproval sends the opposite message.[204]

Not surprisingly, therefore, Justice O'Connor viewed the central question posed by the case as "whether Pawtucket has endorsed Christianity by its display of the crèche."[205] Answering her own question with a resounding "No," she endeavored to justify that response by pointing to two aspects of the facts—one having to do with Pawtucket's purpose, the other with the impact of its display.

With regard to purpose, Justice O'Connor maintained that, by displaying the crèche, the municipality "did not intend to convey any message of endorsement of Christianity or disapproval of nonChristian religions."[206] The city's intent, Justice O'Connor contended, was nothing more than "celebration of the public holiday through its traditional symbols."[207] The concurrence extracted an analogously tame message from the display's "effect," concluding that the presence of the crèche in the display ought not lead reasonable observers to conclude that Pawtucket has communicated the fact that it is endorsing Christianity or disapproving of non-Christian faiths.[208] Like the majority, the concurrence argued that the particular display at issue represented nothing truly different from the sorts of government "acknowledgments" of religion upheld in prior cases as not inconsistent with the anti-establishment principle.[209]

Four members of the Court vigorously dissented, again revealing the deep divisions anti-establishment law had engendered among the justices. In the principal dissent, speaking for all four, Justice Brennan began by observing that "this case appears hard not because the principles are obscure, but because the Christmas holiday seems so familiar and agreeable."[210] Justice Brennan proceeded to explain why, in the view of the dissenters, the standards enunciated in *Lemon* rendered the government-sponsored crèche invalid. Indeed, the dissenters contended that the crèche clashed with each prong of *Lemon*—purpose, effect, and entanglement all.

The reason the inclusion of the crèche in the Pawtucket display failed to satisfy the requirement of a secular purpose, the dissent maintained, centered on the fact that the purported secular purpose of celebrating the Christmas holiday and attracting consumers to the downtown area could have been accomplished just as well without the nativity scene.[211] Moreover, the dissent seized upon some comments in the record to the effect that the municipality had sought to "keep 'Christ in Christmas.' "[212]

The dissent likewise found that the inclusion of the crèche in the municipality's display produced the primary effect of placing Pawtucket's support behind the religious beliefs embodied by the crèche.[213] Put differently, the dissenters concluded that the principal effect of the crèche was to advance the faiths of Christians and to convey to non-Christians the message that their (different) religious beliefs somehow were less worthy of Pawtucket's support.

Entanglement, too, posed a problem for the dissenters. In particular, the dissent contended that, as a result of the Pawtucket display, "Jews and other non-Christian groups . . . can be expected to press government for inclusion of their symbols, and faced with such requests, government will have to become involved in accommodating the various demands."[214]

As the discussion reveals, the high court's important initial confrontation with the issue of precisely what anti-establishment principles say about government-sponsored holiday displays divided the justices into two profoundly different factions. To be sure, five justices in *Lynch* indeed opted to reject the constitutional challenge to the crèche. The conversation the Pawtucket crèche produced among the justices nevertheless left the distinct impression that an unmistakable lack of clarity lay on the horizon for this subspecies of the law.

More Holiday Displays: Crèche in a Courthouse, Menorah on Government Property

Five years after *Lynch* the Court confirmed that impression, returning to the issue of government involvement in religious holiday displays. A pair of holiday displays erected in downtown Pittsburgh afforded the justices the opportunity to continue their squabble and elaborate both on the meaning and lessons of *Lynch* and, more generally, on the proper approach to cases implicating the anti-establishment principle (Allegheny County v. American Civil Liberties Union, 1989).[215] Regrettably, the justices did not use the opportunity to forge an approach to these issues that would produce clarity or predictability in the law.

One display at issue in the case featured a crèche (owned by a Roman Catholic organization) located on the Grand Staircase of the Allegheny County Courthouse. This crèche, not unlike Pawtucket's, included, among other features, figures of the infant Jesus, Mary and Joseph, farm animals, shepherds, and wise men all in the context of a wooden depiction of a manger. The other display under scrutiny consisted of an eighteen-foot Chanukah menorah (owned by a Jewish organization) located adjacent to a Christmas tree more than twice that size accompanied by a sign saluting liberty just outside the principal office building for city and county employees, another publicly owned structure situated a block away from the courthouse. Challengers contended that both the crèche and the menorah violated anti-establishment principles.

Shifting majorities on the sharply fractured Court invalidated the crèche display but rejected the challenge to the menorah. To capture the circumstances of the fracture a bit more vividly: Four justices found no constitutional problem with either display, three found both displays constitutionally flawed, and two believed that the crèche in the courthouse clashed with anti-establishment principles but that the menorah on government property did not. That division produced a result in which five justices held the crèche *unconstitutional* while six reached precisely the opposite conclusion about the menorah.

The five justices who together found the crèche display inconsistent with anti-establishment principles spoke through Justice Harry Blackmun. Their conclusion emerged from two core propositions.

The first of these guiding principles concerned the appropriate tools with which to approach the constitutional problem at issue. For this group of justices, the "no endorsement" view of the anti-establishment guarantee initially articulated by Justice O'Connor in *Lynch* represented a useful approach, one faithful to fundamental constitutional principles. As Justice Blackmun put it:

> In recent years, we have paid particularly close attention to whether the challenged government practice either has the purpose or effect of "endorsing" religion, a concern that has long had a place in Establishment Clause jurisprudence. . . . Whether the key word is "endorsement," "favoritism," or "promotion," the essential principle remains the same. The Establishment Clause, at the very least, prohibits government from appearing to take a position on questions of religious belief or from "making adherence to a religion relevant in any way to a person's standing in the political community." [Quoting the O'Connor concurrence in *Lynch*.][216]

The second, corresponding proposition for the justices speaking through Justice Blackmun drew on the difference of constitutional magnitude these justices discerned between the Pawtucket display upheld five years earlier in *Lynch* and the Allegheny County crèche they believed could not withstand constitutional scrutiny: The latter could not be salvaged constitutionally by virtue of the presence of other, less troublesome holiday paraphernalia surrounding it, such as reindeer pulling Santa's sleigh.[217] Quite the contrary: As Justice Blackmun observed, "[h]ere, in contrast, the crèche stands alone: it is the single element of the display."[218]

Four justices, speaking through Justice Kennedy, devoted considerable energy in *Allegheny County* to expressing their disapproval of the wisdom and usefulness of the "endorsement" approach.[219] One core component of the Kennedy critique rested on the allegation that the "endorsement" approach, applied generally, would reach results inconsistent with traditional historical practices.[220] As examples, Justice Kennedy contended that legislative prayer, the employment of legislative chaplains, presidential proclamations declaring Thanksgiving a day of celebration and prayer, and a host of other long-standing national practices could not withstand scrutiny under the "no endorsement" approach, because, according to Kennedy, such practices—and many others—surely "would cause nonadherents to feel excluded."[221] A second knock on the "endorsement" approach, according to Justice Kennedy, was that the approach "threatens to trivialize constitutional adjudication" by creating "a jurisprudence of minutiae"[222] that requires appellate courts to consider, for instance, whether a municipality has included in a holiday display sufficient and sufficiently secular items—a Santa Claus, talking wishing wells, reindeer, candy canes, and the like—to insulate an indisputably religious item such as a crèche from the charge that it has unconstitutionally "endorsed" a particular set of religious faiths.[223]

After endeavoring to expose the impracticalities of Justice O'Connor's "endorsement" approach, Justice Kennedy proceeded to set out an alternative way to grasp, and be faithful to, the anti-establishment guarantee:

> Our cases disclose two limiting principles: government may not coerce anyone to support or participate in any regulation or its exercise; and it may not, in the guise of avoiding hostility or callous indifference, give direct benefits to religion in such as a degree that it in fact "establishes a [state] religion or religious faiths, or tends to do so." [Quoting the O'Connor concurrence in *Lynch*.][224]

This quartet of justices subscribing to the "no coercion" approach to anti-establishment problems joined with Justices Blackmun and O'Connor to produce the conclusion that the menorah display did not pose a constitutional problem. But the six differed widely on the justification for that conclusion. The Kennedy four expressed the view that the menorah represented nothing more than the city's acknowledgment of the holiday season and decidedly *not* "an effort to proselytize or . . . otherwise the first step down the road to an establishment of religion."[225] Justice O'Connor expressed the view that, despite the menorah's religious significance, its presence alongside a Christmas tree and a sign saluting liberty ultimately combined to convey a message of "pluralism and freedom" rather than an endorsement of religion.[226] Justice Blackmun, by contrast, reached the same conclusion by contending that the displays reflected Pittsburgh's efforts to celebrate both Christmas and Chanukah as "secular holidays," to "recognize[] that both Christmas and Chanukah are part of the same winter-holiday season, which has attained secular status in our society."[227]

This second effort to confront the distinctive anti-establishment issues attendant to religious holiday displays revealed strikingly little consensus among the justices with regard to virtually anything having to do with such issues.

Latin Cross on a Public Square

Six years after *Allegheny County*, the Court confronted the latest of its most recent cases implicating the constitutional status of government-supported religious symbols.

In Capitol Square Review Board v. Pinette (1995),[228] the justices encountered an Ohio law that *both* rendered the ten-acre statehouse plaza in Columbus a forum for the exchange of public discussion *and* empowered a particular organization—the Capitol Square Review and Advisory Board ("the Board")—to regulate public access to the space. Historically the Board had permitted a wide variety of speakers to conduct activities on the Square, and likewise had permitted unattended displays to be erected.

In November 1993, an officer of the Ohio Ku Klux Klan applied to receive the Board's permission to place an unattended cross on the Square for much of the December holiday season. The Board denied the request, informing the Klan that the decision emerged as a result of legal advice seeking to ensure that the Board complied with the state and federal constitutions. It soon became apparent that the Board's action rested on the view that the anti-establishment guarantee forbade it to authorize the placement of the cross on public property.

The Klan proceeded to file suit, seeking an injunction requiring the Board to issue the permit allowing the Klan to erect the cross. The trial court, agreeing with the Klan, concluded that the cross represented private speech that could not reasonably be construed as government endorsement of Christianity.[229] Accordingly, the trial court issued the injunction. The United States Court of Appeals for the Sixth Circuit agreed.[230] So, too, did the high court, with seven justices agreeing on the proposition that allowing the unattended cross equal access to public property with other unattended private displays did not clash with anti-establishment principles.

The seven justices who found the Klan's cross constitutionally unproblematic nevertheless could not muster a consensus on the justification for their conclusion.

Justice Scalia, writing for himself and three others, expressly declined to apply the nonendorsement principle to the facts of *Capitol Square Review Board*.[231] The four-justice plurality made clear that the anti-establishment guarantee serves principally to limit *government* expression and activity, not the "purely private" expression of an organization such as the Klan undertaken on property open to all. For that reason the four-justice plurality observed that, in its view, the extent to which the reasonable observer viewing the Klan's cross would mistake it for the speech of government simply did not matter.

A different three-justice plurality, consisting of Justices O'Connor, Souter, and Breyer, arrived at the conclusion that the scheme did not clash with anti-establishment principles via a strikingly different route. By contrast to their colleagues speaking through Justice Scalia, the three-justice plurality contended that central to the constitutional analysis was the question of whether the reasonable, dispassionate observer viewing the cross display would perceive the display as a government endorsement of religion.[232] As Justice Souter observed, "in some circumstances an intelligent observer may mistake private, unattended religious displays in a public forum for government speech endorsing religion."[233] This trio of justices, in short, believed the Klan's cross display indeed merited the stuff of traditional anti-establishment analysis.

For two reasons, however, the trio ultimately agreed that the Board could have allowed the Klan's cross to be erected without jeopardizing the values underpinning the anti-establishment guarantee. Justice O'Connor offered one such reason, observing that, at bottom, "the reasonable observer would view the Klan's cross display fully aware that Capitol Square is a public space in which a multiplicity of groups, both secular and religious, engage in expressive conduct."[234] Justice Souter offered the other reason, explaining that the Board possessed the authority to obviate any constitutional problem the Klan's display would have engendered by requiring the Klan to affix to the cross a disclaimer message indicating that the display ought not be construed as a governmental endorsement of the Christian faith.[235]

The Court has not delivered a clear or consistent message concerning the role the anti-establishment guarantee plays in the evaluation of holiday displays and other religious symbolism on public property. Indeed, one prominent federal judge has lamented that this slice of the constitutional law of religion "requires scrutiny more commonly associated with interior decorators than with the judiciary."[236] This phenomenon stems in part from a disagreement the justices continue to have concerning precisely what approach to anti-establishment challenges, what legal standards, to apply to these displays. Should judges be seeking to determine the extent to which such displays reflect government "endorsement" of religion? Should they instead be looking for situations in which such displays "coerce" nonbelievers? In short, the inability of the justices to forge consensus on an overarching approach to anti-establishment challenges in part accounts for the jurisprudential chaos pervading the case law devoted to holiday and religious displays.

But the phenomenon perhaps stems as well from the myriad of different displays that crop up across the nation and the difficulty of crafting rules to govern them that will not expose the judiciary to embarrassment or ridicule. Exactly how prominent must the more nonreligious dimensions of a holiday display be in order to neutralize the more fundamentally religious aspects of the display? When does a particular display cross the line between representing little more than an innocuous public recognition of the holiday season and the more problematic sorts of government support for religion or particular religious beliefs and practices? It remains hard to deny that the Court has not been especially helpful in setting out answers to these questions that can serve as a useful guide for municipal officials, organizations, and residents who seek to conform their conduct to the requirements of the law.

THE OTHER SIDE OF THE ANTI-ESTABLISHMENT COIN: PUBLIC ASSISTANCE TO RELIGIOUS INSTITUTIONS AND FAMILIES WHOSE CHILDREN ATTEND RELIGIOUS SCHOOLS

To this point, our focus has been directed at circumstances in which anti-establishment principles have been implicated as a result of some action undertaken by government to invite aspects of religion *into* the institutions of government. At this juncture, we turn to explore the impact of the anti-establishment guarantee when government reaches *out to* support the institutions of religion, usually by extending financial assistance to religious institutions or to families who use such institutions.

The issue of whether, and the extent to which, the anti-establishment guarantee permits public funds to be used for the benefit of religious schools and families who attend such schools has consumed an inordinate amount of judicial time and resources. Unfortunately, the result of this considerable expenditure of time and resources has been a vast body of constitutional law whose principal features include massive inconsistencies, ever-shifting principles, and unconvincing hair-splitting. This section endeavors to impose some order on a body of anti-establishment law worthy of being dubbed many things, but assuredly not orderly.

One other preliminary observation concerning the cases devoted to public assistance to religious schools and the families who attend such schools seems especially appropriate. Today, at the dawn of the twenty-first century, a majority of the nation's high court manifests substantially more sympathy for such financial assistance, and thus more resistance to anti-establishment concerns raised by such assistance, than had been the case two or three decades earlier. Particularly in this aspect of anti-establishment law, therefore, understanding the current status of the law rests to a considerable extent on understanding the way in which the law has evolved.

Financial Assistance to Religion: Assistance to Families Whose Children Attend Religious Schools

Public monies directed to families whose children attend religious schools invariably redound to the benefit of the religious schools themselves. Likewise, financial assistance to religious schools ultimately benefits the families whose children attend such schools. In short, the dichotomy between assistance to families and assistance to schools represents something of a legal fiction. Nevertheless, the distinction has played a meaningful role in some of the most recent case law concerning the implications of anti-establishment principles for financial assistance to religion. For that reason, as well as for purposes of organizational clarity, the materials that follow will discuss the issues of financial assistance along this dichotomy. We begin by exploring the cluster of cases concerning financial assistance to families whose children attend religious elementary and secondary schools.

Transportation of Students

Consideration of the Court's haphazard and seemingly unprincipled treatment of the constitutional issues engendered when government provides financial assistance to religion traditionally begins with a 1947 case out of New Jersey concerning the transportation of students to and from school (Everson v. Board of Education, 1947).[237]

A state law had empowered local school districts to deal with the cluster of issues related to transporting students to and from the schools they attended, both public and not-for-profit private schools. Pursuant to the invitation, the board of education for the township of Ewing authorized parents to be reimbursed for the costs of having their children transported on buses operated by the public transportation system. The result of the Ewing authorization was that parents who sent their children to what the Court referred to as "Catholic parochial schools"[238] received the reimbursement. A taxpayer residing in the district challenged the reimbursement, contending that the anti-establishment guarantee forbade the school board to subsidize the costs of religious education, including the costs of transporting students to Catholic schools. The Court, dividing five to four, disagreed.

Writing for the majority in upholding the practice, Justice Black devoted a considerable portion of the anti-establishment discussion to exploring the historical underbrush of the Constitution's protections for religious liberty. That discussion culminated with the majority expressing two propositions about the anti-establishment guarantee. The first was that, despite the original mischief it set out to foreclose, mischief to be wrought by institutions of the *national* government, the anti-establishment guarantee needed to be construed to bind the states as well.[239] The second, flowing substantially from the first, represented the majority's effort to summarize what the anti-establishment principle was all about:

> The "establishment of religion" clause of the First Amendment means at least this: Neither a state nor the Federal Government can set up a church. Neither can pass laws which aid one religion, aid all religions, or prefer one religion over another. Neither can force nor influence a person to go to or remain away from church against his will or force him to profess a belief or disbelief in any religion. No person can be punished for entertaining or professing religious beliefs, for church attendance or non-attendance. No tax in any amount, large or small, can be levied to support any religious activities or institutions, whatever they may be called, or whatever form they may adopt to teach or practice religion. Neither a state nor the Federal government can, openly or secretly, participate in the affairs of any religious organizations or groups and vice versa. In the words of Jefferson, the clause . . . was intended to erect "a wall of separation between Church and State."[240]

This passage represents perhaps the most famous collection of words in the considerable body of law devoted to the anti-establishment guarantee. The careful reader of this portion of the *Everson* majority opinion could well have anticipated that the majority would proceed to invalidate the New Jersey reimbursement, concluding that it amounted to nothing other than a "tax" being "levied to support . . . religious activities or institutions." That reader, however, would have been in for a surprise.

Instead, the majority labored diligently to uphold the reimbursement and reject the challenge to it. The nub of its defense stemmed from its view that the anti-establishment guarantee requires government "to be a neutral in its relations with groups of religious believers and non-believers; it does not require the state to be their adversary."[241] According to the majority, preventing families who send their children to Catholic schools from receiving the reimbursement would be to exclude these families from receiving a public benefit "*because of their faith*"[242]—a result that, according to the majority, the Constitution simply does not permit. To be sure, the majority observed, the anti-establishment guarantee forbids government to "contribute tax-raised funds to support an institution which teaches the tenets and faith of any church."[243] But the guarantee does *not*, the majority maintained, prevent government from providing a benefit to families of parochial school children that it happens to provide to all families. Accordingly, the *Everson* majority concluded its opinion by asserting as follows: "The First Amendment has erected a wall between church and state. That wall must be kept high and impregnable. We could not approve the slightest breach. New Jersey has not breached it here."[244]

A quartet of dissenting justices essentially accused the *Everson* majority of hypocrisy, of seeking to have it both ways.

On the one hand, the dissenters pointed out, the majority spoke rhapsodically about the "high and impregnable" wall separating government from the institutions of religion and repeatedly observed that the Constitution forbade public monies from supporting religious institutions. On the other hand, the dissenters continued, when the dust from the case settled the result produced by the majority opinion suspiciously resembled precisely that: public monies flowing to the benefit of religious institutions. In the words of Justice Jackson, "the undertones of the [majority] opinion, advocating complete and uncompromising separation of Church from state, seem utterly discordant with its conclusion yielding support to their commingling in educational matters."[245]

Everson revealed that not all public assistance that accrues to the benefit of religious schools and the families of children who attend them will breach the anti-establishment principle. Subsequent cases have sought valiantly—and to a considerable extent unsuccessfully—to clarify the contours of the issue.

Textbooks

Two decades after *Everson* a New York law prompted the Court to explore more deeply the extent to which the anti-establishment principle allows public monies and benefits to flow to religious schools and their families (Board of Education v. Allen, 1965).[246] More specifically, the New York legislature required each local school board to purchase textbooks and to lend them free of charge to all students residing in the district enrolled in grades seven through twelve, including to those students who happened to attend religious schools. Some local school boards challenged the law as a violation of the anti-establishment principle, contending that public monies may not be spent in such a fashion without overstepping that constitutional principle. New York's highest court rejected the challenge. The Supreme Court followed suit, concluding that the practice comported with constitutional constraints.

The analysis set out in the majority opinion of Justice Byron White began with the observation that the New Jersey transportation reimbursement program upheld in *Everson* represented the closest analogue to the facts of *Allen*. From that premise the Court had little trouble upholding the New York practice. Both in *Everson* and *Allen*, the Court noted, the state extended a benefit "to all citizens without regard for their religious affiliation."[247] And in each case, the Court reasoned, the decision to extend such a benefit reflected *both* a genuinely secular purpose—assisting all students in getting to and from school, on the one hand, and strengthening the education that all students receive at school, on the other—*and* a primary effect that neither advanced nor inhibited religion. To be sure, the majority acknowledged, buses indeed are different from books. But the majority emphatically rejected the challengers' argument that, because textbooks implicate the teaching function of religious institutions in a way that transporting students to and from school does not, the anti-establishment guarantee must necessarily be construed to prohibit public monies to be used to supply such textbooks.

That rejection emerged in a variety of replies from the Court, principal among them the fact that the law mandated that the textbooks to be supplied be secular rather than religious in nature. Moreover, the majority made clear that, in its view, the mere fact that government assistance of the sort at issue in the cases may increase the likelihood that some families will send their children to religious schools does not invariably transform an otherwise constitutionally unproblematic practice into one that requires invalidation.

Perhaps the most striking irony of the Court's treatment of the New York textbook scheme at issue in *Allen* concerned a dissent that the case prompted, a dissent authored by, of all people, the very architect of the *Everson* majority two decades earlier. Justice Black dubbed the textbook scheme at issue in *Allen* "a flat, flagrant, open violation" of the anti-establishment principle,[248] and maintained that a constitutional line ought to be drawn between transportation and textbooks. His vigorous and portentous remarks included the following:

> It is true, of course, that the New York law does not as yet formally adopt or establish a religion. But it takes a great stride in that direction and coming events cast their shadows before them. The same powerful sectarian religious propagandists who have succeeded in securing passage of the present law to help religious schools carry on their sectarian religious purposes can and doubtless will continue their propaganda, looking toward complete domination and supremacy of their particular brand of religion. And it nearly always is by insidious approaches that the citadels of liberty are most successfully attacked. . . . It requires no prophet to foresee that on the argument used to support this law others could be upheld providing for state or federal government funds to buy property on which to erect religious school buildings or to erect the buildings themselves, to pay the salaries of the religious school teachers, and finally to have the sectarian religious groups cease to rely on voluntary contributions of members of their sects while waiting for Government to pick up the bills for the religious schools. . . .

I still subscribe to the belief that tax-raised funds cannot constitutionally be used to support religious schools.[249]

This pair of cases—one concerning transportation, the other textbooks—embodies the first phase of the Court's treatment of the issue of financial assistance to religious schools and families. Two features of this phase, each perhaps obvious, nevertheless merit brief comment. First, the Court upheld these expenditures of public monies to assist religious schools and the families who attended them, in each case essentially concluding that such assistance posed no serious conflict with anti-establishment concerns. Second, in each case the dispute engendered among the justices themselves suggested that competing perspectives concerning the application of the anti-establishment principle to issues of financial assistance to religion would persist for a considerable duration of time.

Tax Benefits for the Costs of Tuition

Government assistance sometimes unfolds in the form of tax benefits. Not surprisingly, therefore, the impact the anti-establishment principle holds for tax benefits that redound to the advantage of religious schools and the families who send their children to such schools has been a source of periodic dispute. Two years after *Lemon*, the Court invalidated a New York program that granted tax benefits amounting to tuition grants to families whose children attended nonpublic schools, the vast majority of which were religious schools (Committee for Public Education v. Nyquist, 1973).[250] Ten years later, however, a high court case out of Minnesota revealed a sharply divided Court moving in quite the opposite direction (Mueller v. Allen, 1983).[251]

Minnesota for many years allowed taxpayers to claim a deduction from gross income for some expenses incurred in educating children. Among the expenses permitted to be deducted pursuant to the law were expenses associated with tuition, textbooks, and transportation—expenses almost entirely borne by families sending their children to private schools, the overwhelming bulk of which happened to be religiously affiliated. Accordingly, some taxpayers challenged the tax benefits as a violation of anti-establishment principles. Dividing five to four, the Supreme Court rejected the challenge.

The majority opinion of Justice William Rehnquist purported to evaluate the Minnesota tax scheme against the three-pronged standard set out in *Lemon*. But the evaluation represented at best an exceedingly gentle application of the purpose/effect/entanglement combination.

As for the purpose prong, the majority observed that "little time" need be spent on the question because financial assistance extended by government to the institutions of religion or to families who in turn used the assistance for matters relating to religion traditionally had been found to be rooted in a legitimate secular purpose.[252] Much the same can be said for the Minnesota tax scheme, the majority reasoned:

An educated populace is essential to the political and economic health of any community, and a state's efforts to assist parents in meeting the rising cost of educational expenses plainly serves the secular purpose of ensuring that the state's citizenry is well-educated. Similarly, Minnesota . . . could conclude that there is a strong public interest in assuring the continued financial health of private schools, both sectarian and non-sectarian. By educating a substantial number of students such schools relieve public schools of a correspondingly great burden—to the benefit of all taxpayers. In addition, private schools may serve as a benchmark for public schools in a manner analogous to the "TVA yardstick" for private power companies.[253]

The analysis then proceeded to assess the "effects" prong, an inquiry the majority acknowledged to be "more difficult" given the way in which the Minnesota tax benefit operated.[254] For a variety of reasons, however, the majority concluded that the scheme did not suffer from a *primary* effect of advancing religion.[255]

One reason for this conclusion pointed to by Justice Rehnquist concerned the possibility that the tax benefits extended by the Minnesota legislature served merely to equalize tax burdens on families by softening some of the tax blow experienced by families whose children attended nonpublic schools.[256]

A second reason concerned the fact that the deduction by all terms was available to all families, even those whose youngsters attended public school–notwithstanding the obvious rejoinder that the benefits of the scheme disproportionately accrued to families whose children attended religious schools.[257]

A third reason focused on the way in which the tax scheme worked: By channeling the public benefit to the pocketbooks of families rather than to the coffers of religious schools, the majority contended, the benefit to religion becomes less direct and more attenuated, thus posing less of a problem with *Lemon*'s effects prong.[258]

Finally, the majority expressed the conclusion that the tax scheme posed no substantial entanglement problems.[259] To be sure, Justice Rehnquist observed, state officials need to be certain to disallow deductions improperly taken, such as deductions for religiously oriented instructional books and materials. Nevertheless, the majority reported, such decisions do not implicate entanglement concerns, at least no more so than administrative decisions required to be made by government that had earned previous Court approval, such as ensuring that funds earmarked for textbooks used by children attending religiously affiliated schools get applied only to the secular books. In addition, the Court noted that the sort of political divisiveness of which *Lemon* spoke ought to be understood as confined to circumstances in which government monies flowed directly to religious schools, rather than to families.

A dissenting opinion authored by Justice Thurgood Marshall and joined by three colleagues sought to take the majority to task in two respects.[260]

First, the dissenters expressed their skepticism at what they viewed as the majority's lame effort to distinguish *Nyquist*, the earlier tax case—a distinction that, for the dissenters, rested on the highly formalistic fact that the Minnesota scheme by its terms extended the tax deduction to all families rather than merely to families whose children attended private schools. The costs of tuition continued to represent the bulk of the tax benefit, the dissenters noted, and those costs accrued almost exclusively to families whose children attended private schools, the overwhelming majority of which were religiously affiliated.[261]

These operational realities of the Minnesota tax benefit led to the dissent's more fundamental concern: That the tax deduction scheme clashed with anti-establishment principles and the *Lemon* guidelines because its principal effect was to advance the religious institutions attended by those families who reaped the tax benefit.[262]

The Court's approval of the Minnesota tax benefit—a benefit predominantly accruing to the families of children attending religiously affiliated schools—revealed that a narrow majority of the Court appeared to be forging a consensus around two propositions. The first concerned the notion that governmental assistance flowing in the first instance to families rather than directly from government to religious institutions tended to render the assistance itself less problematic constitutionally. The second concerned the fact that the majority appeared willing to downplay anti-establishment concerns in circumstances in which the formalities of the assistance program at issue failed to make reference to religion, even when the practical realities of the program meant that the vast bulk of the assistance benefited religious institutions and the families who enrolled their children in such institutions.

Assistance to Handicapped Students

The Court consistently has rebuffed governmental efforts to deny assistance to handicapped students merely because the students sought to use that assistance in religiously affiliated schools. Two much discussed cases underscore this theme.

Larry Witters suffered from a deteriorating eye condition. He attended Inland Empire School of the Bible, a Christian college in Spokane, Washington. His studies—designed to prepare him for a career as a pastor, missionary, or youth director—included the Bible, ethics, and church administration. Pursuant to a Washington law, Witters applied to the Washington Commission for the Blind for vocational rehabilitation services, services for which Witters clearly was eligible under the terms of the statute. But the commission declined to provide the assistance, opining that Witters's intention to use the assistance for religious purposes posed an insuperable problem, compelling the commission to deny the assistance. After a variety of administrative and judicial twists and turns, the dispute made its way to the high court (Witters v. Washington Department of Services for the Blind, 1986).[263]

A unanimous Court concluded that nothing in the law of anti-establishment justified the commission's decision to disqualify Witters from the assistance. The majority opinion of Justice Marshall acknowledged that *Lemon*'s second prong, the "effect" inquiry, represented the central issue for resolution of the dispute. The Court sought to justify its conclusion that assistance to Witters would *not* have the primary effect of advancing religion by noting three aspects of the Washington scheme.

First, the majority observed that the payment for vocational assistance proceeded from the state to the individual student, who then transmitted it to a particular school. Accordingly, the majority deemed it important that "[a]ny aid provided under Washington's program that ultimately flows to religious institutions does so only as a result of the genuinely independent and private choices of aid recipients."[264]

Second, and relatedly, the majority paused to note that the program offered assistance generally and without regard to the sectarian or nonsectarian, the public or private, nature of the school ultimately benefited.[265]

Third, the majority opined that, even were assistance to flow to Larry Witters, no substantial portion of the funds coming from the Washington program would end up flowing to religious institutions.[266]

This first pair of themes—on the one hand, the fact that an intervening choice made by a family to bestow a benefit on a religious institution rendered the government assistance less problematic constitutionally and, on the other, the fact that the government assistance flowing to all otherwise eligible recipients (irrespective of whether the recipients used the assistance to benefit secular or sectarian institutions) likewise posed no substantial anti-establishment problem—continues to play an increasingly prominent role in anti-establishment law today.

A case concerning a deaf student seeking a sign-language interpreter for use in a Tucson, Arizona, Roman Catholic high school echoed the approach the Court undertook in *Witters*—although the Arizona case proved substantially more divisive for the Justices (Zobrest v. Catalina Foothills School District, 1993).[267] Pursuant to the federal Individuals with Disabilities Education Act (IDEA) and its Arizona equivalent, James Zobrest, deaf since birth, requested the school district to provide him a sign-language interpreter to accompany him to classes at Salpointe High School, a Roman Catholic high school he attended. The school district refused, contending that anti-establishment principles prohibited it from complying with the request. Five members of the Court disagreed, awarding victory to Zobrest.

The majority opinion of Chief Justice Rehnquist expressed the core principle that led it to its conclusion as follows:

> We have never said that "religious institutions are disabled by the First Amendment from participating in publicly sponsored welfare programs." . . . Given that [such a] rule would lead to absurd results, we have consistently held that government programs that neutrally provide benefits to a broad class of citizens defined without reference to religion are not

readily subject to an Establishment Clause challenge just because sectarian institutions may also receive an attenuated financial benefit. Nowhere have we stated this principle more clearly than in [*Mueller*] and [*Witters*].[268]

The majority elaborated on its reasoning by reporting a range of other factors it deemed germane to the anti-establishment inquiry. One focused on the government program at issue—IDEA—and noted that the program distributes benefits "neutrally" to any qualifying student, irrespective of whether the school the child attends happens to be secular or sectarian. A second factor honed in on the fact that, under the program, *families* determine where to direct the assistance for which a child renders them eligible; *the government*, the majority concluded, thus cannot be said to be responsible for an interpreter turning up in a religious school.

Three dissenting justices discerned a good deal more anti-establishment mischief afoot than did the majority. Speaking through Justice Blackmun, the dissent began by noting that never before had the Court construed anti-establishment principles to "authorize[] a public employee to participate directly in religious indoctrination."[269] That result, they noted, flows inevitably from the majority's decision: An interpreter paid by government would be communicating the material covered in religion class, the substance of the daily masses the school encouraged its students to attend, as well as the secular subjects that, as the dissent put it, the school teaches from a religious perspective. Nor did the dissent find the majority's analogy to *Mueller* and *Witters* especially apt: In those cases, Justice Blackmun contended, government involvement ended with a cash payment or a tax deduction; the facts of *Zobrest*, by contrast, reveal "ongoing, daily, and intimate governmental participation in the teaching and propagation of religious doctrine."[270] Such participation, the dissent noted, "is likely to place the *imprimatur* of governmental approval upon the favored religion, conveying a message of exclusion to all those who do not adhere to its tenets."[271]

Tuition Vouchers and School Choice

The use of government funds to expand the educational opportunities available to poor families otherwise consigned to inner-city public schools has become a prominent political issue around the nation. The issue has forged unusual coalitions on each side of the debate, with racial minorities joining hands with a variety of conservative interest groups in advocating the creation and expansion of such programs and teacher unions providing much of the muscle applied in opposition to such efforts.

Anti-establishment principles enter the fray when government seeks to expand the private schools participating in such "voucher" or "school choice" programs to include religiously affiliated schools. Put simply, the anti-establishment guarantee prompts the question of whether government, consistent with constitutional requirements, may allocate funds to families who in turn use those funds to defray some or all of the costs of attending religiously affiliated elementary or secondary schools. A recent landmark high court case split the Court down the middle, with five justices answering the question in the affirmative (Zelman v. Simmons-Harris, 2002).[272]

The alleged failure of Cleveland's public school system in meeting Ohio's performance criteria prompted the state to enact a scholarship program for families with children in that system. The principal purpose of the program was to expand the educational opportunities for the children in such families. The amount of the scholarship depended upon family income, with the most sizable grants going to families whose income fell below 200 percent of the poverty line. Each family in this category of lowest income could use each scholarship—capped at either $2,250 or 90 percent of the price of tuition, whichever happened to be less—in a variety of ways, including applying the funds toward tuition at one of fifty-six participating private schools within the district, the bulk of which happened to be religious schools. In the most recent academic year for which data existed, 96 percent of students participating in the program attended religious schools, with more than 8 million dollars of public monies going to such schools.

Given such developments, a coalition of plaintiffs—among them taxpayers and the state superintendent of public instruction—not surprisingly challenged the program's inclusion of religious schools, contending that anti-establishment principles forbade such public monies to be used for religious instruction. Dividing five to four, the Court rejected the challenge and upheld the program, doing so for reasons strikingly analogous to those the majority had provided earlier.

The majority opinion authored by Chief Justice Rehnquist explained its conclusion that the anti-establishment guarantee posed no insurmountable problem to such a "religious-school choice" program as follows.

The majority noted, first, that an eminently legitimate secular purpose justified the Ohio program. That purpose the majority expressed as "providing educational assistance to poor children in a demonstrably failing public school system."[273] Because no genuine dispute existed as to the purpose inquiry, the analysis would hinge, the majority reported, on whether the principal effect of the Ohio program impermissibly advanced religion.

Accordingly, the majority then turned to assess the principal effect of the program. Here it undertook a decisive move in the anti-establishment chess game: It observed that, increasingly, an important insight in seeking to determine whether a public assistance program that channels monies to religious endeavors clashes with anti-establishment principles focuses on whether the monies go directly to the religious institutions themselves or, instead, whether the monies ultimately land in the coffers of religious schools only "as a result of the genuine and independent choices of private individuals."[274] Repeating the insight contained in prior cases, the majority reported that financial assistance programs of the former category prove substantially more constitutionally problematic than do those of the latter type. As the chief justice put it,

> [W]here a government aid program is neutral with respect to religion, and provides assistance directly to a broad class of citizens who, in turn, direct government aid to religious schools wholly as a result of their own genuine and independent private choice, the program is not readily subject to challenge under the Establishment Clause. A program that shares these features permits government aid to reach religious institutions only by way of the deliberate choices of numerous individual recipients. The incidental advancement of a religious mission, or the perceived endorsement of a religious message, is reasonably attributable to the individual recipient, not to the government, whose role ends with the disbursement of benefits.[275]

This theme continues to be voiced in the most important recent cases concerning financial assistance to religious institutions and the families whose children attend such institutions.

Finally, the majority concluded that the Ohio choice program being challenged indeed fell into the category of assistance programs in which public monies get directed to religious schools only after private individuals (families) independently opt to use the scholarships in such a fashion. Because of that fact, the majority reasoned, the program cannot be understood to impermissibly advance religion and thus comports with anti-establishment principles. Nor, the majority observed (in a tip-of-the-hat to Justice O'Connor's "no endorsement" approach), would any "reasonable observer" conclude that a program such as the Ohio choice scheme—in which public monies arrive on the doorsteps of religious schools only as a result of the decisions of families to channel the funds in that direction—"carries with it the *imprimatur* of government endorsement."[276]

The majority's disposition of the case occasioned some extensive and wide-ranging dissents. That of Justice Souter, joined by the three other justices who believed that a proper understanding of anti-establishment principles did not permit the Ohio program, represents one of the most significant contributions to the recent constitutional conversation concerning financial assistance programs.

Justice Souter vigorously contended that the failure to invalidate the Ohio program sapped the anti-establishment guarantee of much of its intended substance. He insisted, among other things, that the decision could not be squared with *Everson*, the landmark case announcing that public monies may not be used to support the teaching of religion; that, beginning with *Mueller*, the tuition tax credit case, the Court's approach to anti-establishment challenges began to backslide from welcome realism to unwelcome formalism; and that, contrary to the majority's suggestion, the Ohio program embodied neither neutrality nor genuine choice but instead reflected favoritism toward religious schools. On the latter point, Justice Souter explained that the reason more than 96 percent of the funds spent on the program ended up at religious schools stemmed from the fact that the scheme, rather than being one of neutrality and free choice, suffered from the reality that "too few nonreligious desks are available and few but religious schools can afford to accept more than a handful of voucher students."[277] Justice

Souter closed by observing that "every objective underlying the prohibition on religious establishment is betrayed by this scheme, but something has to be said about the enormity of the violation."[278] Justice Stephen Breyer also submitted a dissent, explaining that, in his view, the Ohio program will engender religious strife and political division along denominational lines—precisely the developments that the anti-establishment guarantee sought to avoid.[279]

The Court's initial consideration of the anti-establishment aspect of the contemporary school choice debate leaves behind two indelible messages. One message can be gleaned from the result: The Court has concluded, by the narrowest of margins, that inviting religious schools into such voucher programs poses no serious anti-establishment problem, to a considerable extent because, in the Court's view, families rather than government ultimately determine whether to direct such monies to religious institutions. The other message emerges from the deep chasm the issue produced among the justices and the intensity of the sentiments expressed by the dissenters: This financial-assistance-that-ultimately-makes-its-way-to-religious-institutions strand of law remains unusually fluid and unstable.

Financial assistance to families whose children attend religious schools represents one set of circumstances in which government undertakes initiatives that redound to the benefit of religious institutions. The body of anti-establishment law devoted to such public assistance reflects division among the justices and inconsistencies in the principles articulated. Without question, a slender majority of the current Court views such assistance as substantially less problematic than did their brethren of two or three decades past.

That slender majority appears to have coalesced around two propositions. One concerns the formal flow of public assistance: Assistance flowing out of government coffers to families—rather to religious institutions themselves—appears to render the assistance less problematic constitutionally, notwithstanding the fact that such assistance ultimately finds its way to religious institutions. The second concerns the nature of the laws containing such assistance: Laws that make no reference to religion or religious institutions likewise appear to pose considerably less anti-establishment concern for these justices. This pair of propositions adhered to by a majority of today's justices produces a contemporary landscape in which government programs that permit families as a result of their own decisions to channel government assistance to religious institutions likely will withstand constitutional challenge.

We now turn our attention to government assistance directed to religious institutions themselves.

Financial Assistance to Religion: Assistance to Religious Schools

Over the course of three decades, the Court has confronted a wide variety of statutory schemes that featured financial assistance finding its way to religiously affiliated elementary and secondary schools. In general, the trajectory of the law has been that the Court has grown increasingly less hospitable to challenges to such schemes grounded in anti-establishment principles and, correspondingly, significantly more tolerant of such assistance. Moreover, even from the outset the Court has been extremely tolerant of assistance to religiously affiliated colleges and universities.

Elementary and Secondary Schools: Salaries, Salary Supplements, and Instructional Materials

Three years after the Court in *Allen* narrowly approved assistance to religious schools, and the children attending them, in the form of textbooks, the justices found a more substantial constitutional problem with a pair of schemes that offered a bit more in the way of governmental assistance (Lemon v. Kurtzman, 1971).[280]

A Rhode Island law required the state to pass along salary supplements in an amount not to exceed 15 percent of salary to many teachers in nonpublic elementary schools, all of whom taught in Catholic schools. Only teachers whose assignments corresponded to courses taught in the public schools could receive such supplements. In addition, the law required each recipient to refrain from teaching a course devoted to religion for the period during which he or she received the supplement. The supplements sought to mitigate what the legislature identified to be a substantial problem: the erosion of educational quality in nonpublic schools triggered by the escalating salaries needed to attract skilled teachers.

An analogous Pennsylvania law provided reimbursement to nonpublic schools—virtually all of which were religious schools—for expenses that included teacher salaries, textbooks, and instructional materials. Like its Rhode Island counterpart, the Pennsylvania law forbade reimbursement for any course that contained religious subject matter. This legislative effort likewise emerged out of a concern for the deleterious effects wreaked by rising costs.

The Court had little difficulty finding a legitimate secular purpose at work in each of the laws. After all, the Court reasoned, improving the quality of secular education, including the secular dimensions of education delivered by otherwise religious institutions, surely satisfies this baseline requirement of anti-establishment law.[281] Nevertheless, the Court invalidated the programs, concluding that they posed an insuperable problem of government "entanglement" with religion.[282] Such unconstitutional entanglement, in the Court's view, could be seen in a variety of aspects of the Rhode Island and Pennsylvania programs.

First and foremost, the Court pointed to the "comprehensive, discriminating, and continuing state surveillance"[283] that would be necessary to ensure that the religious school and teacher recipients of public funds remained faithful to the state-imposed guidelines. In other words, one sort of problematic entanglement that troubled the Court concerned the very operational realities of the programs at issue: Government employees would be carefully monitoring and auditing the conduct, financial records, and accounting principles of religious schools and religious teachers to ensure that such schools and teachers strictly complied with the programs. According to the Court, this inevitable and constitutionally problematic entanglement sprang from the fact that, particularly with regard to the Pennsylvania scheme, public dollars flowed directly to religious *schools*—unlike the transportation and textbook programs approved in *Everson* and *Allen*, in which the benefits had been directed to students and their families.

But the *Lemon* Court identified a very different sort of entanglement that it found constitutionally disturbing as well. It contended that the schemes at issue in the case, precisely because they channeled government funds to religious institutions, would tend to divide the political community along religious lines—a phenomenon that, according to the Court, the anti-establishment guarantee specifically sought to avoid.[284] The core of this provocative aspect of the Court's entanglement argument can be captured in the following insight from Chief Justice Burger:

> Ordinarily political debate and division, however vigorous or even partisan, are normal and healthy manifestations of our democratic system of government, but political division along religious lines was one of the principal evils against which the First Amendment was intended to protect. The potential divisiveness of such a conflict is a threat to the normal political process. To have States or communities divide on the issues presented by state aid to parochial schools would tend to confuse and obscure other issues of great urgency. . . . It conflicts with our whole history and tradition to permit questions of the Religion Clauses to assume such importance in our legislatures and in our elections that they could divert attention from the myriad issues and problems that confront every level of government. . . . The potential for political divisiveness related to religious belief and practice is aggravated in these two statutory programs by the need for continuing annual appropriations and the likelihood of larger and larger demands as costs and populations grow.[285]

In short, the governmental assistance flowing for all intents and purposes "directly" to religious schools and their teachers in *Lemon* posed two quite distinctive types of excessive entanglement. One stemmed from the ongoing monitoring of the recipients that government employees would be required to undertake in order to ensure that the religious institutions and employees who received the assistance continued to comply with the rules and regulations on which the assistance had been conditioned. A fundamentally different concern focused on the potential for direct assistance to religious schools to divide the political community, triggering a struggle among different religious faiths for their respective shares of the public budgetary pie.

Elementary and Secondary Schools: Auxiliary Services and Instructional Materials and Equipment

Four years after *Lemon*, the Court examined a revised Pennsylvania program that channeled a range of assistance to nonpublic schools, the bulk of which were religious schools (Meek v. Pittenger, 1975).[286] One category of such assistance—auxiliary services—included counseling, testing, psychological, and remedial services through which public school employees would perform the services at the religious school. Another category—instructional materials and equipment—included periodicals, maps, recordings, films, and projection and laboratory equipment that, in accordance with the program's provisions, public school officials would lend to religious schools. The Court invalidated these assistance programs. It concluded that the latter resulted in the impermissible effect of advancing religious teachings, because even though the materials and equipment undeniably were secular, their use in pervasively religious schools whose secular and religious functions the Court found "inextricably intertwined" impelled the conclusion that such governmental assistance invariably would assist in religious indoctrination.[287] As to the former—the auxiliary personnel assistance—the Court concluded that the use of public employees in religious schools engendered a level of entanglement between government and religious schools that the anti-establishment guarantee simply did not permit, noting the same sets of concerns that it had recently expressed in *Lemon*.[288]

Elementary and Secondary Schools: Shared Time and Community Education Programs

Two aspects of an assistance program out of Grand Rapids, Michigan, afforded the justices yet another opportunity to confront the impact of anti-establishment principles on such programs (School District of the City of Grand Rapids v. Ball, 1985).[289] The "shared time" aspect of the program featured public school teachers coming into nonpublic (almost exclusively religiously affiliated) schools during the course of the regular school day to offer a variety of courses designed to supplement the core courses required by the state. These supplementary courses included remedial and enrichment courses in mathematics, reading, art, music, and physical education. The typical student devoted approximately 10 percent of his or her time throughout the academic year to these "shared time" courses. The "community education" aspect of the program offered courses to both students and adults in a range of subjects—among them home economics, arts and crafts, gymnastics, yearbook production, chess, and nature appreciation—at the conclusion of the school day. The instructors, teachers otherwise employed by the particular religious schools offering the courses, were deemed part-time employees of the school district. For each aspect of the program, the public school system leased each classroom needed for the programs at a rate of six dollars per week and mandated that, for the duration of the "shared time" or "community education" class, a sign be posted in each classroom expressing the notion that such classroom constituted a public school classroom.

The Court invalidated each aspect of the program, holding that the scheme clashed with *Lemon*'s effect prong. The majority pointed to three ways in which the program could be said to advance religion impermissibly. First, the majority expressed the concern that the teachers delivering instruction in the program could be inculcating students with religious beliefs even as they taught these seemingly secular subjects. As the majority observed, "When conducting a supposedly secular class in the pervasively sectarian environment of a religious school, a teacher may knowingly or unwillingly tailor the content of the course to fit the school's announced goals."[290] Second, the Court opined that the programs at issue forged a disturbing "symbolic link" between government and religion, one that ran the risk of leaving "impressionable youngsters" unable to distinguish between the religious school classes and the public school classes.[291] Third, the majority found that the financial benefit accruing to the religious schools as a result of the programs also clashed with the spirit of anti-establishment principles. As the majority explained, "the programs in effect subsidize the religious functions of the parochial schools by taking over a substantial portion of their responsibility for teaching secular subjects."[292]

Elementary and Secondary Schools: Salaries of Public School Employees Who Teach and Provide Other Services in Religious Schools

A New York City use of federal funds in some respects analogous to the Grand Rapids programs discussed above met a similar fate, and on the same day (Aguilar v. Felton, 1985).[293] New York City used federal funds to pay the salaries of public school employees (teachers, guidance counselors, psychologists, psychiatrists, and social workers) who provided teaching and counseling services to children performing poorly in school. In particular, the assistance provided included remedial reading and other reading skills, remedial mathematics, English as a second language, and a range of guidance services. Pursuant to the federal law, such assistance must be made available to all eligible students, those in private schools no less than those in public schools. With regard to assistance flowing to the private schools and their students, the federal scheme provided that such assistance could benefit students only from low-income families—the vast bulk of whom attended religiously affiliated schools. The Board of Education retained ownership of all materials and equipment used in the program.

A group of taxpayers challenged the part of the municipal operation that featured these public services being provided on the premises of religious schools. A divided Court agreed with the challengers, resulting in an injunction ordering the Board of Education to refrain "from using public funds for any plan or program . . . to the extent that it requires, authorizes or permits public school teachers and guidance counselors to provide teaching and counseling services on the premises of sectarian schools within New York City."[294] In short, the Court's decision required that the assistance flowing to religious schools and their students be halted.

Concerns rooted in the entanglement prong of *Lemon* posed the most prominent problem for the majority. It concluded that because the government assistance at issue takes place in a "pervasively sectarian" environment and features teaching in particular, "ongoing inspection" and "pervasive monitoring" would be necessary to ensure that the public employees refrained from contributing to whatever religious messages the schools otherwise sought to impart.[295] In addition, the majority noted that substantial interaction between administrators of both the school district and the religious schools on matters relating to scheduling, classroom assignments, and a range of other issues exacerbated the entanglement problem.

These cases from the seventies to the middle eighties reveal a Court generally resistant to many forms of assistance flowing from government directly to religiously affiliated schools.

A Change of Tune: The Court Reconsiders

The financial assistance to religious schools cases discussed above reveal that the Court did not hesitate to deploy the tool of anti-establishment to invalidate all sorts of public assistance to religious schools. Sometimes the Court concluded that a particular type of financial assistance to religious schools carried with it the impermissible effect of advancing religion. On other occasions the Court found that particular programs excessively entangled the institutions of religion and government. Nevertheless, the overall message emerging from this cluster of cases very much suggested that financial assistance to religious elementary and secondary schools would be met with a skeptical eye from a majority of the Court.

In 1997, twelve years after the assistance programs from Grand Rapids and New York City in *Ball* and *Aguilar* had been invalidated, a sharply divided Court returned to the identical program that had been at issue in *Aguilar* and came out the other way, overruling the decision in *Aguilar* (and, by implication, the conclusion in *Ball* as well) (Agostini v. Felton, 1997).[296] The slender five-justice majority, speaking through Justice O'Connor, explained its action as a function of the fact that the premises and assumptions set out in some of the earlier cases no longer struck the majority as worthy of continued fidelity.

First, the majority observed that it no longer agreed with the proposition that assigning public employees to duties undertaken on parochial school grounds inevitably leads to state-sponsored indoctrination or amounts to a symbolic union between religion and government.[297]

Second, the majority likewise noted that it no longer agreed with the proposition that all government assistance that directly aids the educational function of religious schools is inconsistent with anti-establishment principles.[298]

Third, the majority expressed disapproval of the way in which the entanglement analysis had been undertaken in *Aguilar* and the conclusion that the scheme evaluated there excessively entangled government and religion.[299] Because, as indicated above, the majority no longer believed it wise to "presume that public employees will inculcate religion simply because they happen to be in a sectarian environment,"[300] it likewise did not agree with the prior conclusion that substantial monitoring would be required to ensure that the teachers and counselors discharging responsibilities remained on the safe side of anti-establishment guidelines. In addition, the majority noted that the entanglement analysis had evolved, and that neither substantial administrative cooperation between public and religious school officials nor the risk of political divisiveness by themselves create excessive entanglement.

Four justices expressed their collective dismay at the change of direction effectuated by the *Agostini* majority. Speaking through Justice David Souter, the dissent lamented both the majority's repudiation of prior anti-establishment law and the fact that its reformulation of constitutional principles would "authorize direct state aid to religious institutions on an unparalleled scale, in violation of the . . . central prohibition against religious subsidies by the government."[301] It elaborated as follows:

> [T]he flat ban on subsidization antedates the Bill of Rights and has been an unwavering rule in Establishment Clause cases. . . . The rule expresses the hard lesson learned over and over again in the American past and in the experiences of the countries from which we have come, that religions supported by governments are compromised just as surely as the freedom of religious dissenters is burdened when the government supports religion.[302]

The tide nevertheless had turned. *Agostini* augured a new era of anti-establishment law, one in which a slender majority on the nine-justice Court would enthusiastically embrace the constitutional legitimacy of financial assistance to religious institutions.

The New Era of Deference

The Court's most recent consideration of financial assistance to elementary and secondary religious schools reflects the sympathy and even gentleness with which the majority of the current Court currently assesses such programs (Mitchell v. Helms, 2000).[303] It also reflects the conspicuous absence of consensus persisting among the justices with regard to the issue of financial assistance to religious schools.

A federal law enacted in 1981 created a program through which federal monies went to local educational agencies to assist students in elementary and secondary schools, both public and private. Such assistance included library services and materials as well as computer software and hardware. To the extent a local agency (typically a school district) extended such assistance to a private school, the law set out a variety of restrictions, among them that the services, materials, and equipment must be "secular, neutral, and nonideological."[304] The local agency for Jefferson Parish, Louisiana, allocated approximately 30 percent of the funds it received from the program to assisting private schools, the overwhelming majority of which were affiliated with the Roman Catholic Church or another religion. Challengers contended that such assistance to religiously affiliated schools violated anti-establishment principles. Six members of the Court disagreed and rejected the challenge, although no rationale offered earned the support of a majority.

The analysis in *Mitchell* focused almost exclusively, as often had been the case, on whether the allocation of public monies to religious schools clashed with the "effect" prong of *Lemon*. In particular, the plurality opinion of Justice Clarence Thomas, speaking for four justices, used as its measuring stick the *Agostini* reformulation of the "effect" inquiry for public assistance cases: whether the assistance results in government-induced religious indoctrination of students; whether the assistance defines its recipients by reference to religion; or whether the assistance creates an excessive entanglement (a matter not at issue in the case).

On the indoctrination point, the plurality concluded that the assistance exhibited no risk of such government-induced religious indoctrination.[305] This conclusion stemmed from three interrelated aspects of the program: the statutory scheme determines eligible recipient schools neutrally, without regard to religion; the assistance flows to schools as a result of choices made by parents and schoolchildren concerning which schools to attend; and the assistance itself (principally computers, computer software, and library books) lacks any impermissible religiously based content.

The second dimension of the "effect" test likewise posed no problem for the plurality. It explained that the federal scheme at issue in the case requires that the assistance be allocated to schools largely on the basis of enrollment, a factor having nothing to do with whether a particular school happens to be religiously affiliated. Accordingly, recipient schools did not receive assistance by virtue of religious criteria.

The plurality, in addition to finding the assistance to religious schools at issue in the case constitutionally unproblematic, passed along two other sets of important observations. One concerned the plurality's lack of enthusiasm for the contention that so-called "direct" assistance to religiously affiliated schools generally will pose an anti-establishment problem. Not so, replied the plurality: Assistance to religious schools that happens to be grounded in neutral, nonreligious criteria and reaches schools only as a result of private choice—even when such assistance does not literally pass through the hands of families—removes the anti-establishment concerns.[306] The second concerned the plurality's observations relating to the argument that assistance to religious schools that runs the risk of being "diverted" to the religious aspects of such schools implicated anti-establishment concerns. Once again, the plurality replied essentially "No. We disagree." Most if not all public assistance can be diverted, the plurality explained. So long as the assistance itself contains no otherwise impermissible religious content, the "divertibility" contention becomes irrelevant to the constitutional analysis.[307]

As noted above, this most recent of encounters with the issue of assistance to religious schools produced a seriously splintered Supreme Court. Justices O'Connor and Breyer—who agreed with the plurality that the program at issue in *Mitchell* did not suffer from anti-establishment flaws—nevertheless took sharp issue with the permissive approach reflected in Justice Thomas's opinion. The pair expressed particular disagreement with the notion suggested by the plurality that financial assistance to religious institutions invariably will withstand constitutional challenge so long as the government program through which the assistance gets distributed treats similarly religious and secular institutions—that is to say, so long as government distributed the assistance "neutrally" without reference to religion. As they put it, "we have never held that a government-aid program passes constitutional muster *solely* because of the neutral criteria it employs as a basis for distributing aid."[308] In addition, Justices O'Connor and Breyer expressed displeasure with the plurality's lack of concern for the prospects that public funds would be diverted to purposes of religious indoctrination. The pair observed that an examination of anti-establishment case law reveals that "we have long been concerned that secular government aid not be diverted to the advancement of religion,"[309] and that such a concern remained eminently justified.

The vast gulf separating the justices on the anti-establishment implications of financial assistance to religious institutions emerged even more strikingly in the dissent of Justice Souter. The dissent, joined by Justices Stevens and Ginsburg, began by observing that the plurality approach "breaks fundamentally" with longstanding anti-establishment principles and represents a "rupture" of principles "painstakingly worked out" over generations of constitutional history.[310] It devoted substantial care to the effort to demonstrate the accuracy of the serious allegations it leveled. Beginning with the simple declaration that the anti-establishment guarantee "bars the use of public funds for religious aid,"[311] the dissent concluded a panoramic review of the case law by observing that, right up until *Mitchell* itself, this principle has continued to served as the centerpiece of our collective understanding of anti-establishment principles. Like the pair of concurring justices, the dissenters expressed vigorous disagreement with *both* the plurality's suggestion that "evenhandedness" in the distribution of public monies to secular and religious schools by itself demonstrates that the assistance satisfies anti-establishment principles *and* its seeming casualness about public monies being diverted to religious use. The dissenters went one step beyond, however, contending that the facts of the case, among them "paltry efforts at [government] monitoring," indicated that the public monies *actually* were being diverted to the religious mission of religious schools, with evidence, for instance, that public monies paid for both religious books and equipment deployed for the purpose of religious indoctrination. The dissent closed on an ominous note:

> [T]here is no mistaking the abandonment of doctrine that would occur if the plurality were to become a majority. . . . [I]n rejecting the principle of no aid to a school's religious mis-

sion the plurality is attacking the most fundamental assumption underlying the Establishment Clause, that government can in fact operate with neutrality in its relation to religion.[312]

Assistance to Higher Education: Construction Grants and General Grants

1. Construction Grants

The Court has suggested that anti-establishment barriers to financial assistance to religiously affiliated institutions of higher education may be a bit more modest than those that attend elementary and secondary schools. A 1963 federal law authorized federal grants and loans to colleges and universities for the construction of academic facilities. The law forbade such funds to be expended for projects that would be used for religious instruction, religious worship, or divinity schools. Nevertheless, the law did not exclude religiously affiliated institutions from the class of potential beneficiaries. The Court proceeded to confront the issue of whether the anti-establishment guarantee allowed such funds to be awarded to religious colleges and universities seeking to build structures such as libraries, art and music centers, science buildings, and language laboratories. The Court concluded that the Constitution posed no such problem (Tilton v. Richardson, 1971).[313]

The plurality's analysis represented the relatively routine application of the *Lemon* three-pronged test: The law reflected the legitimate secular purpose of seeking to secure the welfare of future generations of Americans by enhancing the nation's institutions of higher learning, public and private; the primary effect of the program, rather than strengthening the *sectarian* dimensions of religious colleges and universities, was to enhance the delivery of *secular* education at both public and private institutions; and, finally, no excessively problematic issues on entanglement presented themselves, in part because the grants constituted one-time contributions and thus would not require the persistent monitoring that had been at issue in *Lemon* itself. In the course of the plurality's discussion of entanglement, it passed along the following observation about the difference between religiously affiliated elementary and secondary schools, on the one hand, and those of higher education, on the other:

> There are generally significant differences between the religious aspects of church-related institutions of higher learning and parochial elementary and secondary schools. The "affirmative if not dominant policy" of the instruction in pre-college church schools is to "assure future adherents to a particular faith by having control of their total education at an early age." There is substance to the contention that college students are less impressionable and less susceptible to religious indoctrination. . . . Since religious indoctrination is not a substantial purpose or activity of these church-related colleges and universities, there is less likelihood that religion will permeate the area of secular education. Correspond-

ingly, the necessity for intensive government surveillance is diminished and the resulting entanglements between government and religion lessened.[314]

2. General Grants

Five years after *Tilton*, the Court confronted a Maryland program that provided an annual subsidy to institutions of higher learning, including many religiously affiliated colleges. The grants, initially unrestricted, carried with them a single post-*Lemon* limitation: The funds could not be used "for sectarian purposes." Not surprisingly, a group of Maryland taxpayers and citizens challenged the grants flowing to Roman Catholic colleges—sums that totaled approximately half a million dollars in 1971 and 1972. The Supreme Court rejected the challenge (Roemer v. Board of Public Works of Maryland, 1976).[315]

Justice Harry Blackmun's analysis for the plurality focused principally on the "effect" and "entanglement" prongs of *Lemon*. This increasingly common phenomenon can be attributed to the Court's increasingly common conclusion that assistance to religious schools invariably can be justified through the legitimate secular government purpose of strengthening educational institutions generally.

As to effect, the plurality observed that, typically, a scheme that features public funds flowing to religious schools will tend to withstand challenge under this second prong when two features coalesce: (1) the schools receiving the assistance are able to distinguish the secular aspects of their enterprise from the sectarian aspects, and (2) the public funds flow exclusively to those separate and distinct secular aspects of religious institutions. The Roman Catholic colleges benefiting from the Maryland practice, the plurality concluded, met this standard.[316]

As to the first point—the requirement that recipient schools not exhibit such pervasive sectarianism that the secular aspect of the school cannot be disentangled—the plurality concluded that, all things considered, the recipients of the Maryland monies met that element of the standard—in part because such colleges, despite their religious affiliation, exhibited a substantial degree of institutional autonomy, in part because spiritual development of students represented only "one secondary objective" of the schools, and in part because of the academic freedom that permeated the liberal arts programs.[317]

The plurality likewise found that Maryland tax dollars flowed only to the secular side of the religious institutions receiving such monies. It found this requirement met largely because it assumed the schools would honor the terms of the grant that forbade the monies to be deployed for "specifically religious activity."[318]

The plurality also rejected the argument based on improper entanglement.[319] It especially pointed to two justifications for its conclusion. One had to do with what it presumed to be the fact that the operation of the Maryland subsidy would necessitate only minimal ongoing government supervision. To be sure, the plurality conceded, because the scheme provided for annual grants, "occasional audits" remained a possibility. Such audits, the plurality observed, nevertheless would be "quick and non-judgmental."[320] The second justification concerned the "political divisiveness" aspect of entanglement. The plurality observed that the Maryland scheme did not risk dividing the electorate along religious lines to a considerable degree because the student constituencies of the colleges and universities tended to be more national, and thus more widely dispersed, than happens to be the case at the bulk of elementary and secondary schools.[321]

Financial Assistance to Religion: Grants to Religious Institutions

Much of the public assistance that benefits religious institutions flows to families or religiously affiliated educational institutions. Sometimes, however, government seeks to deploy the assistance of other religious organizations in helping it accomplish objectives the government deems worthy. On such occasions public monies find their way to the coffers of religiously affiliated institutions because particular statutory schemes will include as eligible grantees religious organizations along with secular ones. On such occasions the fact that religious organizations receive public monies often will trigger anti-establishment challenges to such schemes. The Adolescent Family Life Act (AFLA) represents one example of this phenomenon.

In 1981, Congress enacted AFLA. The law provided grants to public or nonprofit private organizations "for services and research in the area of premarital adolescent sexual relations and pregnancy."[322] It required grant recipients to provide two types of services, "care services" and "prevention services."[323] The former consisted of care to pregnant teens and their parents. The latter consisted of efforts to discourage teenage sex and pregnancy. In crafting the legislation, Congress expressed the view that "the problems of adolescent premarital sexual relations, pregnancy, and parenthood [were] multiple and complex."[324] Accordingly, AFLA endeavored to encourage the participation and support of family members, religious and charitable organizations, voluntary associations, and other groups.

A group consisting of federal taxpayers, clergy, and others challenged the inclusion of religious organizations in the scheme, contending that anti-establishment principles forbade public monies to be channeled to such recipients. A divided Court rejected the challenge (Bowen v. Kendrick, 1988).[325]

With *Lemon* as its guide, the majority opinion of Chief Justice Rehnquist concluded, first, that AFLA rested on an eminently secular purpose: reducing the deleterious consequences of teenage sex, pregnancy, and parenthood.[326] The fact that Congress chose to enlist religious organizations in that cause, the majority observed, did not transform an otherwise valid secular purpose into an invalid one.

The majority likewise concluded that the law withstood scrutiny with regard to its principal effect. In so concluding, the majority identified, but rejected, two closely connected arguments made by the challengers to the effect that the law impermissibly advanced religion.

One such argument amounted to the contention that enlisting religiously affiliated organizations in a federally subsidized program by itself represented a violation of anti-establishment principles. The majority countered that, no, Congress evidently believed that some religious organizations were especially well-equipped to assist in the battle against teenage pregnancy, and for that reason the law could not be said to have the principal effect of advancing religion.[327] As the Chief Justice put it, "[n]othing in our previous cases prevents Congress from making such a judgment or from recognizing the important part that religion or religious organizations may play in resolving secular problems."[328]

The other aspect of the effect-prong challenge maintained that, because the law authorized public monies to be directed to religious organizations, the anti-establishment guarantee prohibited the scheme. To this contention the majority replied as follows:

> AFLA defines an "eligible grant recipient" as a "public or nonprofit private organization or agency. . . ." As this provision would indicate, a fairly wide spectrum of organizations is eligible to apply for and receive funding under the Act, and nothing on the face of the Act suggests it is anything but neutral with respect to the grantee's status as a sectarian or purely secular institution.[329]

In sum, the majority essentially reasoned that the fact that AFLA allowed religiously affiliated organizations to be among the many grantees benefited by the law did not undercut the law's neutrality with regard to religious affiliation and thus could not be said to have the primary effect of advancing religion. The majority acknowledged that, despite this rejoinder, the law could have the impermissible effect of advancing religion by directing public monies to "pervasively sectarian" institutions.[330] It nevertheless observed that nothing on the face of AFLA suggested that significant amounts of public monies would be directed to such institutions, or that a risk existed that the religiously affiliated institutions that in fact would receive monies under the law would use such monies for religious indoctrination.[331]

Finally, the majority determined that AFLA posed no excessive entanglement of the institutions of government and religion.[332] In the course of defending this determination the majority conceded that the nature of AFLA would require ongoing governmental supervision of the program and its grant recipients, in order "to ensure that public money is to be spent in a way that comports with the Establishment Clause."[333] But the chief justice dubbed "another Catch-22" the contention that the very government supervision designed to ensure that a program refrained from unconstitutionally advancing religion could be said to transform a federal program into one that renders the program invalid.[334] The majority asserted that it harbored "no reason to fear" that the amount of supervision necessary to ensure that AFLA operated in a constitutional fashion would cause government "to intrude unduly" into "the day-to-day operation" of religiously affiliated grantees.[335]

As has been the case with so many contemporary anti-establishment cases, four members of the nine-person Court dissented. Speaking through Justice Harry Blackmun, the quartet of dissenters contended that AFLA simply could not withstand scrutiny under *Lemon*'s effect prong. The dissent grounded its constitutional objection in the fact that AFLA bestowed on religious groups "a central pedagogical and counseling role without imposing any restraints on the sectarian quality of the participation"[336]—the result being, the dissenters maintained, that the program impermissibly advanced religion. The dissent had no quarrel with the proposition that anti-establishment principles do not foreclose government from subsidizing "secular social-welfare services merely because [such services] are provided by a religiously-affiliated organization."[337] The dissent nevertheless observed as follows:

> There is a very real and important difference between running a soup kitchen or a hospital, and counseling pregnant teenagers on how to make the difficult decisions facing them. The risk of advancing religion at public expense, and of creating an appearance that the government is endorsing the medium and the message, is much greater when the religious organization is directly engaged in pedagogy, with the express intent of shaping belief and changing behavior, than where it is neutrally dispensing medication, food, or shelter.[338]

THE TWILIGHT ZONE: GOVERNMENTAL ACCOMMODATION OF RELIGION AND THE ANTI-ESTABLISHMENT GUARANTEE

The bulk of cases implicating the Constitution's religion clauses fit relatively comfortably into either the anti-establishment or free exercise box. School prayer, religious displays on public property, and financial assistance to religious schools represent fundamentally anti-establishment issues. Whether government is required to carve out an exception from a generally applicable law so as to accommodate the individual whose religious principles prevent him or her from complying with the law represents a classic free exercise issue. To repeat, many, perhaps most issues arising under the First Amendment's religion guarantees can be classified rather easily as anti-establishment matters, on the one hand, or free exercise matters, on the other.

But there remains a category of disputes that falls into something of a twilight zone between anti-establishment and free exercise. The feature common to the disputes in this category can perhaps most accurately be characterized as government reaching out in one way or another to respect the free exercise rights of individuals or groups but then being challenged for its effort at accommodation with the contention that such an effort constitutes an excessively friendly act vis-à-vis religion and for that reason clashes with anti-establishment principles. Accordingly, the central inquiry posed in these cases tends to reduce to this: Has the governmental act grounded in the concern for religion and religious institutions crossed the constitutional line such that it amounts to an impermissible establishment of religion?

Permissible Accommodation: Property Tax Exemption

One such accommodation approved by the Court has been an exemption from the property tax for real estate owned by a religious organization and used for religious purposes, an exemption provided by every state and dating back to the eighteenth century.

Pursuant to a provision in the state's constitution and laws implementing that provision, New York City exempted from its property tax such real estate. A taxpayer challenged the exemption, contending that the exemption amounted to an unconstitutional establishment of religion. One aspect of the challenge concerned the economic contention that the exemption produced a circumstance in which individuals and others ended up essentially being compelled, through their own tax payments, to subsidize religious organizations. The Court rejected the challenge and upheld the exemption (Walz v. Tax Commission, 1970).[339]

Chief Justice Burger began the Court's opinion with a candid acknowledgment of the difficulties that attend efforts to reconcile the competing principles at the roots of the anti-establishment and free exercise guarantees. Burger observed that the Court "has struggled" to chart "a neutral course" between the guarantees.[340] Insofar as property tax exemptions were concerned, however, the Court concluded that neither the purpose nor the effects of such accommodations threatened anti-establishment values. Their purpose, the majority concluded, "is neither the advancement nor the inhibition of religion; it is neither sponsorship nor hostility."[341] Rather, according to the Court, New York, like other states:

> has determined that certain entities that exist in a harmonious relationship to the community at large, and that foster its "moral or mental improvement," should not be inhibited in their activities by property taxation or the hazard of loss of those properties for nonpayment of taxes.[342]

In other words, according to the Court, the purpose of the exemption for such religiously owned property stemmed not from government's aim to advance the cause of religion but, instead, from a perspective that "considers these groups as beneficial and stabilizing influences in community life and [thus considers the exemption] useful, desirable, and in the public interest."[343]

The Court then proceeded to assess whether the effect of such exemptions led to excessive entanglement of the institutions of government and religion. Answering this inquiry in the negative, Chief Justice Burger observed that *taxing* the property of religious organizations would require more frequent and more detailed interaction between government and religion than *exempting* the property from taxation necessitates:

> The exemption creates only a minimal and remote involvement between church and state and far less than taxation of churches. It restricts the fiscal relationship between church and state, and tends to complement and reinforce the desired separation insulating each from the other.[344]

One other factor seemed to play an important role in the Court's conclusion that such tax exemptions for religious organizations represented eminently permissible accommodations: The long-standing and consistent tradition of these exemptions, a tradition going back two centuries, and the absence of any deleterious consequences that would suggest such exemptions will produce a government-sponsored religion. As the chief justice amusingly observed, "[i]f tax exemption can be seen as this first step toward 'establishment' of religion . . . the second step has been long in coming."[345]

Two messages of significance can be extracted from *Walz*. One has to do with the constitutional conclusion the Court reached: Exemptions from the property tax for property owned by religious organizations and used for religious purposes do not clash with anti-establishment principles. The second message has to do with the larger theme of the case: The religion clauses leave government substantial discretion to accommodate the concerns and interests of religious organizations—even when the free exercise guarantee does not *require* such accommodations—without bumping up against anti-establishment concerns.

Permissible Accommodation: Employment Discrimination

Another area in which government has been permitted to accommodate religious organizations without overstepping anti-establishment limits concerns discrimination in employment. Title VII of the Civil Rights Act of 1964 exempts religious organizations from the prohibition on discrimination in employment on the basis of religion that otherwise applies to American employers. Put simply, Congress has authorized religious organizations to consider matters of religion and religious affiliation in connection with the organizations' consideration of employees and prospective employees. Pursuant to this invitation, a Utah gymnasium facility operated by organizations affiliated with the Mormon Church discharged from employment a custodian employed there for sixteen years who failed to demonstrate his eligibility to become a member of the faith. The discharged custodian, along with others, brought suit, contending that in the event a court construed Title VII to authorize the church to take religious issues into account in connection with the employment status of employees who function in nonreligious aspects of a religious organization, Title VII clashed with the anti-establishment guarantee. The justices rejected the argument (Corporation of the Presiding Bishop of the Church of Jesus Christ of Latter-day Saints v. Amos, 1987).[346]

The church and its related organizations had requested the justices to refrain from applying the *Lemon* test, apprehensive that exemption statutes like the one at issue in the case invariably would be found to advance religion and thus fail to withstand scrutiny under the "effect" prong of *Lemon*. The Court essentially replied "not to worry," and proceeded to demonstrate that, in its view, the exemption at issue posed no cause for concern under *Lemon*. It concluded that the purpose animating Congress had much to do with "alleviat[ing] significant governmental interference with the ability of religious organizations to define and carry out their religious missions"[347]—an eminently secular purpose, the Court observed. As for the effect inquiry, the Court acknowledged that the exemption leaves religious organizations "better able to advance their purposes."[348] Nevertheless, the Court contended, anti-establishment principles do not come into play merely because a government action "*allows* churches to advance religion, which is their very purpose."[349] Rather, the "effect" test becomes problematic to satisfy only when "[*g*]*overnment itself*" advances religion, not when government merely allows religion to advance itself.[350] Finally, the Court paused to note the complete absence of "entanglement" concerns. Indeed, the Court indicated that the exemption produces substantially less interaction between government and religion that otherwise would be the case.[351]

In short, employment discrimination represents another aspect of American law in which the liberation of religious institutions from the constraints that operate on other employers has been found to be consistent with anti-establishment principles.

The Court's treatment of the property tax and employment discrimination exemptions discussed above reveals that there exists a twilight zone between the anti-establishment and free exercise guarantees, a zone in which government retains the discretion to accommodate the interests of religious organizations. This twilight zone of permissible accommodation falls between those circumstances in which the free exercise guarantee *requires* government to accommodate free exercise concerns, on the one hand, and those in which government advances religion so considerably that the law under scrutiny cannot withstand anti-establishment scrutiny, on the other.

Despite these contexts in which the Court has proven tolerant of the favored treatment government accords religious institutions, a variety of other governmental efforts at accommodation have met with a high court substantially less tolerant. We turn now to those circumstances in which the Court has concluded that the particular efforts to accommodate religion simply go too far, creating insuperable problems with anti-establishment principles.

Impermissible Accommodation: Empowering Religious Organizations with Governmental Authority—Zoning Decisions Related to Liquor Licenses

A case pitting a Cambridge, Massachusetts, restaurant against a church located just a few feet away provided the Court the opportunity to set some limits on the extent to which government is free to accommodate the interests of religious organizations (Larkin v. Grendel's Den, 1982).[352]

Massachusetts law granted to schools and churches the authority to veto the sale of liquor within five hundred feet of the school or church. Accordingly, when Grendel's Den, a restaurant located just off of Harvard Square, applied for a license to sell alcoholic beverages, the Holy Cross Church exercised the state-granted authority and filed a written objection. (Somewhat ironically, at the time Holy Cross objected to the efforts of the restaurant, there already existed twenty-five liquor licenses within five hundred feet of the church.) Because of the church's objection, Grendel's Den failed to obtain the license it sought. The restaurant then sued the administrative agency responsible for allocating liquor licenses, claiming among other violations that the Massachusetts law clashed with anti-establishment principles. The justices agreed.

The central anti-establishment flaw in the legislative scheme, the Court concluded, stemmed from the fact that governmental authorities essentially had delegated away governmental power to religious organizations.[353] For that reason, the scheme posed problems for each aspect of *Lemon*'s three-pronged approach.

The Court tentatively accepted the argument that the law embodied a secular purpose of protecting certain kinds of institutions—particularly houses of worship and schools—from "the 'hurly-burly' associated with liquor outlets."[354] It nevertheless commented that this legitimate secular objective could be better achieved through an outright ban on liquor licenses within a particular distance of these institutions, as more than half the states had done.

The "effect" and "entanglement" inquiries posed even more substantial problems for the Court. Concluding that the law's primary effect served to advance religion, the Court reasoned that nothing in the statutory scheme protected against churches opting to exercise (or refrain from exercising) their government-granted veto in a manner rooted in explicitly religious goals—say, by "favoring liquor licenses for members of that congregation or adherents of that faith."[355] In short, the Court expressed its skepticism that the power given to houses of worship under the law would ultimately be used only for secular purposes.

The justices likewise found substantial entanglement concerns with the operation of the law. Indeed, the Court began its entanglement analysis by observing that the "fusion of governmental and religious functions" forged by the Massachusetts law ran powerfully counter to the Framers' self-conscious effort to ensure that the power of government not be "delegated to or shared with religious institutions."[356] Unfortunately, the Court explained, that was exactly the situation the Massachusetts law produced: delegating to houses of worship unfettered government power to make decisions about matters that have economic and political consequences for others. Accordingly, the statutory scheme both "enmeshe[d]" religious institutions in government processes and ran the risk of fragmenting the community along religious lines. "Few entanglements," the Court concluded, "could be more offensive to the spirit of the Constitution."[357]

Impermissible Accommodation: Protecting Employees from Compelled Sabbath Work

Another context in which the Court has determined that a state legislature has gone too far in its effort to accommodate religious interests concerns employment protection for observant workers. A Connecticut law provided that an employee who observed a particular day of the week as his or her Sabbath could not be compelled by the employer to work on that day, nor could the employee's refusal to work on that day constitute grounds for dismissal. Donald Thornton, a Presbyterian employee who previously had worked on many Sundays, learned of the law and invoked its protections, informing his employer than no longer would he be willing to work on Sundays. Upon learning the news, the employer sought to transfer Thornton to a Massachusetts store that closed on Sundays, as well as to induce Thornton to accept a demotion to a position that would diminish Thornton's salary. Thornton declined the offers. The employer then unilaterally transferred Thornton to a clerical position, prompting Thornton to resign and file a grievance with state employment officials. The employer defended the grievance in part by alleging that the Connecticut law violated anti-establishment principles. The Supreme Court agreed (Estate of Thornton v. Caldor, 1985).[358]

The Court focused exclusively on the effect of the law, quickly concluding that the law impermissibly advanced religion and thus could not withstand anti-establishment scrutiny. What especially troubled the justices was the fact that, because the legislative accommodation empowered employees not to work on their designated Sabbath day, the law effectively produced a situation in which the religious practices of employees overrode the secular business interests of the employer. The Court noted that the law contained no exceptions for substantial burdens the employer might experience as a result of an employee's election to invoke the statute and take off from work on a particular day—for instance, a schoolteacher whose Sabbath fell on Fridays—nor did it account for any reasonable efforts made by the employer to work out a solution to the quandary.[359] In short, the fact that the law endowed individuals with the unrestrained ability to impose their religious beliefs and practices on the businesses that employed them and the fact that the law required the state's employers to subordinate business needs to the religious interests of their employees together persuaded the Court that this particular accommodation could not be squared with the anti-establishment guarantee.

Impermissible Accommodation: Tax Exemption Exclusively for Religious Publications

Four years after invalidating Connecticut's attempted accommodation for Sabbath-observing employees, the Court again deployed its anti-establishment weaponry, this time declaring unconstitutional a Texas law exempting from its sales and use taxes periodicals published or distributed by a religious faith when such publications consisted of works that promulgated the teaching of the faith or were otherwise deemed sacred by the faith (Texas Monthly, Inc. v. Bullock, 1989).[360] The plurality opinion of Justice Brennan focused heavily on the fact that the Texas legislature had chosen to impose a benefit *solely* on religious organizations and publications rather than to include such organizations and publications in a more expansive class of beneficiaries. As the plurality put it:

> [W]hen government directs a subsidy exclusively to religious organizations that is not required by the Free Exercise Clause and that either burdens nonbeneficiaries markedly or cannot reasonably be seen as removing a significant state-imposed deterrent to the free exercise of religion, as Texas has done . . . it "provide[s] unjustifiable awards of assistance to religious organizations" and cannot but "conve[y] a message of endorsement" to slighted members of the community.[361]

The plurality went on to point out that the breadth of the accommodated class necessary to sustain such an accommodation against an anti-establishment challenge would depend substantially on the precise nature of the secular legislative purpose. In this case, the plurality opined, had Texas extended the benefit to all groups that contributed to the state's cultural, intellectual, and moral betterment, the exemption for religious organizations surely would have withstood anti-establishment scrutiny.

A blistering dissent authored by Justice Scalia, joined by Justice Thomas and Chief Justice Rehnquist, chastised their colleagues for engaging in a "judicial demolition project" that wiped out the long-standing laws of at least fifteen states.[362] The dissent contended that the decision not only could not be squared with *Walz*, but likewise toppled the long-standing assumption that government could be solicitous of religious institutions without implicating anti-establishment concerns. The Court's invalidation of the Texas effort at accommodation, Justice Scalia observed, amounted to a "revolution"[363] in anti-establishment jurisprudence, and the dissent assuredly did not deploy the word as a compliment.

Impermissible Accommodation: Separate and Distinct School District for a Religious Community

Yet another constitutional limit on the extent to which government may accommodate religion emerged out of a highly unusual set of circumstances in which a state enacted a law creating a separate and distinct public school district for a village composed entirely of members of a particular religious faith. The high court concluded that anti-establishment principles did not permit such an accommodation (Board of Education of Kiryas Joel v. Grumet, 1994).[364]

The Satmar Hasidim practice a rigorous and profoundly unassimilated form of Judaism. They speak Yiddish, dress in distinctive garb, segregate the sexes outside of homes, and strictly construe the Torah. In the early seventies, the members of this sect—fewer than ten thousand in all—moved from Brooklyn to an undeveloped subdivision in Monroe, a town in the Catskills. As zoning disputes proceeded to unfold between the Satmars and the town, the Satmars exercised rights under New York law and petitioned the town to carve out a village within the town. In 1977, their effort culminated in success with the creation of the village of Kiryas Joel, a village whose boundaries included only the 320 acres owned and occupied by the Satmars.

Not surprisingly, the minor children in Satmar families attended private religious schools. Satmar families sent their boys to a Talmudic academy where their studies focused on Torah and, to a considerably lesser extent, a smattering of secular subjects. Girls went to school at an affiliated institution at which the central objective of the curriculum was to inculcate them with the skills and wherewithal to assume the duties of marriage and motherhood. These religious schools, however, lacked the personnel and expertise to offer services to handicapped students, services to which both federal and state law made clear the students were entitled—even students attending private schools. Accordingly, beginning in 1984, the Monroe-Woodbury Central School District provided these services for Kiryas Joel students in an annex to the school to which the Satmar families sent their daughters. A year later, however, Supreme Court decisions in *Aguilar* and *Grand Rapids* compelled an end to that short-lived experiment, leaving Satmar families with children who needed such services in an unenviable predicament: continue sending their children to the Satmar schools—which did not offer such services—or move their children to a public school outside the unassimilated community of Kiryas Joel. Those families who opted for the latter alternative soon withdrew their children from public school, finding that the youngsters simply could not function satisfactorily in the secular environment of the American public school. By 1989, therefore, only one Satmar child remained in the Monroe-Woodbury public schools; the other Kiryas Joel children either failed to receive the assistance they needed or used private funds to obtain some of the services.

The New York legislature then stepped in to provide assistance, enacting a law declaring the Village of Kiryas Joel a separate and distinct public school district. Governor Mario Cuomo signed the law, observing that it represented "a good faith effort" to come up with a solution to the seemingly intractable problem of providing special education services to handicapped Kiryas Joel children. Shortly thereafter, however, a range of plaintiffs that included the state association of school boards instituted an action alleging that the law creating the Kiryas Joel public school district clashed with anti-establishment principles.

When the dust settled four years later, a majority of the Supreme Court agreed with plaintiffs.

The unusual facts of the case prompted six of the justices to submit opinions, reflecting the conspicuous lack of consensus that continues to bedevil anti-establishment jurisprudence. Justice David Souter, in a portion of his opinion joined by Justices Harry Blackmun, John Paul Stevens, and Ruth Bader Ginsburg, analogized the facts of the case to the constitutionally problematic circumstances the justices had encountered in *Larkin*. In each set of circumstances, the plurality observed, the State had delegated its discretionary authority over public matters to religious communities. In that prior case, the plurality noted, government essentially transferred to religious organizations the power to make zoning decisions regarding establishments seeking liquor licenses. Similarly, the plurality noted, here the New York legislature essentially delegated to a particular religious community—the Satmar Hasidim—the power to exercise authority over a public school district. In each case, the plurality opined, the impact of the government action amounted to uniting civic and religious authority and thus clashed with the core mandate of anti-establishment principles that government power "must be exercised in a manner neutral to religion."[365]

The Souter plurality appeared to grasp that its invalidation of New York's effort to achieve a satisfactory solution to a truly distinctive problem could be construed as discouraging future government efforts to accommodate the needs of religious communities. Accordingly, it paused to pass along the following insights about the law of permissive accommodation:

> [W]e do not deny that the Constitution allows the State to accommodate religious needs by alleviating special burdens. Our cases leave no doubt that in commanding neutrality the Religion Clauses do not require the government to be oblivious to impositions that legitimate exercises of state power may place on religious belief and practice. . . . [T]here is "ample room under the Establishment Clause for 'benevolent neutrality which will permit religious exercise to exist without sponsorship and without interference.' " . . . But accommodation is not a principle without limits, and what [the Board of Education and the Satmars] seek is an adjustment to [their] religiously grounded preferences that our cases do not countenance.[366]

Three justices, speaking through Justice Scalia, issued a dissent in which they labeled the decision "astounding."[367] The dissent meticulously took apart piece by piece each and every aspect of the opinions declaring the act at issue unconstitutional. With regard to the issue of permissive accommodation, the dissent slammed the decision for ignoring the lengthy tradition of government accommodation of religious beliefs and practices, especially, the dissent noted, the beliefs and practices of minority sects such as the Satmar Hasidim. That longstanding government approach, the dissent observed, represents "the best of our traditions."[368]

CONCLUSION

As this chapter has revealed, a breathtakingly expansive range of circumstances has been found to implicate the ten seemingly uncomplicated words of the anti-establishment guarantee. Recitation of the Pledge of Allegiance, holiday displays, educational instruction devoted to the origins of mankind, government assistance programs, the system of taxation—these and countless other aspects of American life have been challenged as clashing with the anti-establishment injunction. Such challenges have kept the nation's courts hard at work endeavoring to give practical meaning to the ten seemingly uncomplicated words that comprise this First Amendment protection.

A central theme of this chapter has been the striking discord among members of the nation's highest court concerning even the most basic of anti-establishment issues. This discord has manifested itself in case after case in which the justices have deployed their impressive skills and resources to take issue with the premises and reasoning their colleagues bring to bear on the resolution of anti-establishment challenges. Such public debates resonate with importance—not merely for lawyers, scholars, and political and religious activists but for all Americans who care about religious freedom for themselves and those around them.

The appropriate relationship between the institutions of government and religion remains an issue very much up for grabs in America at the dawn of the twenty-first century. Equally difficult to envision is the path down which the constitutional law governing these matters will travel. We nevertheless can say with more than a little assurance that the nation's highest court—and the individuals who serve on it—will continue to play a central role in determining our nation's approach to these matters.

NOTES

1. Lee v. Weisman, 505 U.S. 577 (1992).
2. Allegheny County v. American Civil Liberties Union, 492 U.S. 573 (1989).
3. Zelman v. Simmons-Harris, 536 U.S. 639 (2002).
4. The late Gerald Gunther's influential constitutional law casebook suggested this organizing principle beginning several decades ago. I first encountered the casebook—and thus first begin to muse about the organizing principle—as a college student in 1977. Gerald Gunther, *Constitutional Law: Cases and Materials* (9th ed. 1975).
5. 403 U.S. 602 (1971).
6. *Id.* at 612–13.
7. Engel v. Vitale, 370 U.S. 421 (1962).
8. *Id.* at 422.
9. *Id.* at 424.
10. *Id.* at 425.
11. *Id.* at 429–30.
12. *Id.* at 436.

13. *Id.* at 436.
14. *Id.* at 430.
15. *Id.* at 431.
16. *Id.* at 431.
17. *Id.* at 445 (Stewart, J., dissenting).
18. *Id.* at 445–46 (Stewart, J., dissenting).
19. School District of Abington Township v. Schempp, 374 U.S. 203 (1963).
20. *Id.* at 222.
21. *Id.* at 223.
22. *Id.* at 224–25.
23. *Id.* at 225.
24. *Id.* at 224–25.
25. *Id.* at 222.
26. *Id.* at 230 (Brennan, J., concurring).
27. *Id.* at 308 (Stewart, J., dissenting).
28. *Id.* at 313 (Stewart, J., dissenting).
29. *Id.* at 314 (Stewart, J., dissenting).
30. *Id.* at 316 (Stewart, J., dissenting).
31. Ala. Code 1975 §16-1-20 (1978).
32. *Id.* at §16-1-20.1 (1980).
33. *Id.* at §16-1-20.2 (1982).
34. Wallace v. Jaffree, 472 U.S. 38 (1985).
35. *Id.* at 43.
36. *Id.* at 58.
37. *Id.* at 60.
38. *Id.* at 82.
39. *Id.* at 85 (Burger, J., dissenting).
40. *Id.* at 91 (White, J., dissenting).
41. *Id.* at 92 (Rehnquist, J., dissenting).
42. Lee v. Weisman, 505 U.S. 577 (1992).
43. *Id.* at 581–82.
44. *Id.* at 582.
45. *Id.* at 586.
46. *Id.* at 587.
47. *Id.* at 610 (Souter, J., concurring).
48. *Id.* at 615–16 (Souter, J., concurring).
49. *Id.* at 632 (Scalia, J., dissenting).
50. *Id.* at 644–45 (Scalia, J., dissenting).
51. Santa Fe Independent School District v. Doe, 530 U.S. 290 (2000).
52. *Id.* at 302.
53. *Id.* at 302.
54. *Id.* at 303.
55. *Id.* at 309.
56. *Id.* at 309–10.
57. *Id.* at 310.
58. *Id.* at 318 (Rehnquist, C.J., dissenting).
59. *Id.* at 322 (Rehnquist, C.J., dissenting).

60. *Id.* at 324 (Rehnquist, C.J., dissenting).
61. Elk Grove Unified School District v. Newdow, 124 S. Ct. 2302 (2004).
62. 36 U.S.C. § 172 (1942).
63. 4 U.S.C. § 4 (1998).
64. Cal. Educ. Code § 52720 (1989).
65. *Id.*
66. Newdow v. United States Congress, 292 F.3d 597, 600 (9th Cir. 2002).
67. *Id.* at 607–08.
68. *Id.* at 608.
69. *Id.* at 609.
70. *Id.*
71. *Id.* (quoting 100 Cong. Rec. 8618 (1954)).
72. *Id.* at 610.
73. *Id.*
74. *Id.*
75. Adam Liptak, *Judges Decide Father Has Right to Challenge Pledge in Court*, N.Y. Times, December 5, 2002, at A3; Evelyn Nieves, *Judges Ban Pledge of Allegiance from Schools, Citing "Under God,"* N.Y. Times, June 27, 2002, at A1.
76. Newdow v. United States Congress, 328 F.3d 466 (9th Cir. 2003).
77. Elk Grove Unified School District v. Newdow, 124 S. Ct. 384 (2003).
78. *See* Elk Grove Unified School District v. Newdow, 124 S. Ct. 2301 (2004).
79. One justice, Antonin Scalia, recused himself from the case after making off-the-bench remarks critical of the Ninth Circuit's ruling. *See* David Savage, *Justices Keep "God" in Pledge of Allegiance*, L.A. Times, June 15, 2004, at A1.
80. Elk Grove v. Newdow, 124 S. Ct. 2301.
81. *Id.* at 2312 (Rehnquist, C.J., concurring).
82. *Id.* at 2319–20 (Rehnquist, C.J., concurring).
83. *Id.* at 2321 (O'Connor, J., concurring).
84. *Id.* (O'Connor, J., concurring).
85. *Id.* at 2322 (O'Connor, J., concurring).
86. *Id.* at 2323 (O'Connor, J., concurring).
87. *Id.* at 2323–24 (O'Connor, J., concurring).
88. *Id.* at 2325 (O'Connor, J., concurring).
89. *Id.* at 2326 (O'Connor, J., concurring).
90. *Id.* (O'Connor, J., concurring).
91. *Id.* at 2328 (Thomas, J., concurring).
92. *Id.* at 2327 (Thomas, J., concurring).
93. *Id.* at 2330 (Thomas, J., concurring).
94. *Id.* at 2330–31 (Thomas, J., concurring).
95. *Id.* at 2331 (Thomas, J., concurring).
96. *Id.* at 2332 (Thomas, J., concurring).
97. Epperson v. Arkansas, 393 U.S. 97 (1968).
98. *Id.* at 99.
99. *Id.* at 103.
100. *Id.* at 106.
101. Edwards v. Aguillard, 482 U.S. 578 (1987).
102. *Id.* at 586–87 ("While the Court is normally deferential to a State's articulation

of a secular purpose, it is required that the statement of such purpose be sincere and not a sham.").

103. *Id.* at 591.

104. *Id.* at 587.

105. *Id.* at 588.

106. *Id.* at 590.

107. *Id.* at 591.

108. *Id.* at 622–25 (Scalia, J., dissenting).

109. *Id.* at 627 (Scalia, J., dissenting).

110. *Id.* at 627 (Scalia, J., dissenting).

111. *Id.* at 634 (Scalia, J., dissenting).

112. Stone v. Graham, 449 U.S. 39 (1980).

113. *Id.* at 39 n.1.

114. Stone v. Graham, 599 S.W. 157 (Ken. 1980).

115. *Stone*, 449 U.S. at 41.

116. *Id.* at 41–42.

117. *Id.* at 45 (Rehnquist, J., dissenting).

118. *Id.* at 45–46 (Rehnquist, J., dissenting).

119. *Id.* at 43 (Rehnquist, J., dissenting).

120. *Id.* at 47 (Rehnquist, J., dissenting).

121. *Id.* at 43 (Stewart, J., dissenting).

122. American Civil Liberties Union v. McCreary County, 354 F.3d 438 (6th Cir. 2003), *cert. granted*, 2004 WL 2059432 (U.S. Oct. 12, 2004) (No. 03-1693). On the same day the Court announced its decision to hear *McCreary* it also announced its acceptance of a second case implicating the anti-establishment aspects of governmental display of the Ten Commandments, Van Orden v. Perry, 351 F.3d 173 (5th Cir. 2003), *cert. granted*, 2004 WL 2282082 (U.S. Oct. 12, 2004). *Van Orden* concerns a granite display of the Ten Commandments on the grounds of the Texas Capitol in Austin. The Fifth Circuit concluded that the display served a secular purpose and that the reasonable observer cannot conclude that the display evinces the state's endorsement of religion.

123. *Id.*

124. *Id.* at 443.

125. *Id.* at 444.

126. 145 F. Supp.2d 845 (E.D. Ky. 2001).

127. *McCreary County*, 354 F.3d at 438.

128. *Id.* at 445.

129. *Id.* at 446–54.

130. *Id.* at 448–49.

131. *Id.* at 453.

132. *Id.* at 454.

133. *Id.* at 457.

134. *Id.* at 446.

135. *Id.* at 458–61.

136. *Id.* at 461.

137. *Id.* at 463 (Ryan, J., dissenting).

138. *Id.* at 474 (Ryan, J., dissenting), quoting *Stone*, 449 U.S. 43, 47 (Rehnquist, J., dissenting).

139. *Id.* at 474–75 (Ryan, J., dissenting).
140. *Id.* at 446–47.
141. *Id.* at 477–78 (Ryan, J., dissenting).
142. *Id.* at 480 (Ryan, J., dissenting).
143. McCollum v. Board of Education, 333 U.S. 203 (1948).
144. *Id.* at 210.
145. *Id.* at 239.
146. Zorach v. Clauson, 343 U.S. 306 (1952).
147. *Id.* at 308.
148. *Id.* at 313.
149. *Id.* at 315.
150. *Id.* at 317 (Black, J., dissenting).
151. *Id.* at 323 (Frankfurter, J., dissenting).
152. Widmar v. Vincent, 454 U.S. 263 (1981).
153. *Id.* at 274.
154. *Id.* at 274–75.
155. Board of Education v. Mergens, 496 U.S. 226 (1990).
156. Lamb's Chapel v. Center Moriches Union Free District, 508 U.S. 384 (1993).
157. *Id.* at 389.
158. *Id.* at 395.
159. Rosenberger v. Rectors and Visitors of the University of Virginia, 515 U.S. 819 (1995).
160. *Id.* at 825.
161. *Id.* at 840–41.
162. *Id.* at 874–75.
163. *Id.* at 875.
164. *Id.* at 892.
165. Good News Club v. Milford Central School, 533 U.S. 98 (2001).
166. *Id.* at 103.
167. *Id.* at 113.
168. *Id.*
169. Marsh v. Chambers, 463 U.S. 783 (1983).
170. *Id.* at 786.
171. *Id.*
172. *Id.* at 788.
173. *Id.* at 791.
174. *Id.*
175. *Id.* at 796 (Brennan, J., dissenting).
176. *Id.* at 796–97 (Brennan, J., dissenting).
177. *Id.* at 802 (Brennan, J., dissenting).
178. *Id.* at 796 (Brennan, J., dissenting).
179. *Id.* at 797 (Brennan, J., dissenting).
180. *Id.* at 798 (Brennan, J., dissenting).
181. *Id.* at 799–800 (Brennan, J., dissenting).
182. *Id.* at 800–01 (Brennan, J., dissenting).
183. *Id.* at 803 (Brennan, J., dissenting).
184. *Id.* at 803–04 (Brennan, J., dissenting).

185. *Id.* at 804 (Brennan, J., dissenting.
186. *Id.* at 805 (Brennan, J., dissenting).
187. *Id.* at 822–23 (Stevens, J., dissenting).
188. *Id.* at 823 (Stevens, J., dissenting).
189. Lynch v. Donnelly, 465 U.S. 668 (1984).
190. *Id.* at 671.
191. Donnelly v. Lynch, 525 F.Supp. 1150, 1178 (D.R.I. 1981) and Donnelly v. Lynch, 691 F.2d 1029 (1st Cir. 1982).
192. *Donnelly,* 465 U.S. at 672.
193. *Id.* at 673.
194. *Id.* at 676.
195. *Id.* at 678.
196. *Id.*
197. *Id.* at 679.
198. *Id.* at 681.
199. *Id.* at 681–82.
200. *Id.* at 682.
201. *Id.* at 684.
202. *Id.*
203. *Id.*
204. *Id.* at 687–88 (O'Connor, J., concurring).
205. *Id.* at 690 (O'Connor, J., concurring).
206. *Id.* at 691 (O'Connor, J., concurring).
207. *Id.* (O'Connor, J., concurring).
208. *Id.* at 692 (O'Connor, J., concurring).
209. *Id.* at 692–93 (O'Connor, J., concurring).
210. *Id.* at 696 (Brennan, J., dissenting).
211. *Id.* (Blackmun, J., dissenting).
212. *Id.* (Blackmun, J., dissenting).
213. *Id.* (Blackmun, J., dissenting).
214. *Id.* at 702 (Brennan, J., dissenting).
215. Allegheny County v. American Civil Liberties Union, Greater Pittsburgh Chapter 492 U.S. 573 (1989).
216. *Id.* at 592–94 (quoting *Lynch*, 465 U.S. at 692 (O'Connor, J., concurring)).
217. *Id.* at 598.
218. *Id.*
219. *Id.* at 669 (Kennedy, J., concurring in the judgment in part and dissenting in part).
220. *Id.* at 668–74 (Kennedy, J., concurring in the judgment in part and dissenting in part).
221. *Id.* at 670–71 (Kennedy, J., concurring in the judgment in part and dissenting in part).
222. *Id.* at 674 (Kennedy, J., concurring in the judgment in part and dissenting in part).
223. *Id.* (Kennedy, J., concurring in the judgment in part and dissenting in part).
224. *Id.* at 659 (Kennedy, J., concurring in the judgment in part and dissenting in part).
225. *Id.* at 664 (Kennedy, J., concurring in the judgment in part and dissenting in part).
226. *Id.* at 634 (O'Connor, J., concurring in part and concurring in the judgment).
227. *Id.* at 616.
228. Capitol Square Review & Advisory Board v. Pinette, 515 U.S. 753 (1995).

229. Capitol Square Review & Advisory Board v. Pinette, 844 F.Supp. 1182, 1184 (S.D. Ohio 1993).

230. Capitol Square Review & Advisory Board v. Pinette, 30 F.3d 675 (6th Cir. 1994).

231. *Capitol Square Review Board*, 515 U.S. at 763.

232. *Id.* at 582 (O'Connor, J., concurring in part concurring in the judgment).

233. *Id.* at 785 (Souter, J., concurring in part and concurring in the judgment).

234. *Id.* at 782 (O'Connor, J., concurring in part and concurring in the judgment).

235. *Id.* at 794 (Souter, J., concurring in part and concurring in the judgment).

236. American Jewish Congress v. City of Chicago, 827 F.2d 120, 129 (1987) (Easterbrook, J., dissenting).

237. Everson v. Board of Education of the Township of Ewing, 330 U.S. 1 (1947).

238. *Id.* at 3.

239. *Id.* at 15.

240. *Id.* at 15–16.

241. *Id.* at 18.

242. *Id.* at 16. Emphasis added.

243. *Id.*

244. *Id.* at 18.

245. *Id.* at 19 (Jackson, J., dissenting).

246. Board of Education of Central School District No. 1 v. Allen, 392 U.S. 236 (1968).

247. *Id.* at 242.

248. *Id.* at 250 (Black, J., dissenting).

249. *Id.* at 251–53 (Black, J., dissenting).

250. Committee for Public Education and Religious Liberty v. Nyquist, 426 U.S. 736 (1973); *Lemon*, 403 U.S. 602 (1971).

251. Mueller v. Allen, 463 U.S. 388 (1983).

252. *Id.* at 394.

253. *Id.* at 395.

254. *Id.* at 396.

255. *Id.*; *Lemon*, 403 U.S. at 622–23.

256. *Mueller*, 463 U.S. at 396.

257. *Id.* at 397.

258. *Id.* at 402.

259. *Id.* at 403.

260. *Id.* at 404 (Marshall, J., dissenting).

261. *Id.* at 405 (Marshall, J., dissenting).

262. *Id.* at 408 (Marshall, J., dissenting).

263. Witters v. Washington Department of Services for the Blind, 474 U.S. 481 (1986).

264. *Id.* at 487.

265. *Id.* at 488.

266. *Id.*

267. Zobrest v. Catalina Foothills School District, 509 U.S. 1 (1993).

268. *Id.* at 8.

269. *Id.* at 18.

270. *Id.* at 22.

271. *Id.*

272. Zelman v. Simmons-Harris, 536 U.S. 639 (2002).

273. *Id.* at 649.
274. *Id.*
275. *Id.* at 652.
276. *Id.* at 655.
277. *Id.* at 707.
278. *Id.* at 711.
279. *Id.* at 717.
280. *Lemon*, 403 U.S. 602 (1971).
281. *Id.* at 613.
282. *Id.* at 623–24.
283. *Id.* at 619.
284. *Id.* at 622.
285. *Id.* at 622–23.
286. Meek v. Pittenger, 421 U.S. 349 (1975).
287. *Id.* at 366.
288. *Id.* at 370–72.
289. School District of the City of Grand Rapids v. Ball, 473 U.S. 373 (1985).
290. *Id.* at 388.
291. *Id.* at 385.
292. *Id.* at 397.
293. Aguilar v. Felton, 473 U.S. 402 (1985).
294. Agostini v. Felton, 521 U.S. 203, 212 (1997) (quoting App. to Pet. for Cert. in No. 96–553, pp. A25–A26).
295. *Aguilar*, 473 U.S. at 412.
296. Agostini v. Felton, 521 U.S. 203 (1997).
297. *Id.* at 223.
298. *Id.* at 225.
299. *Id.* at 234.
300. *Id.*
301. *Id.* at 240 (Souter, J., joined by Stevens and Ginsburg, JJ., and joined in part by Breyer, J.).
302. *Id.* at 243 (Souter, J., dissenting).
303. Mitchell v. Helms, 530 U.S. 793 (2000).
304. *Id.* at 802.
305. *Id.* at 809.
306. *Id.* at 811–13.
307. *Id.* at 822.
308. *Id.* at 839 (O'Connor, J., joined by Breyer, J., concurring in the judgment).
309. *Id.* at 840 (O'Connor, J., joined by Breyer, J., concurring in the judgment).
310. *Id.* at 869 (Souter, J., joined by Stevens and Ginsburg, JJ., dissenting).
311. *Id.* at 868 (Souter, J., joined by Stevens and Ginsburg, JJ., dissenting).
312. *Id.* at 913 (Souter, J., joined by Stevens and Ginsburg, JJ., dissenting).
313. Tilton v. Richardson, 403 U.S. 672 (1971).
314. *Id.* at 685–87.
315. Roemer v. Board of Public Works of Maryland, 426 U.S. 736 (1976).
316. *Id.* at 755.
317. *Id.* at 755–56.

318. *Id.* at 752.
319. *Id.* at 763.
320. *Id.* at 764.
321. *Id.* at 765, citing Tilton v. Richardson, 403 U.S. at 688–89.
322. Bowen v. Kendrick, 487 U.S. 589, 593 (1988).
323. *Id.* at 593.
324. *Id.* at 595.
325. *Id.* at 589.
326. *Id.* at 602.
327. *Id.* at 607.
328. *Id.* at 606.
329. *Id.* at 608.
330. *Id.* at 609.
331. *Id.* at 610–11.
332. *Id.* at 615–17.
333. *Id.* at 615.
334. *Id.*
335. *Id.* at 616.
336. *Id.* at 626.
337. *Id.* at 640.
338. *Id.* at 641.
339. Walz v. Tax Commission of New York, 397 U.S. 664 (1970).
340. *Id.* at 668.
341. *Id.* at 672.
342. *Id.*
343. *Id.* at 673.
344. *Id.* at 676.
345. *Id.* at 678.
346. Corporation of the Presiding Bishop of the Church of Jesus Christ of Latter-day Saints v. Amos, 483 U.S. 327 (1987).
347. *Id.* at 335.
348. *Id.* at 336.
349. *Id.* at 337.
350. *Id.*
351. *Id.* at 339.
352. Larkin v. Grendel's Den, Inc., 459 U.S. 116 (1982).
353. *Id.* at 122.
354. *Id.* at 123.
355. *Id.* at 125.
356. *Id.* at 126–27.
357. *Id.* at 127.
358. Estate of Thornton v. Caldor, Inc., 472 U.S. 703 (1985).
359. *Id.* at 709–10.
360. Texas Monthly, Inc., v. Bullock, 489 U.S. 1 (1989).
361. *Id.* at 15.
362. *Id.* at 29.
363. *Id.* at 38.

364. Board of Education of Kiryas Joel Village School District v. Grumet, 512 U.S. 687 (1994).

365. *Id*. at 704.

366. *Id*. at 705–06.

367. *Id*. at 752.

368. *Id*. at 744.

3

The Free Exercise Guarantee

"Congress shall make no law respecting an establishment of religion, or prohibiting the free exercise thereof;"

INTRODUCTION

As we have seen, the typical set of circumstances raising the specter of the First Amendment's anti-establishment guarantee finds government (be it national, state, or local) undertaking an activity that, in the view of some complaining party, places government too far on the side of religion (be it a particular religious faith, on the one hand, or religious institutions generally, on the other). Moment-of-silence practices at the beginning of the elementary or secondary public school day at which school officials encourage students to pray, a holiday crèche supported by municipal funds or located on municipal property, state tax dollars being directed to families to help defray the costs of participation in voucher programs that include religiously affiliated schools—such circumstances represent the stuff of typical contemporary anti-establishment scenarios. This is emphatically *not* to say, of course, that scenarios such as those set forth in the trio of examples invariably will be found to clash with the anti-establishment prohibition. It is to say, however, that such scenarios often prompt courts to confront core issues as to the meaning of the anti-establishment guarantee.

The typical set of circumstances implicating the free exercise guarantee differs considerably from that of the anti-establishment paradigm. In the free exercise arena, the most common complaint is that government has stepped over the constitutional line by placing its authority *against* religion and religious practices—almost invariably those religions and practices belonging to a minority of the citizenry. More specifically, the typical free exercise challenge seeks to take government to task for refusing to carve out an exception to a generally applicable law, for failing to accommodate the special, distinctive practices of a particular individual's religious faith.

May government, consistent with free exercise principles, deny unemployment compensation to an individual who claims her unemployment status results from a religious conviction that compelled her to decline an employment opportunity because the job required her to work on a day of the week that her religion holds sacred? Or, instead, does free exercise require that the individual be granted an exception? May government, consistent with free exercise principles, require commercial activity to grind to a halt on Sunday in the face of an objection by some business owners that the law places them at a substantial competitive disadvantage because their religious convictions require them to shut down on a day other than Sunday? Or, instead, does the guarantee require government to allow the Saturday worshipers to keep their businesses open on Sunday? Such requests that government create exceptions from generally applicable laws in order to respect the religiously driven choices of individuals—requests whose rejection by government not infrequently leads to litigation seeking to establish the constitutional legitimacy of the requests—represent much of the day-to-day stuff of the free exercise guarantee.

For this reason, therefore, perhaps the central issue in the evolution of the constitutional law of free exercise—not the only issue, as the materials that follow make clear, but the central one—has been the extent to which this particular constitutional guarantee requires government to liberate a complaining individual from the constraints of a law with which others must comply. Or, to invoke the language of the constitutional discussion itself, the central free exercise issue capturing the attention of American courts concerns the extent to which this constitutional guarantee requires government to make exceptions for, to "accommodate," the particular religious practices of its citizenry when such practices render it problematic for individuals to comply with generally applicable laws.

The bulk of this chapter will explore the core free exercise issue noted above. Constitutional commentators tend to refer to this core issue as the issue of "mandatory," or "compelled," or "required" accommodation. Such commentators deploy this jargon because, stripped to its basics, the issue inevitably reduces to whether the free exercise guarantee requires government to make an exception from a widely applicable law so as to liberate the religiously motivated conduct of a particular individual from the constraints of the law.

But not all free exercise challenges implicate this core concern. For that reason, our discussion in this chapter also will include a range of less common and less controversial free exercise matters.

EARLY DEVELOPMENTS IN FREE EXERCISE: A NINETEENTH-CENTURY SNAPSHOT, BELIEFS VS. ACTIONS, AND THE SUBSTANTIAL DEFERENCE TO GOVERNMENT

Polygamy and the *Reynolds* Case

Discussion of the free exercise guarantee, and especially discussion of whether the guarantee requires government to carve out "accommodations" to those who violate (or seek to violate) generally applicable laws, often begins with a nineteenth-century case concerning the bigamy prosecution of George Reynolds, a Mormon residing in the Utah territory (Reynolds v. United States, 1878).[1] To be sure, the underlying facts of the *Reynolds* case tend to strike contemporary observers as quaint, far removed from the cultural, political, and religious realities of today. Yet the constitutional issue at the core of the case resounds with relevance for today's free exercise analysis.

In 1862, Congress had enacted a law rendering bigamy a crime, subject to fine and imprisonment, in all territory over which the United States possessed exclusive jurisdiction. George Reynolds sought to defend against the charge in part through the contention that, as a member of the Church of Latter-day Saints (also known as the Mormon Church), his religious faith compelled him and other males to practice polygamy or else risk penalties that included "damnation in the life to come."[2] Reynolds demonstrated at trial, moreover, that Mormon authorities *both* granted permission for Reynolds to marry his second wife *and* performed the marriage ceremony that produced the very polygamous marriage for which government sought to hold Reynolds accountable. Given these facts, Reynolds argued that, because his second marriage stemmed from a duty owed to his religious faith, government lacked the power to punish him for entering into such a marriage. Territorial courts rejected the contention and imposed a fine of five hundred dollars, the maximum set out in the statute, as well as imprisonment at hard labor for two years.[3]

The nation's highest court likewise rejected Reynolds's arguments. In so doing, Chief Justice Morrison Waite's opinion for the justices made two principal points concerning the free exercise arguments pressed by Reynolds.

First, the Court observed that, at least prior to the establishment of the Mormon Church, polygamy long had been deemed "odious" throughout the bulk of what the Court appeared to consider the civilized world—with the result that the marriage subsequent in time, the Court advised, long had been deemed "always void."[4] Only the "Asiatic" and "African people,"[5] Chief Justice Waite expressly noted, constituted the exceptions to this general rule. Because of this long-standing hostility to the practice of polygamy, the Court concluded, Congress assuredly can lay claim to authority to forbid polygamy in places over which the national government has jurisdiction.[6]

The Court then turned to confront the contention that George Reynolds's religious beliefs afforded him a legal excuse, a constitutional justification, to refrain from complying with the anti-polygamy law. Rejecting the contention, the Court elaborated as follows:

> [T]he only questions which remains is . . . whether those who make polygamy a part of their religious beliefs are exempted from operation of the statute. If they are, then those who do not make polygamy a part of their religious belief may be found guilty and punished, while those who do, must be acquitted and go free. This would be introducing a new element into criminal law. Laws are made for the government of actions, and while they cannot interfere with mere religious beliefs and opinions, they may with practices. Suppose one believed that human sacrifices were a necessary part of religious worship, would it be seriously contended that the civil government under which he lived could not interfere to prevent a sacrifice? Or if a wife religiously believed it was her duty to burn herself upon the funeral pile of her dead husband, would it be beyond the power of the civil government to prevent her carrying her belief into practice?
>
> . . . To permit this would be to make the professed doctrines of religious belief superior to the law of the land, and in effect to permit every citizen to become a law unto himself. Government could exist only in name under such circumstances.[7]

This explanation by the Court, not surprisingly, has prompted commentators to construe the central message of *Reynolds* as amounting to the proposition that the constitutional guarantee of free exercise, whatever its precise contours, allows government substantially more room to regulate human *action* than human *belief*.[8] Indeed, the *Reynolds* Court left the strong impression that the free exercise guarantee posed little or no limit on government's power to regulate human action—a fact that, if true, would dramatically circumscribe the scope of the constitutional guarantee. Elsewhere in the Court's opinion, separate and apart from the language set forth above, Chief Justice Waite suggested such an idea in the course of exploring the origins of the religion guarantees, declaring that "Congress was deprived of all legislative power over mere opinion, but was left free to reach actions which were in violation of social duties or subversive of good order."[9]

In short, the experiences of George Reynolds and the early judicial confrontation with the free exercise guarantee in the case that bears his name—irrespective of whether one likes or dislikes the result the Court reached, whether one views the case as properly or improperly decided—prompted one conclusion to emerge with unmistakable clarity: Individuals seeking relief under the free exercise guarantee from laws that apply generally (such as prohibitions on polygamy) will have an uphill battle persuading courts to afford them that relief, especially if such laws address core aspects of the way American society is structured (such as marriage).

Beyond *Reynolds*: *Cantwell*

The *Reynolds* case, as noted above, embodied and reflected the notion that the free exercise guarantee posed at most an insubstantial obstacle to government efforts to regulate human behavior that clashed with widely applicable rules and regulations (for instance, the ban on polygamy). That notion persisted long after *Reynolds*, and, as we shall see after exploring some of the twists and turns in the constitutional road, persists to a considerable extent in the law today.

Six decades after articulating in *Reynolds* the differing constitutional treatment for regulating religious beliefs, on the one hand, and conduct rooted in such beliefs, on the other, the Supreme Court returned to underscore and elaborate on the distinction. The occasion for doing so concerned a Connecticut case about three Jehovah's Witnesses charged with, among other statutory and common-law violations, improper door-to-door solicitation in a neighborhood described by the Court as "about ninety per cent . . . Roman Catholic" (Cantwell v. Connecticut, 1940).[10] In particular, a Connecticut statute required that individuals undertaking certain forms of solicitation do so only after obtaining the approval of a particular state official. Newton, Jesse, and Russell Cantwell undertook a variety of acts of solicitation, including seeking to sell religious materials and playing a phonograph record characterized by the Court as "anti-Catholic" in a public street, without complying with the statutory requirement.

The Cantwells contended, among other things, that the guarantee of free exercise rendered unconstitutional the statutory scheme. The Court essentially agreed, reversing the convictions. For the law of free exercise, however, the *Cantwell* Court's words mattered more than its deeds. Justice Owen Roberts, writing for the Court, contributed the following observations about the constitutional guarantee of free exercise, more particularly, the guarantee's different implications for beliefs and actions:

> [The free exercise of religion] embraces two concepts,—freedom to believe and freedom to act. The first is absolute but, in the nature of things, the second cannot be. Conduct remains subject to regulation for the protection of society. . . . In every case the power to regulate must be so exercised as not, in attaining a permissible end, unduly to infringe the protected freedom.[11]

These observations underscored two aspects of the Court's approach to free exercise cases in the century after *Reynolds*.

First and most conspicuously, the Court continued to employ the dichotomy between beliefs and actions, and continued to manifest a commitment to the notion that the dichotomy had a central role to play in the evolving case law devoted to the free exercise guarantee. The very fact that the *Cantwell* majority paused to note these "two concepts" reveals the enduring power of the dichotomy for the high court.

But these words from *Cantwell*, especially the final sentence, suggested something else as well. That sentence reflected the fact that the Court's commitment to the view that religiously motivated *conduct* earned little if any constitutional protection from the free exercise guarantee might be softening. Indeed, the fact that Justice Roberts cautioned lawmakers not to "unduly infringe" upon rights of free exercise in the course of regulating human conduct suggested that the Court acknowledged limits on the power of lawmakers to "infringe" on such free exercise rights in the course of regulating conduct without exceeding the boundaries of permissible legislation. Put differently, the *Cantwell* Court unquestionably acknowledged that laws regulating conduct could and would clash with the constitutional guarantee of free exercise.[12]

Sunday "Blue" Laws: *Braunfeld*—More of the Same, Accompanied by Whispers of Skepticism

The Court continued to ground its free exercise decisions in the distinction between beliefs and actions for nearly a century after *Reynolds*. In Braunfeld v. Brown (1961),[13] the justices reviewed a Pennsylvania law mandating that the bulk of commercial activity shut down on Sundays. Abraham Braunfeld and other Orthodox Jewish merchants from the Philadelphia area challenged the law as an unconstitutional deprivation of their right to free exercise. In particular, the challengers contended that the state law imposed a substantial and undue hardship on them, a hardship produced by the confluence of their religious beliefs (which required them to refrain from work on *Saturdays*) and the law itself (which mandated that they shut down on *Sundays*). In short, the challengers contended that the law both undermined their efforts to earn a living and afforded their commercial competitors an unfair economic advantage.

A divided Court rejected the challenge. In so doing, the plurality opinion of Chief Justice Earl Warren relied heavily on the dichotomy between belief and action forged for free exercise purposes in *Reynolds*. Citing *Reynolds* and *Cantwell*, Chief Justice Warren observed that "[t]he freedom to hold religious beliefs and opinions is absolute. . . . However, the freedom to act, even when the action is in accord with one's religious convictions, is not totally free from legislative restrictions."[14] As the quotation reveals, the *Braunfeld* Court persisted in clinging to the distinction between harboring religious beliefs, on the one hand, and undertaking conduct consistent with those beliefs, on the other. Yet the quotation reveals something more as well. The observation contained in the second sentence—the observation to the effect that "the freedom to act . . . in accord with one's religious convictions . . . is not totally free from legislative restrictions"—reflects an approach to free exercise that had evolved in the ensuing century since *Reynolds*. After all, the *Reynolds* Court had suggested that, whatever else the free exercise guarantee meant, it did not mean to protect religiously motivated conduct, such as polygamy. By contrast, the language of *Braunfeld* eight decades later indicated unmistakably that religiously motivated conduct, though not "totally free" from regulation, nevertheless had acquired some measure of constitutional protection.[15]

Chief Justice Warren proceeded to justify the rejection of Braunfeld's free exercise claim by noting a consideration that, in the plurality's view, militated against allowing the *Braunfeld* plaintiffs to escape the constraints of the Pennsylvania law. That consideration, according to the plurality, was that "the statute . . . does not make unlawful any religious practices of appellants; [it] simply regulates a secular activity and [thus] operates to make the practice of their religious beliefs more expensive."[16] In other words, the chief justice sought to explain the Court's rejection of the free exercise claim in *Braunfeld* as rooted in part in the fact that the constraints imposed by the law rendered no religious practice *illegal* but, instead, merely increased the costs of observing such practices. The chief justice also expressed the identical thought in a slightly different way, dubbing the Sunday prohibition at issue in the case merely "an indirect burden"[17] on the exercise of religion precisely because the law did not outlaw any religious practice. Importantly, the plurality proceeded to note that the characterization of a law as representing merely "an indirect burden" on free exercise rights did not necessarily translate to the conclusion that the law posed no constitutional problem. As the plurality put it:

> to hold unassailable all legislation regulating conduct which imposes solely an indirect burden on the observance of religion would be a gross oversimplification. If the purpose or effect of the law is to impede the observance of one or all religions or is to discriminate invidiously between religions, that law is constitutionally invalid even though the burden may be characterized as being only indirect.[18]

The problem with the plurality's observation, of course, was that to a considerable extent the *Braunfeld* challengers claimed precisely that "the purpose or effect" of the Sunday prohibition was to "impede the observance of" their religion. The plurality nevertheless rejected the contention, doing so in large measure out of the view of the free exercise guarantee it expressed as follows:

> [I]f the state regulates conduct by enacting a general law within its power, the purpose and effect of which is to advance the State's secular goals, the statute is valid unless the State may accomplish its purpose by means which do not impose such a burden.[19]

The legislative goal of reaping the benefits of a weekly and uniform respite from commercial activity, the chief justice explained, represented just such a secular goal. Moreover, the legislature may well have concluded that the costs of carving out an exception to accommodate those practitioners who observed their day of rest on Saturday risked substantially undermining the secular goal. According to the plurality, therefore, the free exercise guarantee did not render the statutory scheme unconstitutional.

The disposition of the free exercise claim brought by Abraham Braunfeld and his fellow merchants, however, was hardly unanimous. The case produced an important pair of dissents, dissents that would contribute substantially to the evolution of free exercise law.

Justice William Brennan devoted the bulk of his dissent to an issue that would prove both crucial and immensely divisive in the half century that followed. That issue, central to the constitutional analysis of claims implicating individual liberty in general, but especially so in the realm of free exercise, concerned the appropriate level of scrutiny the free exercise guarantee required a court to apply when challengers such as Abraham Braunfeld or George Reynolds claimed that an act of government infringed on their religious exercise.[20]

For Justice Brennan, his colleagues' approach to the plight of the *Braunfeld* challengers reflected a disturbing deference to government decision makers and an analogously problematic indifference to the claims of religious liberty. The proper manner in which to approach the claim at issue in the case, Justice Brennan argued, was to require the state to satisfy the standard commonly referred to as "strict scrutiny" in order to determine whether its law could withstand the challenge that it imposed a substantial burden on the free exercise of religion. And, according to Brennan, the mere "convenience" of a day relatively free of commercial activity simply did not rise to the level of a compelling state interest.

Justice Potter Stewart, expressing his agreement with the observations of Justice Brennan, likewise dissented. Justice Stewart observed that the Pennsylvania law presented "a cruel choice," a choice that "compels an Orthodox Jew to choose between his religious faith and his economic survival."[21]

The discussion set forth above seeks to illuminate two propositions about the early development of the constitutional guarantee of free exercise. One proposition—the more conspicuous of the pair—is that, as late as the middle of the twentieth century, the nation's highest court self-consciously had refrained from infusing the free exercise guarantee with the sort of content that would enable the guarantee to be used as a serious weapon against generally applicable laws that worked hardship on the religious practices of religious minorities. The second proposition—the more subtle of the pair—is that some members of the Court had begun to urge a change in this long-standing status quo, to express a vision of the free exercise guarantee as more protective of religious practices, and less deferential of government action that impinged on such practices, than the vision that previously had prevailed.

Over time, stability and predictability in the law would require that one of these propositions ultimately surrender to the other. To the surprise of many, however, such a surrender would unfold not once but twice over the course of the next forty years.

As discussed at the outset of this chapter, cases in which individuals seek release from the constraints of generally applicable laws because their religious practices clash with such laws represent a considerable portion of free exercise cases. But not all free exercise cases appear on the judicial stage wrapped in this costume. Some of the least thorny of free exercise matters represent outright attempts by government to interfere with beliefs and practices attendant to religious freedom. Two examples of such interference follow.

Interference with Political Candidates

One example of government seeking to meddle unconstitutionally in matters of religious belief stems from the middle of the twentieth century. The governor of Maryland appointed Roy Torcaso to the office of Notary Public. Torcaso shortly thereafter refused to declare his belief in God. For that precise reason, the state refused to allow Torcaso to assume the office, citing the following provision of the Maryland constitution: "[N]o religious test ought ever to be required as a qualification for any office of profit or trust in this State, *other than a declaration of belief in the existence of God*" [emphasis added].[22] Torcaso sought to have the state courts of Maryland intercede, contending among other things that the free exercise guarantee forbade the state to deny him public office by virtue of his refusal to acknowledge a belief in God's existence. The state courts rejected the argument, concluding that such a requirement did not clash with free exercise principles. In particular, Maryland's highest court reasoned that the state requirement posed no First Amendment problem because "[Torcaso] is not compelled to believe or disbelieve, under threat of punishment or other compulsion. True, unless he makes the declaration of belief he cannot hold public office in Maryland, but he is not compelled to hold office."[23] Displeased both with this reasoning and the result it produced, Torcaso then petitioned the nation's highest court for assistance.

In Torcaso v. Watkins (1961),[24] the Supreme Court held for Roy Torcaso, invalidating the Maryland requirement and with it the state's efforts to enforce the requirement against him. The brief majority opinion authored by Justice Hugo Black suggested that the Court found the issue raised by the case straightforward and uncomplicated, and the Maryland requirement conspicuously inconsistent with the First Amendment. Indeed, the Court appeared to find the case sufficiently easy that it did not feel compelled to discuss at length principles relating to free exercise or any other aspect of religious freedom, though Justice Black did pause to observe that Article VI of the United States Constitution contains a provision expressly forbidding in connection with offices of the *national* government the sort of oath that Maryland required for prospective *state* officials such as Roy Torcaso.

The *Torcaso* Court nevertheless expressed the animating principle of the case in terms that resounded with free exercise concerns:

> We repeat and again reaffirm that neither a State nor the Federal Government can constitutionally force a person 'to profess a belief or disbelief in any religion.' . . . This Maryland religious test for public office unconstitutionally invades [Torcaso's] freedom of belief and religion and therefore cannot be enforced against him.[25]

In short, the *Torcaso* Court had little problem identifying the central flaw in the Maryland law as the state's purposeful interference with the religious beliefs of aspiring officeholders.

Interference with Clergy

As noted above, the Maryland law at issue in *Torcaso* sought to keep out of state government individuals who did not believe in the existence of God. The nation's highest court rebuffed the effort, concluding that free exercise as well as related constitutional principles took such power away from the state.

A Tennessee law sought to keep out of state government a strikingly different class of individuals, some of whom we can safely assume—quite unlike the targets of the law invalidated in *Torcaso*—believed rather intensely in the existence of God: members of the clergy. In McDaniel v. Paty (1978),[26] the high court rebuffed this effort as well.

Beginning in 1796, Tennessee law featured a state constitutional provision disqualifying ministers and other clergy members from serving in the legislature. By the middle of the twentieth century that prohibition applied equally to clergy seeking to serve as delegates to a constitutional convention. In 1976, Paul McDaniel, a Baptist minister from Chattanooga, filed as a candidate for delegate to an upcoming constitutional convention. Selma Cash Paty, McDaniel's opponent, instituted an action in state court to disqualify McDaniel, relying on the prohibition.

The trial court refused to disqualify McDaniel, citing the free exercise guarantee. As a result, the election unfolded, and voters selected McDaniel to serve as a delegate. Shortly thereafter, however, Tennessee's highest court reversed, holding that countervailing concerns outweighed any infringement on free exercise. In particular, that court relied heavily on two propositions to justify its conclusion. One was that the state law posed no free exercise problem because the disqualification focused not on McDaniel's religious *beliefs* or religious *practices* but, instead, on his choice of careers. The second was that the law steered clear of free exercise concerns because it left McDaniel entirely free to discharge his duties as a minister and impaired only his ability to run for office.

The Supreme Court emphatically disagreed. And although the justices could not entirely agree on the basis for their conclusion, their conclusion nevertheless was unanimous.

Three members of the Court—Justices Brennan, Marshall, and Stewart—deemed the facts and principles of religious freedom implicated by the case analogous to those of *Torcaso*. Justice Stewart, for instance, observed:

> [e]xcept for the fact that Tennessee bases its disqualification not on a person's statement of belief, but on his decision to pursue a religious vocation as directed by his belief, that case is indistinguishable from this one—and that sole distinction is without constitutional consequence.[27]

Justice Brennan echoed such sentiments:

[b]ecause the challenged provision establishes as a condition of office the willingness to eschew certain protected religious practices, [*Torcaso*] compels the conclusion that it violates the Free Exercise Clause. [*Torcaso*] . . . expressly disavow[ed] "the historically and constitutionally discredited policy of probing religious beliefs by test oaths or limiting public offices to persons who have, or perhaps more properly profess to have, a belief in some particular kind of religious concept." That principle equally condemns the religious qualification for elective office imposed by Tennessee.[28]

The plurality opinion of Chief Justice Burger nevertheless found the comparison between the constitutional principles at stake in *Torcaso* and *McDaniel* a bit more nuanced.[29] It concluded that the principle that had rendered unconstitutional the Maryland law in *Torcaso*—the notion that "[t]he Free Exercise Clause categorically prohibits government from regulating, prohibiting, or rewarding religious beliefs as such"[30]—did not carry over to invalidate the Tennessee circumstances set forth in *McDaniel*. The reason for such a disconnect, the plurality reasoned, had to do with the fact that the Tennessee clergy-prohibition law sought to punish not the *beliefs* of clergy members but the *status* of clergy members.

That distinction led the plurality to observe that the essential constitutional flaw in the Tennessee regulation of clergy had to do not with the fact that the law interfered with the exercise of religious *beliefs* of clergy, or even the ability of clergy to formulate or harbor such beliefs. Rather, the unconstitutional interference engendered by the Tennessee law had to do with the fact that it compelled Paul McDaniel and other clergy to surrender one right (the right to serve as ministers, priests, rabbis, and the like) in order to pursue another (the right to run for political office). The compelled "surrender" imposed by the Tennessee law, the plurality found, represented the substantial infringement on free exercise; that infringement, in the wake of *Yoder*, *Sherbert*, and other precedents, required a state interest of the highest order in order to withstand scrutiny.

Tennessee officials contended that the ban on clergy from positions of public office rested on the view that, once in office, clergy politicians will have a deleterious impact on both politics and religion, that such clergy politicians "will necessarily exercise their powers and influence to promote the interests of one sect or thwart the interests of another, thus pitting one [religion] against the others."[31] Whatever the merits of the argument, the plurality refused to buy it. In rejecting it, Chief Justice Burger concluded as follows:

However widely that view may have been held in the 18th century by many, including enlightened statesmen of the day, the American experience provides no persuasive support for the fear that clergymen in public office will be less careful of anti-establishment interests or less faithful to their oaths of civil office than their unordained counterparts.[32]

* * *

Together, *Torcaso* and *McDaniel* reveal some conspicuous limits on the power of government to shape the religious composition of its political representatives. Constitutional principles simply do not permit government to render a belief in God a prerequisite to securing political office. Nor do such principles permit government to exclude from office those who have chosen to pursue the path of religion. To be sure, electoral politics may have much to say about the likelihood of success for a candidate who opts to publicly deny God's existence, or one who seeks to obtain political office after a career as a member of the clergy. Nevertheless, the Constitution forecloses the authority of any government to make such decisions for its constituents.

THE EMERGENCE OF INTENSIFIED SCRUTINY

As noted earlier, the Brennan dissent in *Braunfeld* chastised the Court for its insufficiently rigorous scrutiny of laws that burden the exercise of religion. A mere two years after Justice Brennan leveled that critique the insight bore constitutional fruit.

Unemployment Compensation—*Sherbert*

A case out of South Carolina represented the first of many high court cases linking free exercise liberties and unemployment compensation (Sherbert v. Verner, 1963).[33] The case also portended the justices' deep contemporary divisions over fundamental questions implicating the free exercise guarantee.

Adell Sherbert, a Seventh-day Adventist, found herself discharged from employment when she refused to work on Saturday, the Sabbath day of her faith. She failed to obtain alternative employment for much the same reason. Accordingly, she sought unemployment compensation pursuant to the laws of South Carolina, but met with rejection because authorities found that she lacked "good cause" under the statutory scheme to refuse the alternative employment offered to her. South Carolina courts refused to accept the contention that such treatment infringed upon Sherbert's free exercise rights. Sherbert appealed to the nation's highest court, and prevailed.[34]

Three features of the majority's treatment of Adell Sherbert's claim stand out.

First, the majority underscored the obvious fact that the South Carolina law and its application to Sherbert constituted a burden of free exercise. As Justice Brennan's majority opinion observed, the plaintiff's purported ineligibility for unemployment compensation was rooted exclusively in her religious practices. The administrative ruling, the majority concluded, "forces her to choose between following the precepts of her religion and forfeiting benefits, on the one hand, and abandoning one of the precepts of her religion in order to accept work, on the other hand."[35] Such a choice, the majority explained, imposed "the same kind of burden" on Adell Sherbert as if the state had imposed a fine on her for worshiping her religion on Saturday.[36]

Second, the majority, heeding the argument Justice Brennan had issued in dissent in *Braunfeld*, expressly paused to remark that burdens on the free exercise guarantee will withstand constitutional scrutiny only if they are supported by genuinely weighty public interests. As the Court put it, "in this highly sensitive constitutional area, 'only the gravest abuses, endangering paramount interest, give occasion for permissible limitation.' "[37] In short, the *Sherbert* Court served public notice that government lawyers seeking to defend laws burdening the exercise of religion were going to experience an increasingly difficult time winning their arguments.

Third, the majority made clear that, for at least two reasons, the government purpose underpinning the South Carolina "good cause" exception in the context of Ms. Sherbert's circumstances failed to measure up to this stringent level of scrutiny required in free exercise cases and thus mandated that the law be struck down.[38] First and foremost, the Court expressed skepticism as to whether the state's purported justification for the "good cause" exception—diminishing the prospects for fraudulent or spurious claims for unemployment compensation by individuals purporting to be Sabbatarians—represented a sufficiently compelling justification to account for the scheme and the treatment doled out to Sherbert under it. Second, the Court found absolutely no support in the record to support that purported justification.

The justices nevertheless were far from unanimous in their views of the proper disposition of Adell Sherbert's claim.

Justice Stewart, agreeing that the South Carolina scheme at issue in the case was constitutionally problematic, passed along a pair of cogent insights.

One was that the Court's invalidation of the South Carolina scheme for the benefit of Adell Sherbert simply did not square with its refusal two years earlier to provide Abraham Braunfeld and his fellow Philadelphia area merchants the same level of accommodation. Indeed, Justice Stewart observed that, if anything, the burden imposed on the challengers in *Braunfeld*—a burden that could well drive the plaintiffs out of business—exceeded the deprivation imposed on Adell Sherbert, who would forfeit a maximum of twenty-two weeks worth of unemployment insurance. Justice Stewart thus urged that *Braunfeld* be overruled.[39]

The second, equally probing criticism deployed by Stewart concerned the relationship between the Court's free exercise and anti-establishment jurisprudence. More specifically, Justice Stewart mused that the result mandated by the free exercise guarantee in *Sherbert*—a result that would compel South Carolina to accommodate Adell Sherbert's Sabbatarian practices (to repeat, a result with which Stewart agreed)—clashed with what he dubbed the Court's "insensitive," "positively wooden," "sterile," and "mechanistic" approach to the anti-establishment guarantee in the early school prayer cases of *Engel* and *Schempp* (not surprisingly, an approach with which he disagreed).[40] In particular, Justice

Stewart expressed frustration at the ironic juxtaposition of the school prayer cases—cases that spoke fervently about the constitutional ban on governmental financial support to religious institutions—with the free exercise result in *Sherbert*, which, according to Justice Stewart, essentially *required* government to support Adell Sherbert's religious practices. For Justice Stewart, the proper course of action required the Court to rethink its approach to the anti-establishment guarantee.

Justices John Harlan and Byron White expressed a more unvarnished concern with the Court's performance in *Sherbert* and the implications of that performance for the evolution of free exercise law. In a dissent authored by Justice Harlan, the pair took serious issue with the majority's conclusion that the free exercise guarantee *required* South Carolina to carve out an exception from its law for the religiously-motivated conduct of Adell Sherbert.[41] To be sure, the dissenters made clear that, in their view (by contrast to that of Justice Stewart), South Carolina had *the discretion* to carve out such an exception, such an accommodation, in the event the state's political representatives deemed such an exception wise. But the state's failure to go that route, the dissenters claimed, posed no free exercise problem.

Compulsory Education—*Yoder*

Less than a decade after *Sherbert* the Court reiterated its commitment to searching, skeptical review of laws claimed to impose substantial burdens on religious exercise. This time the factual context of the review, far from the complexities and technicalities of a system of state unemployment compensation featured in *Sherbert*, concerned the family unit and the education of minor children.

Wisconsin's compulsory attendance law required youngsters to attend public or private school until they reached the age of sixteen. Jonas Yoder, a member of the Old Order Amish faith, refused to send his fifteen-year-old daughter Frieda to school beyond the eighth grade. Yoder's refusal was rooted in the Amish belief that sending children to high school would both undermine principles close to the core of the Amish faith—among them self-reliance, a commitment to physical work and manual labor at the expense of classroom learning, and devotion to community welfare rather than individual achievement—and risk the family's salvation. The appropriate school district administrator proceeded to file a complaint, alleging that Yoder's refusal violated state law.

The trial court convicted Jonas Yoder and imposed on him a fine of five dollars, the minimum amount set out in the statute. In so doing, the court candidly acknowledged that the Wisconsin requirement interfered with the freedom of the Yoders and other Amish families to carry out their sincerely held religious beliefs. The trial court nevertheless concluded that Wisconsin's "reasonable" exercise of government power should trump the countervailing religious practices of the Amish. Wisconsin's highest court did not agree, holding instead for the Yoders and their Amish codefendants.[42]

In Wisconsin v. Yoder (1972),[43] the nation's highest court likewise held for the Yoders, concluding that the guarantee of free exercise liberated the Amish from the post-eighth grade aspect of Wisconsin compulsory attendance law. The unfocused majority opinion authored by Chief Justice Warren Burger neither broke new constitutional ground nor made especially clear how free exercise principles recently set out in *Sherbert* applied to the different facts of *Yoder*. But a few observations that appear to form the core of the majority's reasoning can be extracted from the kaleidoscopic opinion of the chief justice.

First, the *Yoder* majority paused to deny the usefulness and vitality of the dichotomy between beliefs and actions forged back in *Reynolds*.[44] Put more precisely, the majority opinion of Chief Justice Burger paused to observe that the Court rejected the contention that " 'actions,' even though religiously grounded, are outside the protection of the First Amendment"[45]—a contention that, according to the majority, Wisconsin authorities pressed in *Yoder* and to which some state courts continued to give credence. Quite the contrary, the chief justice retorted:

> [O]ur decisions have rejected the idea that religiously grounded conduct is always outside the protection of the Free Exercise Clause. . . . It is true that activities of individuals, even when religiously based, are often subject to regulation by the States in the exercise of their undoubted power to promote the health, safety, and general welfare, or the Federal Government in the exercise of its delegated powers [citing, e.g., *Braunfeld* and *Reynolds*]. . . . But to agree that religiously grounded conduct must often be subject to the broad police power of the State is not to deny that there are areas of conduct protected by the Free Exercise Clause of the First Amendment and thus beyond the power of the State to control, even under regulations of general applicability [citing, e.g., *Sherbert* and *Cantwell*].[46]

Quite simply, the *Yoder* majority made clear that the Court's free exercise jurisprudence had undergone substantial evolution since the days of *Reynolds*. Chief Justice Burger captured that evolution with a straightforward declarative sentence that could not have been more at odds with *Reynolds*: "A regulation neutral on its face may, in its application, nonetheless offend [constitutional principles] if it unduly burdens the free exercise of religion."[47]

Second, the majority echoed the theme that animated *Sherbert* a decade earlier by reminding that courts will examine searchingly governmental action alleged to constitute a substantial burden on free exercise.[48] The Court observed that, to withstand such scrutiny, the action challenged must be grounded in "a state interest of sufficient magnitude" to override the interest undergirding the free exercise side of the particular factual dispute, an interest "of the highest order . . . and not otherwise served."[49]

Third, the *Yoder* Court demonstrated its commitment to the pair of principles set forth above by soundly rejecting Wisconsin's efforts to justify the application of its compulsory education law to the Amish.[50] The majority did not quibble with the state's argument that some degree of education is indispensable both in preparing youngsters for the challenges of good citizenship and for instilling self-reliance and self-sufficiency. It nevertheless replied that an additional year or two of formal education for Amish youngsters "would do little to serve those interests" given the principally agrarian community inhabited by the Amish and the fact that, in the Court's view at least, the record revealed that the community had been "a highly successful social unit within our society."[51] In addition, the majority denigrated as excessively speculative the state's argument that such additional schooling is important because some Amish minors will opt to leave the community and that absent some time in high school such expatriates would be "ill-equipped for life."[52]

Justice William Douglas provided the sole dissenting voice in *Yoder*. Douglas offered a view of the case that diverged sharply from that of his brethren, although that divergence of opinion concerned free exercise matters only tangentially.

At bottom, the Douglas dissent took the majority to task on two grounds. Most important, Justice Douglas decried the fact that the *Yoder* case proceeded through the American legal system without eliciting the views of Amish youngsters, both those whose families triggered the dispute and others upon whose rights the Court's disposition would have a substantial impact.[53] Justice Douglas contended that no judicial decision on the merits of the constitutional question should be reached until the minors whose rights were in issue had been given an opportunity to express their views on the matter.

Justice Douglas also expressed skepticism at the clean-as-a-whistle picture of the Amish community painted in Chief Justice Burger's majority opinion.[54] In a footnote, Justice Douglas indicated that the picture of the "idyllic agrarianism" of the Amish rests on myth, citing an academic study that reported alcohol problems among Amish youth and "preoccupation with filthy stories" along with "significant rowdyism and stress" in the Amish community generally.[55]

Together, *Sherbert* and *Yoder* worked a fundamental change in the law of free exercise. More precisely, these high court efforts worked *two* fundamental changes in free exercise law. One such change concerned the fact that the justices essentially relinquished the notion that the free exercise guarantee existed to protect beliefs rather than conduct. The other concerned the enunciation of a new and clear standard with which to assess government actions alleged to burden rights of free exercise—the strict scrutiny standard—and the corresponding burden this new standard would impose on government action alleged to burden free exercise principles. Quite simply, the pair of important cases revealed a Court profoundly more sympathetic to challenges grounded in free exercise than had been the case in prior generations.

THE CALM BEFORE THE STORM OF *SMITH II*: FREE EXERCISE CHALLENGES IN PARTICULAR CONTEXTS

The central message to be gleaned from *Sherbert* and *Yoder*, as explored in the preceding pages, appeared to be that laws posing substantial burdens on rights of free exercise of religion would prompt relatively intensive judicial examination. That intensive examination—as *Sherbert* and *Yoder* themselves made clear—would create circumstances in which such laws would run the serious risk of judicial invalidation.

The two decades following *Sherbert* and *Yoder* revealed that this central message would be underscored in some contexts but undercut a bit in others.

Unemployment Compensation

The unemployment compensation context has been a fertile source of free exercise challenges. Individuals seeking redress in the law of free exercise from denials of unemployment compensation flowing from religiously motivated conduct have found the nation's highest court sympathetic and receptive, especially in the era prior to *Smith*. The experiences of Eddie Thomas, Paula Hobbie, and William Frazee underscore the point.

Eddie Thomas, a Jehovah's Witness living in Indiana, had worked in a roll foundry helping to fabricate sheet steel. The foundry shut down, prompting the employer to transfer Thomas to a department that, Thomas quickly learned, fabricated turrets to be used on military tanks. Because the employer had no job for Thomas that did not implicate the production of weapons, and because Thomas's religious beliefs forbade him to undertake such work, Thomas requested the employer to fire him. The employer refused to do so, prompting Thomas to quit and seek unemployment compensation from the appropriate Indiana authorities. When the administrative dust had settled Indiana's highest court had rejected Thomas's claim, seeking to justify that rejection in a variety of ways, among them that personal philosophy rather than religious conviction accounted for Thomas's choices, that the burden placed on his free exercise rights by denying him unemployment compensation amounted to a modest one, and that the state's interests in preserving the integrity of its insurance fund and maintaining a stable work force trumped any harm the denial imposed on Thomas.

The Supreme Court disagreed (Thomas v. Review Board, 1981).[56] The majority opinion of Chief Justice Burger dubbed the circumstances in which Eddie Thomas found himself "indistinguishable"[57] from those that had produced Adell Sherbert's landmark case, observing that, in each of the cases, "the termination flowed from the fact that employment, once acceptable, became religiously objectionable because of changed circumstances."[58] Then, after pausing to repeat the principle set out in *Yoder* that "only those interests of the highest order . . . can overbalance legitimate claims to the free exercise of religion,"[59] the majority quickly concluded that the interests put forward by Indiana in its effort to justify the burden of Eddie Thomas's religious exercise proved insufficiently compelling.

The receptivity of his brethren to Eddie Thomas's free exercise claim did not sit especially well with Justice William Rehnquist. In particular, the sympathy his colleagues displayed for that claim and the implications of that sympathy for the future of free exercise law prompted Justice Rehnquist to issue a forceful dissent—a dissent that, a decade after its publication, would achieve a measure of triumph.

Speaking only for himself in *Thomas*, Justice Rehnquist expressed the view that the Court's free exercise jurisprudence had gone "far astray."[60] The dissent made it abundantly clear exactly where and how it believed the train of free exercise law had derailed: by insisting in *Sherbert* that laws of general applicability need to withstand strict judicial scrutiny whenever an individual claims that such a law interferes with the exercise of his or her religious convictions. As Justice Rehnquist observed:

> Just as it did in *Sherbert* . . . the Court today reads the Free Exercise Clause more broadly than is warranted. As to the proper interpretation . . . I would accept the decision in *Braunfeld* and the dissent in *Sherbert*. . . . Likewise in this case, it cannot be said that the State discriminated against Thomas on the basis of his religious beliefs or that he was denied benefits *because* he was a Jehovah's Witness. Where, as here, a State has enacted a general statute, the purpose and effect of which is to advance the State's secular goals, the Free Exercise Clause does not in my view require the State to conform that statute to the dictates of religious conscience of any group.[61]

In short, the Rehnquist dissent in *Thomas* challenged directly and without reservation the central premise that had animated free exercise law since *Sherbert* and *Yoder*: that an individual such as Eddie Thomas could insist that a generally applicable government action alleged to burden the exercise of religion, such as Indiana's unemployment compensation scheme, be measured against a standard of scrutiny that few government actions could withstand. At the time, the Rehnquist challenge appeared to have strikingly little impact on his colleagues in *Thomas*. A decade later, however, with the stunning arrival of *Smith II*, such an argument would emerge as the law of the Constitution.

In the interim, the Court continued to award victories to individuals who deployed the free exercise weapon to challenge state denials of unemployment compensation. The experiences of Paula Hobbie echoed those of Eddie Thomas. Hobbie had worked in a Florida jewelry store for more than two years when she informed her employer that she intended to be baptized into the Seventh-day Adventist Church and thus for religious reasons could no longer work from sundown on Friday to sundown on Saturday. Several weeks after such notification the store's general manager informed Hobbie that she had a choice to make: either work the shifts the employer assigned her (including some that would require working on her day of rest) or resign. Finding the options less than satisfying, Hobbie refused the offer; the employer then fired Hobbie. Hobbie shortly thereafter sought unemployment compensation, a claim that met with repeated rejection from Florida administrative and judicial authorities.

Fortunately for Paula Hobbie—as earlier had proven fortuitous for Adell Sherbert and Eddie Thomas—the nation's highest court displayed considerably more sympathy for her plight than did her employer or Florida authorities (Hobbie v. Unemployment Appeals Commission, 1987).[62] The majority opinion of Justice Brennan, holding that Florida had trampled unconstitutionally on Hobbie's free exercise rights, announced the conspicuous absence of any "meaningful distinction" among the three sets of circumstances. The opinion concluded, "Here, as in *Sherbert* and *Thomas*, the State may not force an employee 'to choose between following the precepts of her religion and forfeiting benefits . . . and abandoning one of the precepts of her religion in order to accept work.' "[63]

Two years after Paula Hobbie had earned a place in free exercise lore, William Frazee joined her. Frazee turned down a temporary position with Kelley Services, doing so because the job would have demanded him to work on Sundays, a demand he could not fulfill because Frazee, a Christian, believed Sunday represented "the Lord's day." He then applied for unemployment compensation benefits, an application that met with rejection in part because both the administrative agency and Illinois courts concluded that Frazee's failure to be a member of a particular "church, sect, or denomination" undercut his claim for a religiously grounded justification for failing to secure employment.

Once again, however, the Supreme Court awarded the challenger a free exercise victory in the context of unemployment compensation (Frazee v. Illinois Department of Employment Security, 1989).[64] The majority opinion authored by Justice White reflected scant regard for the argument that had served to deny benefits to William Frazee:

> It is true, as the Illinois court noted, that each of the claimants [Adell Sherbert, Eddie Thomas, and Paula Hobbie] was a member of a particular religious sect, but none of those decisions turned on that consideration or on any tenet of the sect involved that forbade the work the claimant refused to perform. Our judgments in those cases rested on the fact that each of the claimants had a sincere belief that religion required him or her to refrain from the work in question. Never did we suggest that unless a claimant belongs to a sect that forbids what his job requires, his belief, however sincere, must be deemed a purely personal preference rather than a religious belief.[65]

The experiences of Eddie Thomas, Paula Hobbie, and William Frazee make clear that the unemployment compensation context has proven a rich source of free exercise law. Indeed, as will become apparent later on in this chapter, the single most important recent development in the constitutional law of free exercise—the 1990 Supreme Court decision of Employment Division v. Smith—emerged as a result of yet another denial of unemployment compensation benefits. That development, as we will see, would ensure that, at least for the duration of the reign of *Smith II*, subsequent courts would be substantially less hospitable to future claimants in circumstances analogous to those of Eddie Thomas, Paula Hobbie, and William Frazee.

Taxation

Individuals and entities seeking relief from the impact of generally applicable *tax* laws in the safe harbor of free exercise principles have experienced a good deal less success than their compatriots in the unemployment compensation context. This fact stems in part from the importance the Supreme Court has attached to various aspects of the American system of taxation. But it stems as well from the magnitude of the difficulties the justices have indicated would emerge were they to accommodate free exercise concerns in the context of tax laws. Three examples of this judicial approach follow.

The case of Edwin Lee captures well these developments (United States v. Lee, 1982).[66] Lee, a member of the Old Order Amish faith living in Pennsylvania, worked as a farmer and carpenter, and employed workers to assist both on the farm and in the carpentry shop. In his capacity as employer Lee refused to withhold social security from his employees' paychecks, refused to file the quarterly social security tax returns required of employers, and refused to pay the employer share of social security taxes. Lee claimed that the religious beliefs held by him and his employees—beliefs rooted in the notion that members of the Amish faith have an obligation to care for the sick and elderly and thus a corresponding obligation to refrain from contributing to, or receiving assistance from, the national social security system—compelled him to resist all requirements of that system.

The Supreme Court rejected Lee's free exercise claim. Speaking through Chief Justice Burger, the majority sought to account for that rejection in a range of ways. First, the Court observed that a comprehensive national social security that allowed employers and employees to opt in or out "would be almost a contradiction in terms and difficult, if not impossible to administer. Thus, the Government's interest in assuring mandatory and continuous participation in and contribution to the social security system is very high."[67] Second, the Court concluded that the harm to be wrought by the tax system were it to accommodate the beliefs of Lee, his employees, and other members of the Amish faith—both the particular social security system implicated by the facts of the case as well as the wider set of rules and regulations governing American tax law—simply represented too high a price to pay for religious freedom. In this regard, the opinion noted that "the tax system could not function"[68] were members of different religious faiths allowed to prevail in their respective contentions that government happened to be spending tax dollars in ways that clashed with principles of such faiths.

The uphill battle encountered by individuals and institutions seeking to use the free exercise guarantee to gain relief from widely applicable tax regulations likewise can be gleaned from a high court case concerning the propriety of tax-exempt status for universities that discriminate on the basis of race (Bob Jones University v. United States, 1983).[69]

A pair of private schools—Bob Jones University in South Carolina, serving students from kindergarten through college and graduate school, and Goldsboro Christian Schools in North Carolina, educating students from kindergarten through high school—each conducted its school in a manner that took account of the race of its students. One school essentially accepted only Caucasian applicants; the other, which previously had excluded African-American applicants, forbade interracial dating and marriage among students. In each instance the school's policy stemmed from its view of biblical injunctions concerning the races.

The Internal Revenue Service, purporting to construe tax regulations enacted by Congress, denied tax-exempt status to each institution. It grounded its determination in its view that regulations germane to charitable organizations rendered schools that discriminated on the basis of race ineligible for such favorable treatment. The schools countered that, because religious convictions impelled their conduct regarding the races, the free exercise guarantee rendered the IRS determinations unconstitutional.

The Supreme Court, consistent with its approach in *Lee*, rejected the free exercise argument. The majority opinion of Chief Justice Burger demonstrated with ample clarity that the Court's justification for the rejection focused on the overriding importance of the government's interest in discouraging discrimination on the basis of race:

> On occasion this Court has found certain governmental interests so compelling as to allow even regulations prohibiting religiously based conduct. . . . The governmental interest at stake here is compelling. . . . Government has a fundamental, overriding interest in eradicating racial discrimination in education. . . . That governmental interest substantially outweighs whatever burden denial of tax benefits places on [the schools'] exercise of their religious beliefs. The interests asserted by [the schools] cannot be accommodated with that compelling governmental interest.[70]

The majority likewise noted that the impact the IRS determination would have on the schools, though not insubstantial financially, nevertheless would not "prevent" the schools from continuing to "observe" the dictates of their religious convictions.[71]

A third case—this one implicating the sales and use taxes—likewise reflects the lack of success often resulting when challengers to government action seek to use the free exercise guarantee as a weapon against tax laws (Jimmy Swaggart Ministries v. Board of Equalization, 1990).[72]

Jimmy Swaggart Ministries (JSM), a Louisiana nonprofit corporation, conducted evangelical crusades and sold a range of religious and nonreligious merchandise at these crusades, approximately two dozen of which occurred in California. California authorities advised the organization that both the state sales tax (applicable to sales of personal property) and use tax (applicable to out-of-state purchases of personal property by in-state residences) applied to JSM, as it did to essentially all sellers and purchasers. JSM replied that, among other things, the free exercise guarantee forbade California to impose these generally applicable taxes on JSM's religious activities.

Once again, the Court rejected the argument grounded in free exercise. In so doing, the majority opinion of Justice Sandra Day O'Connor sought to justify its conclusion in a range of ways, noting, first, that the California sale and use tax treated similarly all personal property and thus could not be understood to single out religious activities for disadvantage; second, that religious principles animating JSM did not clash with the organization's payment of the taxes at issue; and third, that as a result the sales and use taxes worked "no constitutionally significant burden" on JSM's religious practices or beliefs.[73]

In short, free exercise principles have not proven especially useful in enabling taxpayers to elude the financial obligations government imposes generally on individuals and entities.

The Military

Courts give enormous deference to military institutions in constitutional cases, only rarely overturning exercises of military authority in the name of constitutional freedoms. Indeed, a recurring theme running through constitutional law generally concerns the reluctance of judicial institutions to second-guess decisions emerging from the military context. A much-discussed case underscores this theme in the context of free exercise principles (Goldman v. Weinberger, 1986).[74]

Simcha Goldman, a rabbi and Orthodox Jew, served in the Unites States Air Force as a clinical psychologist working at a mental health clinic on a base in California. For several years while in service Goldman wore a yarmulke (skull cap) along with his uniform, donning his service cap over the yarmulke whenever he went outside. After Goldman testified on behalf of the defense during a court-martial hearing while wearing the yarmulke, however, events began to unfold that jeopardized Goldman's ability to continue wearing the yarmulke, particularly when he ventured away from the clinic. In sum, a superior officer ultimately ordered Goldman to stop wearing the yarmulke, even in the clinic, citing a regulation that forbade headgear from being worn indoors except by armed military police.

Goldman then instituted a lawsuit, contending that the free exercise guarantee protected his right to wear his yarmulke while in uniform. The trial court held for Goldman, ordering the Air Force to back off. The appellate court reversed, observing that "the Air Force's interest in uniformity [of appearance] renders the strict enforcement of its regulation permissible."[75] Goldman then took his case to the Supreme Court, where by the narrowest of margins, five to four, the justices informed Simcha Goldman that he was very much out of luck.

In rejecting Goldman's claim, the majority opinion authored by Justice Rehnquist reasoned that the lessons of *Sherbert*, *Yoder*, and a variety of other free exercise cases favorable to claimants simply did not carry weight in the military context. Instead, the Court expressed the following insights about the relationship between free exercise rights and military authority:

> [W]e have repeatedly held that "the military is, by necessity, a specialized society separate from civilian society." . . . Our review of military regulations challenged on First Amendment grounds is far more deferential than constitutional review of similar laws or regulations designed for civilian society. The military need not encourage debate or tolerate protest to the extent that such tolerance is required of the civilian state . . . ; to accomplish its mission the military must foster instinctive obedience, unity, commitment, and esprit de corps. . . . The essence of military service "is the subordination of the desires and interests of the individual to the needs of the service."[76]

With that foundation, the majority not surprisingly proceeded to opine that free exercise principles did not require the Air Force to accommodate Simcha Goldman's desire to wear his yarmulke. The Air Force's interest in striving for uniformity of appearance among its personnel, Justice Rehnquist and the majority concluded, merits substantial judicial deference, even at the expense of Simcha Goldman's desire to wear a headcovering required by his religion.[77]

As mentioned above, four members of the Court parted company with the majority, expressing the view that, properly understood, free exercise principles led to the conclusion that Goldman should prevail.

Justice Brennan, joined by Justice Marshall, accused the majority of "abdicat[ing] its role as principal expositor of the Constitution and protector of individual liberties in favor of credulous deference to unsupported assertions of military necessity."[78] In particular, the pair contended that the military's own regulations and practices, which permit jewelry and other manifestations of difference, undercut the Air Force argument grounded in uniformity of appearance and worked a special and distinctive harm on Orthodox Jews, ultimately affording members such as Goldman "a painful dilemma—the choice between fulfilling a religious obligation and serving their country."[79] The Brennan dissent closed by urging Congress to step in and undo the wrong perpetrated by the Air Force and the Rehnquist majority.[80]

Justice Harry Blackmun likewise disagreed with the majority's disposition of the matter. But the Blackmun dissent stemmed from a concern more basic than that of Justice Brennan: the concern that Simcha Goldman's request represented one sufficiently rare and unusual that the Air Force simply had no basis to reject it for fear that it would unleash a flood of analogous requests.[81]

Justice O'Connor, also joined by Justice Marshall, contributed to the chorus of dissent. Justice O'Connor observed, among other things, that no justification existed for the failure to apply basic free exercise principles in the military context and that the appropriate application of such principles should prompt the Court to require the Air Force to accommodate Goldman's religious beliefs and practices.[82]

The justices indeed divided sharply over the merits of Simcha Goldman's free exercise claim. Yet, when the dust settled, the case represented another link in the lengthy chain of disputes in which the nation's highest court rejected a challenge to the exercise of military discretion rooted in the individual rights guarantees of the Constitution.

Prisons

The *Goldman* case illuminated both the Court's distinctive approach to free exercise issues in the military context and the sharp divisions on the Court concerning that approach. A year after *Goldman* another free exercise case produced sharp divisions on the Court. This time, however, the institution we know as the American prison provided the context for the dispute (O'Lone v. Shabazz, 1987).[83]

Ahmad Uthman Shabazz and Sadr-Ud-Din Nafis Mateen, members of the Islamic faith, resided in a New Jersey prison. Changes in the rules and regulations governing prisoners, engendered in part as a result of overcrowding and the security issues attendant to that problem, produced a situation in which Shabazz, Mateen, and other Muslim prisoners assigned to details away from the principal structure that housed prisoners no longer were permitted to return to that particular building during the course of the day. As a result, such prisoners found themselves prevented from attending Jumu'ah, a weekly Islamic service that the Koran requires be conducted shortly after noontime on Fridays. As the trial court observed, the Jumu'ah service represents a ceremony as important to Islam as Saturday service is to Judaism or Sunday worship to Christianity. Shabazz and Mateen claimed that this deprivation imposed on them by prison officials clashed with their free exercise rights. Dividing five to four, the Supreme Court disagreed.

The central message of the *Shabazz* majority—a message that strikingly echoed the message delivered in *Goldman* in the context of the military, and that again was conveyed by a majority opinion authored by Justice Rehnquist—concerned the substantial deference the Court would pay to the decisions of prison officials in circumstances in which prisoners allege deprivation of constitutional rights. Stripped to the bone, that message essentially went like this: Incarceration invariably leads to the loss or diminution of many rights, including rights of free exercise. It naturally follows, the majority reasoned, that restrictions on the rights of prisoners need not withstand the stringent scrutiny to which limits on the constitutional rights of other individuals tend to get subjected. Moreover, the majority reminded, another corollary flowing from the diminished rights of prisoners happens to be reflected in the "appropriate deference" courts will afford "the considered judgment" of the government officials whose very professional task it is to secure the safety of prison facilities—in short, the reluctance of courts to overturn such judgments so long as they "'reasonably relate[] to legitimate penological interests.'"[84]

This deferential approach—applied to the distinctive facts of the New Jersey prison, Muslim inmates, and the weekly Jumu'ah ritual—led to a hardly surprising result. The majority concluded that the rules and regulations governing work outside the main prison facility, including the policy that forbade prisoners to return to that facility during the course of the day, emerged out of legitimate concerns for the risks and burdens to which a more permissive set of policies would have exposed prison administrators, prison resources, and other prisoners. The majority likewise concluded that the free exercise guarantee did not require prison officials to sacrifice these legitimate concerns in order to honor the religious practices of incarcerated Muslims, even if the consequences meant that prisoners such as Shabazz and Mateen lost their ability to attend Jumu'ah.

Four members of the Court, speaking through Justice Brennan, expressed vigorous disagreement with the deferential "reasonableness" standard articulated by the majority and the consequences that standard engenders for the constitutional freedoms of individuals housed in prisons around the nation.[85] The dissenters instead urged the Court to invoke a more rigorous standard for contexts in which the constitutional freedoms of prisoners happen to be at stake. In particular, that more rigorous standard, they contended, would take account of whether the activity in which the prisoner seeks to engage represents a "presumptively dangerous" one (if so, the dissenters acknowledged that more deference should attach to the decision of prison administrators) and whether the inmate has been "completely deprived" of the right to engage in the activity (if so, the dissenters suggested that less deference attach to the decision circumscribing the freedom).[86] When the dust settled, the dissenters concluded that prison officials had failed to justify adequately the deprivation imposed on Muslims incarcerated at the New Jersey facility.

Despite the seemingly intractable division among the justices exemplified by the divergent approaches in *Shabazz*, the American prison, like that of the military, remains a context in which free exercise principles typically produce substantial deference to government officials. As a result, prisoners frequently find themselves on the short end of the free exercise stick.

The Administration of Government

By its very nature, the typical free exercise challenge consists of a grievance about something government happens to be doing *to* the complaining party. The typical grievant contends that the particular government action at issue poses a distinctive burden on the grievant's ability to conduct herself in a manner faithful to her religious beliefs. As we have seen, sometimes such a burden amounts to government imposition of a penalty on an act the grievant insists her religion requires faithful adherents to undertake (say, the act of refusing to have minor children participate in formal education beyond a certain age). In other instances, the burdens amount to government rendering the grievant ineligible for a particular benefit because she has undertaken an action that the grievant contends she undertook in order to be faithful to her religious beliefs (say, rejecting an employment opportunity). To repeat, challenges grounded in the free exercise guarantee—most especially those that command the attention of the justices who work out of our nation's capital—typically appear on stage garbed in such costume.

Occasionally, however, a free exercise challenge presses the limits of the conventional format. One aspect of a case in which Native American parents sought to prevent government from linking their daughter with a social security number represents a notable example of this phenomenon (Bowen v. Roy, 1986).[87]

Stephen Roy's ancestors belonged to the Abenaki Tribe. Conversations with an Abenaki chief underscored in Roy and his wife, Karen Miller, the belief that technology "robs" the human spirit. Accordingly, in order to preserve the uniqueness of their two-year-old daughter, Little Bird of the Snow, and maximize Little Bird's prospects for spiritual growth, Roy and Miller insisted that government not use a social security number to identify Little Bird, essentially because such use would serve to rob Little Bird of her spirit.

The Court rejected the claim. Chief Justice Burger's majority opinion explained—in terms conspicuously unsympathetic to the request—the problem with the constitutional claim of Little Bird's parents:

> Roy may no more prevail on his religious objection to the Government's use of a Social Security number for his daughter than he could on a sincere religious objection to the size or color of the Government's filing cabinets. The Free Exercise Clause affords an individual protection from certain forms of government compulsion; it does not afford an individual a right to dictate the conduct of the Government's internal procedures.[88]

This explanation may well be susceptible to criticism both for its harshness—in equating the religious claim to one about filing cabinets—and for the possibility that it distorted the claim itself by minimizing the extent to which Stephen Roy believed that government use of a social security number for Little Bird would harm Little Bird's spiritual development. The explanation nevertheless captures an important truth: Courts will not readily permit the free exercise guarantee to be deployed as a weapon in a battle whose principal aim is merely to induce government to change its methods of internal "recordkeeping" or "administration."

Road Construction

The reluctance the Court evinced in *Roy* to use the constraints of free exercise to work changes in the internal operations of government reemerged shortly thereafter in a context that on first blush appeared materially different: road construction planned to take place on land owned by the national government but deemed sacred and used for religious purposes by adherents of a particular faith (Lyng v. Northwest Indian Cemetery Protective Association, 1988).[89]

By the late 1970s, the national government already had completed much of the work necessary to create a paved road linking two California towns separated by seventy-five miles. Between two completed portions of the project lay a six-mile stretch through the Chimney Rock section of Six Rivers National Forest. Unfortunately for all concerned, the Chimney Rock section—the area necessary to complete the project—for centuries had been used for religious purposes by the Yurok, Karok, and Tolowa Indians. Indeed, a study commissioned by the United States Forest Service determined that the Chimney Rock area "is significant as an integral and indispensable part of Indian religious conceptualization and practice."[90] Administrative efforts undertaken by the tribes and others to stop the construction nevertheless proved unsuccessful. Not surprisingly, therefore, a lawsuit unfolded, one in which the free exercise guarantee figured prominently.

The Supreme Court's majority opinion, authored by Justice O'Connor, rested on the premise that internal administrative use of a social security number and a road construction project presented closely analogous circumstances. More precisely, that opinion concluded that, insofar as the free exercise guarantee was concerned, the road construction at issue in *Lyng* "cannot meaningfully be distinguished" from the use of a social security number at issue in *Roy*.[91] The majority endeavored to justify the conclusion with the following exercise in reasoning:

> In both cases, the challenged Government action would interfere significantly with private persons' ability to pursue spiritual fulfillment according to their own religious beliefs. In neither case, however, would the affected individuals be coerced by the Government's action into violating their religious beliefs; nor would either governmental action penalize religious activity by denying any person an equal share of the rights, benefits, and privileges enjoyed by other citizens.[92]

In short, as this important passage reveals, the *Lyng* majority took the position that the free exercise guarantee should be construed as conveying the notion that its principal concern rests with government action that threatens to induce individuals into changing *their* course of conduct and undertaking activity inconsistent with *their* religious beliefs. The guarantee ought not be twisted and judicially rewritten, the majority cautioned elsewhere, into one that encourages individuals to "exact" involuntary concessions from government that compel government to change the way it does its business in order "to satisfy every citizen's religious needs and desires."[93] The majority likewise placed particular emphasis on the word "prohibit" featured in the text of the guarantee, suggesting that the self-conscious use of the word underscored the fact that the free exercise right had to do principally with what government could do to individuals.

Three members of the Court dissented in *Lyng*, vigorously taking issue with the free exercise analysis. Justice Brennan, writing for the trio, dubbed the majority approach to the claim "astonishing"[94]—and he assuredly did not invoke that adjective as a compliment. The dissenters objected especially to the majority's "inability" to distinguish between the internal administrative use of a social security number and road construction:

> I find this inability altogether remarkable. In *Roy*, we repeatedly stressed the "internal" nature of the Government practice at issue. . . . [W]e likened the use of such recordkeeping numbers to decisions concerning the purchase of office equipment. When the Government processes information, of course, it acts in a purely internal manner, and any free exercise challenge to such internal recordkeeping in effect seeks to dictate how the Government conducts its own affairs.
>
> Federal land-use decisions, by contrast, are likely to have substantial external effects that government decisions concerning office furniture and information storage obviously will not. . . . [This fact] is demonstrated by the cruelly surreal result [the majority] produces here: governmental action that will virtually destroy a religion is nevertheless deemed not to "burden" that religion.[95]

A substantial volume of free exercise law emerged in the nearly two decades between the high court's enunciation of the heightened scrutiny standard in *Sherbert* and *Yoder* and the retreat from that standard to be announced in 1990. This middle era of free exercise law revealed a Court increasingly eager to limit the practical implications of its recently-announced proposition that substantial burdens on rights of free exercise bear a presumption of constitutional illegitimacy and thus will withstand constitutional scrutiny only if *both* justified by the weightiest of considerations *and* crafted so as to burden free exercise rights only to the extent necessary to advance those weightiest of considerations.

The justices comprising the majorities in these cases deployed two principal analytic tools to effectuate their goal in this middle era. First, they identified a range of contexts in which the general proposition simply would not be applied. Prisons and the military represented two such contexts. Second, they applied the strict scrutiny standard to some subcategories of free exercise claims with a bit less muscle than the standard gets applied in other aspects of constitutional law. The tax cases represent a prominent example of this phenomenon. To be sure, the standard retained significant bite in some other aspects of free exercise law—

for instance, the context of denials of unemployment compensation. In retrospect, however, it seems unmistakable that, increasingly throughout this era, a majority of justices increasingly looked for reasons either to set aside entirely the strict scrutiny standard or to apply it in such a way as to render it substantially less hospitable to individual challengers than previously had been the case.

Looking back, therefore, perhaps the momentous impending development of *Smith II* should not have been quite so surprising.

THE RETREAT FROM INTENSIFIED SCRUTINY: EMPLOYMENT DIVISION V. SMITH

As noted above, the central issue in the case law devoted to the free exercise guarantee has been the extent to which the Constitution requires government to accommodate the distinctive religious practices of particular individuals by providing such individuals an exemption, an out, from laws that apply generally throughout society. By any standard, the most important recent statement from the high court on the matter is the watershed case of Employment Division v. Smith (1990) ("*Smith II*").[96]

Prior to *Smith II*, as we have seen, the justices had crafted a body of free exercise law whose central animating principle represented the notion that, with exceptions here and there, laws substantially burdening rights of free exercise would withstand constitutional challenge only if they satisfied the strict scrutiny standard. With the arrival of *Smith II*, however, a narrow majority of justices abandoned this strict scrutiny standard. In its place the majority left behind a standard strikingly less sympathetic to the claims of religious minorities. Accordingly, in the wake of *Smith II* a pair of new principles animates free exercise law. One is that, for the most part, an individual's religious beliefs or practices will not excuse her from compliance with an otherwise valid generally applicable law. The second is that generally applicable laws alleged to work substantial burdens on free exercise rights for the most part need not even be subjected to intensive judicial scrutiny.

We turn now to examine *Smith II* and its implications.

The (Not Uncomplicated) Facts of *Smith II*

Alfred Smith and Galen Black worked for a drug rehabilitation organization in Oregon. Each of the men ingested (that is to say, ate) peyote—a small cactus that the state classified as a controlled substance—at religious ceremonies sponsored by the Native American church. Their employer discharged them from employment because of this fact, prompting the pair to seek unemployment compensation.

The state administrative processes began promisingly enough for Smith and Black, with a referee concluding that each was entitled to unemployment compensation. To a considerable extent this initial decision traced back to *Sherbert* and its message that government efforts to burden the exercise of religion needed to withstand searching scrutiny. Unfortunately for Smith and Black, however, the appeals board disagreed with the referee, prompting the state to deny the claims. The board justified its conclusion in a variety of ways, among them that Oregon indeed had a compelling interest in denying benefits in these circumstances—that interest being the statewide prohibitions attending illegal drugs—and the corresponding fact that the state statute permitted unemployment benefits to be denied in the event employment had been terminated for "misconduct connected with work."[97]

Smith and Black proceeded to take their concerns to the Oregon state court system. They contended, among other things, that the sacramental use of meager quantities of peyote represented a constitutionally protected activity, and that free exercise principles forbade Oregon to deny them unemployment compensation because of such religiously driven conduct.

Lawyers for Oregon contended, by contrast, that the context at hand should lead to a different conclusion from that reached by the *Sherbert* court, and for two reasons, each rooted in the assumption that the conduct undertaken by Smith and Black constituted a crime. One contention was that the free exercise guarantee imposed no obligation on Oregon to carve out an exception from its criminal law for religiously motivated conduct. The other was that, in light of the importance of laws regulating drug use and possession, Oregon had satisfied the stringent constitutional test set out in *Sherbert* by which to evaluate laws alleged to burden religious exercise. In sum, unlike the status of Sabbath observance confronting South Carolina authorities in *Sherbert*, the state argued, Oregon's self-conscious categorization of peyote possession as a crime and the obvious importance of anti-drug laws provided the "compelling" public interest for refusing to accommodate the religiously motivated conduct of Black and Smith.

When the dust settled, Oregon's highest court reversed the administrative decision and awarded victory to Smith and Black. In so doing, that court pointed to *Sherbert* and the compelling governmental interest standard that case endorsed as both the appropriate test for free exercise challenges and the explanation for its result. In particular, the court explained that, in its view, Oregon lacked a sufficiently "compelling" interest to justify its denial of unemployment benefits to the pair. The reason this was so, the court explained, had to do with the fact that, in its opinion, the law of free exercise did not permit Oregon to go outside the boundaries of its law of unemployment compensation to justify the denial of unemployment compensation benefits. Because the applicable unemployment compensation laws *themselves* made no reference to denying benefits on the basis of criminal conduct such as drug use or possession, the court reasoned, Oregon could not put forth such an explanation as its constitutionally "compelling" interest. Stripped of perhaps their most powerful rhetorical weapon, state authorities had little in reserve; all that remained of the purported state interest in denying benefits to Black and Smith, the court noted, was the interest in preserving the financial integrity of the state's system of unemployment compensation. But that concern, the court opined, represented an interest insufficiently compelling to justify the burden imposed on religious practices.

The state then appealed to the nation's highest court, prompting the case to land there for the first of its two dockings (Employment Division v. Smith, 1988 ("*Smith I*")).[98] Unfortunately for all concerned, the free exercise issue at the core of the case received scant attention, as the justices found themselves distracted by other matters.

In particular, the justices wholeheartedly agreed with Oregon's contention that the criminal status of religiously inspired peyote consumption under state law was central to the determination of the free exercise issue. Surprisingly, however, the Court announced that it needed assistance from Oregon's highest court in answering that question before the justices could turn to the central free exercise issue. As Justice John Paul Stevens put it for the Court in *Smith I*:

> Neither the Oregon Supreme Court nor this Court has confronted the question whether the ingestion of peyote for sincerely held religious reasons is a form of conduct that is protected by [free exercise principles] from the reach of the state's criminal laws. . . . It is inappropriate [for us to proceed] without first receiving further guidance concerning the status of the practice as a matter of Oregon law. A substantial number of jurisdictions have exempted the use of peyote in religious ceremonies from legislative prohibitions against the use and possession of controlled substances. If Oregon is one of those states, [the conduct of Black and Smith] may well be entitled to constitutional protection. On the other hand, if Oregon does prohibit the religious use of peyote, and if that prohibition is consistent with [free exercise principles], there is no federal right to engage in that conduct in Oregon. If that is the case, the State is free to withhold unemployment compensation from [Black and Smith] for engaging in work-related misconduct, despite its religious motivation. Thus, [we first must obtain] . . . an understanding of the legality of their conduct as a matter of state law.[99]

Accordingly, the Court remanded the case to the Oregon Supreme Court, essentially instructing it to determine whether the sacramental use of peyote constituted a crime under Oregon law.

On remand, the Oregon court issued two notable conclusions—one that Justice Stevens and his colleagues in the high court majority had self-consciously elicited and one that the high court had not. The Oregon justices reluctantly reported that Oregon law made no exception in its criminal laws for the sacramental use of peyote. In addition, they passed along their view that First Amendment free exercise principles nevertheless insulated religiously inspired peyote use from criminal prohibition, that is to say, that the free exercise guarantee *required* Oregon to accommodate the religiously inspired peyote use of Black and Smith and refrain from imposing on them the state criminal prohibition.[100]

With the Oregon justices having completed their assignment, the case returned to Washington, where Justice Antonin Scalia proceeded to author an opinion for the majority that has dramatically reworked the law of free exercise.

The *Smith II* Majority: Good-bye to the Compelling Government Interest Test

The opening step for the *Smith II* majority—a rhetorical step of no small importance—was to seek to capture the history and current status of free exercise law. This discussion culminated in a striking two-part conclusion, one boding poorly for the proponents of expansive protection for religious exercise.

One part of the conclusion was the Court's announcement that "[w]e have never held that an individual's religious beliefs excuse him from compliance with an otherwise valid law prohibiting conduct that a State is free to regulate."[101] According to the majority, in short, the history of free exercise from *Reynolds* onward reflected a rejection of the proposition that an individual can use her religious faith as a constitutional trump card to elude the constraints of an otherwise valid law through the invocation of the demands of her religion.

Not surprisingly, the other part of this conclusion consisted of the majority's imaginative reformulation of the meaning of *Sherbert*, *Yoder*, and other cases in which the Court had seemed to forbid government to ensnare religiously motivated individuals within the confines of generally applicable laws.[102] According to Justice Scalia, however, those cases ought not have been construed to mean what those who decided them may have thought they meant. Instead, the *Smith II* majority sought to distinguish such cases, to rob them of their otherwise powerful precedential value, by declaring that such cases emerged out of something *other than* pure free exercise concerns. Understood properly, the *Smith II* majority contended, the facts of these prior "hybrid" cases implicated constitutional rights *above and beyond* mere free exercise concerns, such as free speech rights or the rights of parents to direct the education of their children. It was the existence of these other constitutionally protected rights, the majority advised, that accounted for the Court's receptivity to such claims.[103] In short, the *Smith II* majority delivered an opening gambit that rocked the foundation of free exercise law by fundamentally redefining the entire body of law that had preceded it.

The next move for the *Smith II* majority came as no surprise. The majority turned to confront the facts and constitutional claim at issue in the case—facts and a claim rooted in the religiously inspired use of peyote—and proceeded to explain why such circumstances do not fit into this special category of "hybrid" claims worthy of special constitutional solicitude. Quite simply, the majority noted, the religiously inspired use of peyote presents no such connection to constitutional rights above and beyond those of free exercise, such as rights attendant to free speech or raising a family. For that reason, the majority concluded, free exercise principles impose no obligation on Oregon to accommodate those who seek an exemption from the state's criminal law on the basis of such religiously inspired conduct.[104]

Despite the considerable importance of this opening step of the *Smith II* majority, a judicial act of even greater explosiveness awaited in the remainder of the opinion. There the majority proceeded to confront—and shatter—a premise that had been central to free exercise law at least since *Sherbert*: The premise that substantial government-imposed burdens of free exercise would receive searching constitutional scrutiny and would withstand such scrutiny only if, among other things, justified by a compelling interest.

Not so, informed the majority. Such an approach to the free exercise guarantee, Justice Scalia explained for the five-justice *Smith II* majority, exposes the legal system to dangers that far outweigh its benefits.[105] In particular, the majority explained that such an approach "would be courting anarchy"[106] in the administration and enforcement of the law because the approach essentially amounts to the creation of "a private right to ignore generally applicable laws."[107] Moreover, Justice Scalia elaborated, the ever-increasing religious diversity of the American citizenry ensures that the costs and dangers of imposing the compelling government interest standard on government each time it seeks to enforce a law of general application on an individual who claims a religiously driven exception to that law likewise will be ever-increasing. As the majority observed:

> Precisely because "we are . . . made up of people of almost every conceivable religious preference" . . . and precisely because we value and protect that religious divergence, we cannot afford the luxury of deeming *presumptively invalid*, as applied to the religious objector, every regulation of conduct that does not protect an interest of the highest order. [Such a notion] would open the prospect of constitutionally required religious exemptions from civil obligations of almost every conceivable kind—ranging from compulsory military service . . . to the payment of taxes . . . to health and safety regulations such as manslaughter and child neglect laws . . . compulsory vaccination laws . . . drug laws . . . and traffic laws; to social welfare legislation such as minimum wage laws . . . child labor laws . . . animal cruelty laws . . . environmental protection laws . . . and laws providing for equality of opportunity for the races. . . . The First Amendment's protection of religious liberty does not require this.[108]

Quite simply, the *Smith II* majority concluded that free exercise principles required Oregon *neither* to accommodate religiously inspired peyote use through an exemption from its generally applicable criminal prohibition *nor* to provide unemployment compensation to individuals who lost their jobs because of such religiously inspired use.

In short, the *Smith II* majority trumpeted a new era for free exercise law—one that promised to be decidedly less hospitable to individuals seeking relief on free exercise grounds from the constraints of generally applicable laws.

The O'Connor Concurrence

As noted above, five members of the Court—Justices Scalia, White, Stevens, and Kennedy, along with Chief Justice Rehnquist—comprised the *Smith II* majority, joining in the landmark opinion authored by Justice Scalia. The four remaining members—Justices Brennan, Marshall, Blackmun, and O'Connor—combined to issue sharp rebukes of the handiwork wrought by their colleagues. This fact alone made it abundantly clear that core free exercise principles would continue to divide the Court into the twenty-first century.

One of the four justices who parted company with the majority—Justice Sandra Day O'Connor—nevertheless did agree with the bottom line of the majority opinion that, on the facts of the case, the constitutional guarantee of free exercise did not require Oregon to accommodate the religious practices of peyote users. Ironically, however, it just so happened to be the remarks and analysis set out in that justice's separate opinion for the four that exposed the depth and intensity of the disagreement among the justices.

In an opinion whose most important and enduring sections earned the support of colleagues Brennan, Marshall, and Blackmun, Justice O'Connor assailed the work of the *Smith II* majority on three particular fronts. First, the O'Connor four contended that the majority's interpretation of the constitutional text itself proved seriously flawed.[109] Second, they accused the majority of playing fast and loose with the history of free exercise precedent.[110] Third, they highlighted the disturbing consequences to be experienced by religious minorities as a result of the Court's decision to abandon searching scrutiny of laws that substantially burden religious exercise.[111]

The quartet's expression of dissatisfaction with the majority's understanding of the constitutional language of free exercise proceeded essentially as follows. In order to *exercise* one's religion, to be faithful to one's religious beliefs, they noted, individuals often must engage in, as well as refrain from, particular sorts of conduct. The very constitutional language of free exercise, they observed, reflects an awareness of this self-evident truth. The proof, in short, can be found in the textual pudding: The language of free exercise, they pointed out, conspicuously and self-consciously refuses to distinguish between government action that impinges on religious belief and government action that impinges on religiously motivated conduct. This textual language, they reminded, refuses to tell government that the restraints the guarantee imposes on it are limited to circumstances in which government seeks to intrude on religious beliefs. In short, the very language of free exercise, the O'Connor four maintained, reveals that conduct motivated by religious belief, no less than the belief itself, earns presumptive constitutional protection. A law forbidding a person to undertake an act that constitutes an act of religious worship for the person, they contended, unquestionably amounts to "prohibiting the free exercise" of religion. For that reason, Justice O'Connor maintained, the text of the guarantee itself requires such a law to be examined with rigorous skepticism rather than nonchalant deference.

O'Connor and colleagues likewise took to task the *Smith II* majority for manipulating beyond recognition prior free exercises cases. In particular, they challenged Justice Scalia's representation that nowhere in the free exercise precedents can be found examples of the Court excusing religiously motivated individuals from compliance with generally applicable laws. Not true, the O'Connor four retorted: At the very least *Yoder* and *Cantwell* reflect precisely that phenomenon. The majority's effort to demean the importance of such cases, to slip them under the judicial table by slapping the label "hybrid" on them, Justice O'Connor suggested, lacks credibility.

Finally, the O'Connor four paused to lament the real-world impact of *Smith II* for religious minorities. As explained earlier, the *Smith II* majority readily acknowledged the fact that, in its view, "an 'unavoidable consequence' "[112] of the American form of government happens to be that individuals who belong to minority religious faiths must depend to a considerable extent on the kindness of the political process to accommodate the practices of such minority faiths.[113] Justice O'Connor replied to this devil-may-care treatment of religious minorities with a stinging rebuke:

> In my view, however, the First Amendment was enacted precisely to protect the rights of those whose religious practices are not shared by the majority and may be viewed with hostility. The history of our free exercise doctrine amply demonstrates the harsh impact majoritarian rule has had on unpopular or emerging religious groups such as the Jehovah's Witnesses and the Amish.[114]

In short, the O'Connor quartet made clear the vast gulf that separated the understanding of free exercise subscribed to by its members from that of the *Smith II* majority. Reconciliation would not be forthcoming anytime soon.

THE RESPONSE TO *SMITH II*

Politics, the Constitution, and Free Exercise: The Religious Freedom Restoration Act of 1993 (RFRA)

The news of *Smith II* promptly triggered widespread outcries, nowhere more prominently than on the floor of Congress. Looking back, perhaps such a response ought not have been entirely unexpected. After all, it required scant effort to extract from *Smith II* that the Court's rejection of the "compelling government interest" standard would usher in an era that exposed the practices of religious minorities and others to substantial risk, placing such practices at the mercy of legislative majorities both in state capitals around the nation as well as in Congress. Indeed, acknowledgments contained in both the Scalia majority and the O'Connor critique explicitly noted the fact, the former explaining that such was the price to be paid for democratic rule and the latter bemoaning the in-your-face scorn of core constitutional principles alleged to be reflected in that very majority opinion.

But members of Congress did more than merely criticize *Smith II*'s elimination of the compelling government interest standard. They sought to change through legislation this watershed development in free exercise law wreaked by *Smith II*. The method they chose to effectuate that change—the Religious Freedom Restoration Act of 1993 (RFRA), signed into law by President William Clinton in November of his initial year in office—could not have been more unequivocal in its pursuit of this objective.

As the text of the statute itself revealed, RFRA's express purposes included the following:

(1) to restore the compelling government interest test set forth in *Sherbert v. Verner* and *Wisconsin v. Yoder* . . . and to guarantee its application in all cases where free exercise of religion is substantially burdened; and (2) to provide a claim or defense to persons whose religious exercise is substantially burdened by government.[115]

In other words, Congress, joined by President Clinton, sought to undo *Smith II*, to overturn via legislative action the high court's interment of the compelling government interest standard. And Congress sought to do so with unmistakable particularity, mandating that any substantial burden on free exercise rooted in a state or national rule of general applicability withstand constitutional scrutiny only in the event such a rule *both* furthers a compelling governmental interest *and* furthers such an interest through the least restrictive means conceivable. In short, Congress could not have been more straightforward in its effort to obliterate the work of its coequal branch of the national government.

Nor did Congress seek to soften the justification for its unusual action. That justification, too, could be found in the law's text:

(1) the framers of the Constitution, recognizing free exercise of religion as an unalienable right, secured its protection in the First Amendment to the Constitution;

(2) laws "neutral" toward religion may burden religious exercise as surely as laws intended to interfere with religious exercise;

(3) governments should not substantially burden religious exercise without compelling justification;

(4) in [*Smith II*] the Supreme Court virtually eliminated the requirement that the government justify burdens of religious exercise imposed by laws neutral toward religion; and

(5) the compelling interest test as set forth in prior Federal court rulings is a workable test for striking sensible balances between religious liberty and competing prior governmental interests.[116]

According to Congress, quite simply, the proper standard of judicial scrutiny to be applied in matters in which free exercise liberties were at stake represented an issue on which reasonable minds could not disagree. The *Smith II* majority had gotten it wrong—just plain wrong—and that wrong needed to be righted. Thus spoke Congress.

The Fate of RFRA: City of Boerne v. Flores

But Congress did not get its way for long. Instead, four years after RFRA's passage the high court got what for now at least seems the last laugh: The justices struck down the law as exceeding the powers of Congress (City of Boerne v. Flores, 1997).[117] In so doing, the majority opinion of Justice Anthony Kennedy grounded its decision in aspects of the Constitution quite different from those portions devoted to religious freedom. For this reason, the *City of Boerne* majority contributes little to the actual development or understanding of the free exercise guarantee.

The case nevertheless served to reignite the *Smith II* debate between Justices Scalia and O'Connor implicating core issues of free exercise interpretation.

Justice O'Connor, dissenting in *City of Boerne*, persisted in the contention that the *Smith II* majority had wrongly decided the issue central to that case (an error, she explained, that lay at the root of its mistake in *City of Boerne*).[118] Justice O'Connor urged the Court to revisit the issues central to *Smith II* and by so doing enable the train of free exercise law to get "back on course."[119]

The bulk of the O'Connor dissent in *City of Boerne* represented an effort to use history to buttress the argument that *Smith II* had been wrongly decided. Whereas her dissent in *Smith II* itself had focused principally on a range of other not insubstantial reasons to part company with the Scalia majority, Justice O'Connor turned in *City of Boerne* to deploy the weapon of historical analysis to the anti-*Smith II* battle. She began with the following declaration:

> The historical evidence casts doubt on the Court's current interpretation of the Free Exercise Clause. The record instead reveals that its drafters and ratifiers more likely viewed the Free Exercise Clause as a guarantee that government may not unnecessarily hinder believers from freely practicing their religion, a position consistent with our pre-*Smith* jurisprudence.[120]

The dissent proceeded to examine a variety of historical sources that in its view supported the arguments for constitutionally required accommodation, among them state-specific documents springing up in the prerevolutionary colonies; the prevailing understanding of free exercise in the minds of those who framed the Constitution and the Bill of Rights; the postrevolutionary experiences in drafting state constitutions; and the writings of influential American figures throughout the nation's formative period in the late eighteenth and early nineteenth centuries, including Madison, Jefferson, Washington, and Henry. Dispassionate analysis of these historical sources, Justice O'Connor maintained, led to but one conclusion: "[T]he Free Exercise Clause is properly understood as an affirmative guarantee of the right to participate in religious activities without impermissible governmental interference, even where a believer's conduct is in tension with a law of general application."[121]

The O'Connor critique in *City of Boerne* of *Smith II* and its approach to free exercise issues attracted the support of two colleagues who had joined the high court subsequent to *Smith II*: Justices Stephen Breyer and David Souter. Justice Breyer added his name to all that O'Connor had to say about the weight of historical evidence cutting decidedly in favor of the argument that a central purpose of the free exercise guarantee was to make it difficult for government to interfere with religious practices even through laws of general application. Justice Souter, for his part expressing "serious doubts" about the correctness of *Smith II*, acknowledged that O'Connor's historical tour in *City of Boerne* had "intensified" those doubts.[122] Souter concluded that, because of *Smith II*, the constitutional law of free exercise remained "marked by an 'intolerable tension.' "[123]

Not surprisingly, Justice Scalia did not sit by silently in *City of Boerne* and allow colleagues to undercut his *Smith II* labors. Justice Scalia instead submitted a concurrence that confronted and sought to reply to the historical evidence put forward by Justice O'Connor, a concurrence that dubbed "extravagant" the O'Connor claim that the weight of such historical evidence undermined the approach of *Smith II*.[124]

The central theme of the Scalia concurrence was that the evidence mustered by Justice O'Connor simply did not lead where she contended it led, to the conclusion that the framers *intended* the free exercise guarantee to require government to exempt religiously driven conduct from the constraints of laws of general application. Quite the contrary, Justice Scalia replied: The evidence adduced by O'Connor suggests that, consistent with the approach of *Smith II*, the Framers understood rights of free exercise to extend only insofar as the individuals exercising such rights kept their religious practices from clashing with laws of general applicability. The fact that, on occasion, both colonial and postrevolutionary state legislatures enacted specific accommodations for the practices of religious minorities, Justice Scalia observed, ought not prompt us to jump to the erroneous conclusion that such accommodations were "understood to be constitutionally *mandated* by the Free Exercise Clause."[125] Indeed, Justice Scalia contended, the very absence of any case from early American history in which a court refused to enforce a generally applicable law against a religious believer because such a law failed to make an appropriate accommodation for the believer provides "telling" support for the conclusion of the *Smith II* majority that the free exercise guarantee does not require such accommodations.[126]

The extraordinary effort of Congress and President Clinton to undo through legislation the core of *Smith II*—and, in so doing, to return the strict scrutiny standard to its central role in free exercise jurisprudence—met with defeat at the hands of the very Court that animated the effort in the first place. In the aftermath of that defeat, one overarching question remains: Where exactly does that leave the constitutional law of free exercise? We turn now to that question.

THE AFTERMATH OF *SMITH II*: THE PRESENT, AND FUTURE, OF FREE EXERCISE LAW

Smith II changed the course of free exercise jurisprudence. Prior to *Smith II*, laws implicating free exercise principles typically needed to withstand strict judicial scrutiny in order to survive constitutional challenge. With *Smith II*, however, the majority rejected the deployment of strict scrutiny, consigning antecedent cases to a "hybrid" bundle.

After *Smith II*, how much deference does the free exercise guarantee require courts to pay to generally applicable government actions that burden religious practices? After *Smith II*, how likely are the prospects that individuals will be able to prevail, as Adell Sherbert and the Yoder family did a generation ago, in court efforts to compel government to make exceptions from such laws for religiously driven conduct? For now, the answers to these questions are not especially difficult: a considerable amount of deference, and not very likely to prevail.

Yet, as the discussion set forth above suggests, the dawn of the twenty-first century finds this most central aspect of free exercise law surrounded by considerable clouds of uncertainty. The differences of opinion dividing the justices on these issues reflect a good deal more than quibbles at the margin. Such differences, instead, implicate the most basic principles of free exercise law and interpretation.

For this reason, the path the law of free exercise will follow over the course of the next few generations remains perilously difficult to predict. Will the advocates of stringent scrutiny for laws that pose substantial burdens on religious exercise—advocates such as Justice O'Connor and some of her colleagues on the current Court—ultimately win out? Or, instead, will the Court continue to hew to the approach reflected in the *Smith II* majority, an approach rooted in the view that government ought not be required to make exceptions for religiously driven conduct and ought not be required to withstand searching scrutiny into its justification for laws of general applicability merely because such laws pose problems for some individuals whose religious practices differ from those of majority faiths?

Generally Applicable and Facially Neutral Laws

As the discussion set forth above reflects, *Smith II* effectuated a dramatic shift in the manner in which courts go about assessing constitutional challenges grounded in free exercise principles. Two trends in particular reflect this dramatic shift. First, as a consequence of the less searching standard of review adopted by the majority in *Smith II*, the vast bulk of free exercise challenges meets with rejection, with the challenged laws being upheld as constitutional. Second, courts have partitioned free exercise challenges into a variety of subclassifications in order to manage and resolve the different sort of challenges arising in the post-*Smith II* era.

In the wake of *Smith II*, the central proposition animating the disposition of free exercise cases appears to be that a generally applicable and facially neutral law will withstand the claim that free exercise requires an accommodation to be made for the religiously based conduct trapped within the law's constraints so long as the challenged law advances a legitimate governmental objective. In general, therefore, the burden imposed on religious practices by a generally applicable and facially neutral law has been rendered essentially irrelevant. What matters in the post-*Smith* era, instead, is whether the law is generally applicable and facially neutral.

A case out of Rhode Island provides a poignant example of the practical impact of *Smith II* (Yang v. Sturner, 1990).[127] In *Yang*, a Hmong couple brought a lawsuit against Rhode Island's medical examiner for performing an autopsy on their son without parental consent. The autopsy clashed with the Yangs' religious convictions, convictions that equated an autopsy with mutilation and embodied the belief that an autopsy would enslave the spirit of the dead body and prompt that spirit to return to take another person from the family.

The trial court initially found for the Yangs. After the high court handed down *Smith II*, however, the trial court reversed itself, noting that the Rhode Island law requiring an autopsy constituted a law that satisfied the *Smith II* standards of general applicability. The trial court expressed its "deep regret"[128] that the intervening high-court decision prompted it to recall its prior opinion. The trial court observed that, in its view, *Smith II* had "distorted long-standing precedent"[129] in its eagerness to conclude, as Justice Blackmun put it in his *Smith II* dissent, that "strict scrutiny of a law burdening the free exercise of religion is a 'luxury' that a well-ordered society cannot afford, and that the repression of minority religions is an 'unavoidable consequence' of democratic government."[130] Nevertheless, the trial court expressed the view that the *Smith II* majority left it no choice. Because the Rhode Island law governing autopsies applied generally and could not be said to be targeted at particular religiously inspired conduct, *Smith II* precluded the court from holding for the Yangs, despite the fact that, as the trial court noted, the law obviously amounted to a substantial burden on the Yangs' exercise of their religion.

In addition to obviating a court's "substantial burden" analysis, *Smith II* likewise precludes a court from granting special treatment from a generally applicable and facially neutral law—an exemption, if you will—to an individual holding unusual religious beliefs. A recent case out of Oklahoma underscores this point (Swanson v. Guthrie Independent School District, 1998).[131]

In *Swanson*, a couple who home-schooled their daughter Annie for religiously motivated reasons petitioned the local school district to create an exemption to allow their daughter to attend public school part-time. The reason for the petition lay in the belief of the Swanson parents that the public school's pedagogic expertise in certain subject matter areas—especially foreign languages, vocal music, and some sciences—exceeded their own, and thus that their daughter's attendance would enhance her preparation for college. The district policy in effect at the time of the request permitted part-time attendance only for fifth-year seniors and special education students. Accordingly, a new superintendent denied the request, concluding that Annie Swanson fell into neither category of exceptions to the policy. The Swansons challenged the denial, contending that it clashed with their rights of free exercise. The trial court, citing *Smith II*, awarded victory to the school district. The United States Court of Appeals for the Tenth Circuit affirmed.

The appellate court began its analysis with a concise statement of the applicable post-*Smith II* standard: "As a general proposition, a law (or policy) that is neutral and of general applicability need not be justified by a compelling governmental interest even if that law incidentally burdens a particular religious practice."[132] The court proceeded to apply this standard to the facts of Swanson's challenge. It concluded—as courts invariably do in the post-*Smith II* world—that the challenged policy satisfied constitutional standards, in this case because the policy reasonably related to the district's objective as preserving scarce educational resources.[133]

In short, the post-*Smith II* judicial landscape reveals a terrain in which individuals who seek exemptions from laws of general applicability for religiously inspired conduct confront a rugged, uphill climb in their efforts to prevail on their free exercise claims. With *Smith II* on the books, generally applicable laws alleged to burden the exercise of religion will not be subjected to strict judicial scrutiny. As a result, such laws invariably will withstand constitutional attack.

The vestiges of pre-*Smith II* jurisprudence linger, however, in connection with a variety of government classifications. As a result, courts continue to subject to strict scrutiny laws alleged to burden free exercise rights in a range of distinctive circumstances. Each such bundle of circumstances represents a situation in which, for one reason or another, courts deem the challenged government classification sufficiently problematic—because of what courts view as the decidedly nonneutral way in which the classification treats religion—as to remove the bundle from the vast bulk of laws that in the post-*Smith II* world need to withstand mere minimal judicial examination. These bundles of circumstances that continue to receive searching scrutiny include the following: (1) where the challenged law includes secularly driven but not religiously driven exemptions; (2) where the challenged law includes an "individualized" exemption that government applies in a manner so as to disadvantage religion; (3) where the challenged law targets a particular religious practice; and (4) where the challenged law—though by its terms generally applicable and facially neutral—gets applied by government in a manner discriminatory toward religion. The discussion that follows elaborates on these and related matters.

Laws Containing Exemptions

Laws containing exemptions may be partitioned into two categories: laws containing legislatively created *religious* exemptions and laws containing legislatively created *secular* exemptions.

Insofar as the first is concerned, government remains free in the aftermath of *Smith II* to carve out religious exemptions from generally applicable and facially neutral laws, provided, of course, that the exemptions refrain from discriminating *among* religions. Likewise, government remains free to carve out exemptions in situations in which otherwise neutral laws would threaten to burden particular religious practices. In short, the political process remains available to religious minorities in their efforts to ward off the potentially deleterious consequences of a government classification.

Secular exemptions likewise dot the post-*Smith II* landscape. Secular exemptions come in two varieties: "categorical" and "individualized." Categorical exemptions represent sweeping exemptions that apply to a cluster of people falling within a particular category (for instance, those male police officers who, against the requirements of a general policy, wear beards as a result of a shared medical condition). Individualized exemptions, by contrast, represent circumstances in which government has excused from compliance no category of individuals or entities but, instead, has doled out the exemption on an ad hoc basis.

Despite the differences between the two categories of secular exemptions, courts remain skeptical whenever government carves out *secular* exemptions while refusing *religiously based* claims for a similar exemption. Accordingly, to the extent a statutory scheme includes *secularly driven* exemptions, free exercise principles disable government from refusing to create *religiously driven* exemptions absent a justification of overriding importance. The judicial process comes into play, in short, in circumstances in which government has carved out some *nonreligious* exemptions to an otherwise generally applicable and facially neutral law but the law continues to burden the religious practices of individuals not benefited by an exemption. In such circumstances, courts will subject the law to stringent scrutiny, insisting that the law advance interests of the highest order in a manner narrowly tailored to achieving the governmental objective. The discussion that follows elaborates on this bundle of post-*Smith II* law.

Legislatively Created Religious Exemptions

As noted above, lawmakers around the nation remain free to carve out exemptions from their laws that accommodate religious needs and practices. Laws that do so typically withstand constitutional scrutiny. A California case illustrates such a legislative effort (Catholic Charities of Sacramento, Inc. v. Superior Court of Sacramento County, 2004).[134]

A California law required employers who provided their employees with health insurance that included prescription drug benefits to include prescription contraceptives within the coverage. The statutory scheme permitted "religious employers" to opt out of providing the otherwise mandatory coverage for prescription contraceptives. Catholic Charities, which conceded that it did not meet the statutory criteria for receiving an exemption, objected to the law as offensive to its organizational principles, principles to the effect that contraception is "a sin."[135] It also claimed that the narrowness of the statutory definition of "religious employer" amounted to discrimination against it, justifying strict judicial scrutiny of the classification. The court disagreed, concluding that both the law itself, intended to eliminate insurance practices that disadvantaged women, and the accommodation to religious employers, which applied equally to diverse faiths, satisfied free exercise principles.

Likewise, religiously accommodating exemptions pass constitutional muster in the event a generally applicable law otherwise would threaten to burden religious practices. Put differently, free exercise principles permit government to endeavor to ward off *potential* harm to religiously driven conduct even in circumstances in which the statutory scheme does not impose *actual* harm on such conduct. Once again, a California law drives home the point.

A California law granted an exemption to religious organizations from the state's landmark designation laws. Plaintiffs challenged the law, claiming that it improperly bestowed an economic benefit on religious groups. The court disagreed, observing that the exemption merely sought to relieve religious organizations from *potential* burdens on free exercise (East Bay Asian Local Development Corp. v. California, 2000).[136]

Legislatively Created Secular Exemptions

When government creates exemptions from the constraints of statutory schemes for secular reasons, it generally cannot refuse to carve out an analogous exemption for those burdened by the scheme on account of religion. A useful example of this phenomenon concerns a recent Virginia case (Horen v. Commonwealth, 1997).[137]

Timothy and Diane Horen were convicted of possession of wild bird feathers, a misdemeanor under the law of Virginia. The law allowed for a variety of secular exemptions to the prohibition—among them taxidermy, museum display, and research. The Horens contended that their Native American religion required the use of feathers in religious practices such as prayer, cleansing, purification, consecration, and healing. The Horens made clear that they did not believe in killing birds; the feathers in their home came from dead birds.

The Virginia appellate court overturned the conviction, concluding that the law infringed upon the Horens' free exercise rights. In so doing, the court concluded that the presence within the statutory scheme of a variety of *secularly based* exemptions coupled with the absence of any exemption for *religiously based* conduct robbed the law of the deference that ordinarily accompanies post-*Smith II* challenges by rendering the law nonneutral. In short, the fact that the law contained exemptions for nonreligious conduct while at the same time substantially burdening religious practices trapped within the law's constraints meant that strict judicial scrutiny was appropriate. As the court put it: "Where the state creates a mechanism for legitimate . . . exceptions but fails to include religious uses among these legitimate exceptions, discriminatory intent may be inferred."[138] The court proceeded to require the state to demonstrate a compelling interest in regulating the Horens' possession of wild bird feathers. The state replied that the statutory scheme endeavored to protect and preserve wild birds. Because, as noted above, the trial court had found that the Horens used only stray feathers and the feathers of dead birds in their religious practices, the appellate court concluded that the state's interest in protecting wild birds simply would not be advanced by ensnaring the Horens within the constraints of the law.[139]

"Categorical" Secular Exemptions

When government opts to carve out "categorical" exemptions for secular reasons, free exercise principles typically forbid government to refuse to create an analogous exemption for religiously based conduct. A recent case out of New Jersey reinforces the principle in the context of public employment (Fraternal Order of Police of Newark Lodge No. 12 v. City of Newark, 1999).[140]

The Newark Police Department forbade its male employees to wear beards. The policy emerged out of the department's desire to promote uniformity of appearance among its officers and, in turn, to convey the image of a disciplined force with readily identifiable officers. The department nevertheless exempted from the ban beards necessitated by medical reasons.

A pair of Muslim officers contended that fidelity to their religious principles required them to grow beards. The department resisted, prompting a lawsuit by the pair of officers. A federal appellate court held that the department's refusal to permit a religiously based exception to its ban while at the same time allowing a secularly based medical exception triggered heightened judicial scrutiny. Because, in the court's view, the officers wearing beards for religious reasons posed no more substantial threat to uniformity and safety than those officers wearing beards for medical reasons, the court ordered the department to allow the pair of Muslim officers to wear beards on the job.[141]

"Individualized" Secular Exemptions

Courts also apply strict scrutiny where government crafts individualized exemptions that work to harm religiously based conduct. A federal case from Maryland offers an example of free exercise principles at work in such circumstances (Keeler v. Mayor & City Council of Cumberland, 1996).[142]

Catholic church leaders intended to demolish an outdated monastery and chapel in order to replace them with more modern facilities. Before destroying the buildings, however, municipal law required the church to receive permission from local authorities, because the buildings occupied an historic part of the city.

Pursuant to a local ordinance, the city denied the church's application, justifying the denial on the grounds that the buildings were of "unusual importance and no economically feasible plan can be formulated for their preservation."[143] The church sued. The court ruled for the church.

Two facts accounted for the result. First, the ordinance provided for exemptions in some circumstances. As a result, the court concluded:

> [t]he ordinance embodie[d] a legislative judgment that the City's interest in historic preservation should, under certain circumstances, give way to other interests, such as furthering major development and protecting property owners from financial hardship.[144]

The court reasoned that, in light of such a legislative judgment, free exercise principles required it to extend a similar exemption to the church unless a compelling justification existed for failing to do so.

Second, the city failed to proffer a compelling reason for denying the church's application. To be sure, the city sought to justify its refusal to accommodate the church's request through a range of arguments—among them a concern for property values, the preservation of historic districts, and the fostering of civic beauty. But the court found none of the proffered justifications sufficiently compelling.[145]

Targeting the Practices of a Particular Religious Faith

Non-Generally Applicable, Non-Facially Neutral Laws

Exceedingly rare these days is the occasion in which government goes out of its way to interfere deliberately with the practices of a particular religious faith. When government does pursue such an unusual course, however, the free exercise guarantee tends to serve as the constitutional weapon unleashed on the offending law, with invalidation amid talk of impermissible motivation likely to follow. A recent, provocative high court case arising in Florida serves as a useful example (Church of the Lukumi Babalu Aye v. Hialeah, 1993).[146]

Central to the controversy at issue in the case is the fact that the Santeria religion employs animal sacrifice as a core aspect of its worship. Animals sacrificed in connection with Santerian worship include chickens, pigeons, ducks, guinea pigs, and turtles. Because of persecution in their native Cuba, thousands of Santerians fled to Florida throughout the second half of the twentieth century. In 1987, the city of Hialeah learned that the Santerians planned to establish a house of worship and a range of related structures within the municipality. What seems to have especially troubled the city was the fact that Santerians planned to make more conspicuous the ritual of animal sacrifice that plays such a central role in their faith.

Accordingly, the city council called an emergency session to confront these impending developments. Out of the emergency session materialized a range of resolutions, including those that trumpeted the "great concern regarding the possibility of public ritualistic animal sacrifices"[147] animating city residents, the fact that such sacrifices clashed with state law, and the warning that those who insisted on undertaking such animal sacrifices should expect to be prosecuted. Shortly thereafter the city council enacted ordinances purporting to deal further with the issue, ordinances that together rendered unlawful the ritual sacrifice of an animal for purposes other than food consumption and exposed to fine and imprisonment those who proceeded to violate such ordinances.

Not surprisingly, the church and its leadership, including President Ernesto Picardo, himself a Santerian priest, instituted an action in federal district court in Florida, alleging that the municipality's actions infringed upon the free exercise freedoms of Santerians. The trial court and appellate court each concluded that the ordinances did not infringe upon such rights. A unanimous Supreme Court disagreed, awarding victory to the Santerians.

The central challenge the case posed for the justices in the aftermath of *Smith II* concerned the extent to which the newfangled deference to government burdens on free exercise reflected in *Smith II* carried over to the facts of *Lukumi*. Justice Kennedy, writing for the majority, approached that question by restating the lesson of *Smith II* as follows:

> In addressing the constitutional protection for free exercise of religion, our cases establish the general proposition that a law that is neutral and of general applicability need not be justified by a compelling governmental interest even if the law has the incidental effect of burdening a particular religious practice [citing *Smith II*]. . . . A law failing to satisfy these requirements must be justified by a compelling governmental interest and must be narrowly tailored to advance that interest. These ordinances fail to satisfy the *Smith* requirements.[148]

Hialeah's efforts fell short of earning the deference that attaches to most laws of general applicability in the post-*Smith II* world, the majority explained, because such efforts satisfied *neither* the neutrality requirement *nor* the requirement that laws burdening rights of free exercise be laws of general applicability.

Insofar as the necessary neutrality was concerned, the majority found the Hialeah laws and the events prompting them conspicuously lacking. Justice Kennedy explained that the ordinances "had as their object the suppression of religion," that the municipality's lawmaking efforts purposefully sought to "target" the religious conduct of Santerians and were undertaken " 'because of,' not merely 'in spite of,' " the impact such efforts would have on Santerian practices.[149] Neutral lawmaking endeavors, the majority made clear, do not set out deliberately to undercut some category of religious practices.

Likewise unsatisfied in the majority's view was the *Smith II* requirement that laws burdening free exercise earn judicial deference only after demonstrating that they represent laws of general applicability. Indeed, according to Justice Kennedy, the underinclusivess of the ordinances—exceptions abounded for killing animals for food; exterminating mice, rats, insects, and other pests; fishing; and animal euthanasia—suggested that they trapped within their constraints essentially only those individuals and institutions who sought to kill animals for religious reasons. As the majority put it, "The ordinances 'ha[ve] every appearance of a prohibition that society is prepared to impose upon [Santeria worshippers] but not itself.' This precise evil is what the requirement of general applicability is designed to prevent."[150]

The majority's conclusion that the Hialeah lawmaking endeavor embodied neither neutrality nor general applicability meant that the judicial deference mandated by *Smith II* for most laws that burden free exercise simply did not apply. As a result, the majority proceeded to subject the ordinances to a sort of *Sherbert*-like strict scrutiny, finding them entirely inadequate for reasons noted above.

In short, laws that target specific religious practices will be subject to searching judicial scrutiny, with invalidation likely to follow.

Generally Applicable and Facially Neutral Laws Enforced in a Discriminatory Manner

Courts likewise will apply searching scrutiny in circumstances in which government administers otherwise neutral and generally applicable laws in a manner that discriminates against religious conduct. A New Jersey case demonstrates how free exercise principles constrain such government action (Tenafly Eruv Association v. Borough of Tenafly, 2002).[151]

The municipality of Tenafly had on its books an ordinance prohibiting any sign or advertisement from being displayed in a public place without prior municipal approval. The ordinance on its face forbade officials to make exceptions to the law. Municipal officials nevertheless frequently permitted exceptions—for address numbers affixed to telephone poles; for signs indicating that pets had been lost; for orange ribbons signifying protests; for holiday decorations adorning public property during the Christmas season. When a group of Orthodox Jews sought to demarcate an *eruv* by placing small ribbons on utility poles, however, the borough balked, forcing the group to remove the ribbons.

The tenets of Orthodox Judaism forbid members to push or carry objects on the Sabbath. By convention, however, such activities may be performed within a ceremonial area called an *eruv*. Absent an *eruv*, therefore, many Orthodox Jews who are disabled or have small children are essentially prevented from attending synagogue on the Sabbath. For that reason, Orthodox Jews in Tenafly endeavored to create such an *eruv* by attaching *lechis*—thin black plastic strips—to utility poles within the borough. After municipal officials compelled the group to remove the strips, the group instituted a lawsuit contending that such government action deprived its members of their constitutional rights.

The United States Court of Appeals for the Third Circuit observed that the Tenafly ordinance represented a facially neutral generally applicable law. It nevertheless held for the challengers, concluding that the city had administered the otherwise neutral law in a manner unfair to the religiously inspired conduct. As the court noted:

> Because the Borough has tolerated equally permanent house numbers, it hardly has a compelling interest in refusing to allow the inconspicuous *lechis* on the ground that they are permanent. Further, it is hard to see how the allegedly permanent nature of the unobtrusive *lechis* somehow undermines [the ordinance's] objective of avoiding visual clutter and maintaining control over municipal property more than items like bright orange ribbons and lost animal signs. Moreover, even if the Borough had a compelling interest in preventing permanent fixtures on its utility poles, its decision to remove the *eruv* while allowing the house numbers is not narrowly tailored to promote that interest.[152]

Accordingly, the court held that the Borough's selective enforcement of an otherwise neutral and generally applicable law deprived plaintiffs of their free exercise rights.

Hybrid Claims

The *Smith II* majority purported to distinguish the facts before it from cases such as *Yoder* by categorizing those earlier cases as "hybrid claims" implicating "not the Free Exercise Clause alone, but the Free Exercise Clause in conjunction with other constitutional protections."[153] The hybrid nature of these pre-*Smith II* cases, Justice Scalia contended, accounted for why earlier courts had invoked strict scrutiny. In short, *Smith II* relegated seemingly prominent high court cases to a special purpose category of free exercise jurisprudence, suggesting that only circumstances falling within such a category would trigger strict judicial scrutiny and thereby require government to put forth a compelling interest to justify its refusal to accommodate religiously inspired conduct.

Courts have struggled mightily to come to grips with the practical significance of this aspect of *Smith II*. Some courts have construed this aspect of *Smith II* as nonbinding dicta, a sort of suggestive set of musings distinct from the core of the case. Some courts have acknowledged the precedential weight of hybrid claims. Some courts have rejected altogether the notion of hybrid claims. In short, little consensus has emerged in the aftermath of *Smith II* as to how exactly to identify a hybrid claim. Not surprisingly, therefore, few successful hybrid claims dot the landscape. A case out of California provides a glimpse into a typical post-*Smith II* effort to make use of the "hybrid" notion (Ventura County Christian High School v. City of San Buenaventura, 2002).[154]

A religiously affiliated high school leased its property from the local school district. The high school sought to install modular classrooms on the property while its larger physical structure underwent renovation. The school district approved the plan. Unfortunately for the school, after it had obtained the modular classrooms the city informed it that a city use permit would be required in order to proceed with installation. The school replied that the city had allowed other private organizations to build similar modular units without obtaining a permit and also contended that the permit requirements were arbitrary and burdensome. Haggling ensued between the city and the school, prompting a lawsuit by the school.

In particular, the school alleged that the city had violated its free exercise *and* equal protection rights. Because of this "hybrid" nature of its claim, the school argued, the court should invoke strict scrutiny and require the city to demonstrate a compelling justification for the additional permit requirement. The city countered that it did not discriminate against the high school and that all land uses must comply with city permits.

The trial court concluded that the school had not been denied equal treatment. Accordingly, it held that the likelihood of the school prevailing on its equal protection claim was slim. The court then turned to the school's free exercise claim. It readily conceded that, consistent with *Smith II*, hybrid claims tend to demand strict judicial scrutiny. It nevertheless held that, because the school had not demonstrated a colorable equal protection claim, its free exercise claim could not properly be categorized as "hybrid." The court proceeded to hold for the city on the free exercise claim, wielding the deferential scrutiny reminiscent of *Smith II* rather than the more powerful weapon of heightened scrutiny.

The Ministerial Exception

One body of law implicating religious freedom that remains largely unaffected by *Smith II* concerns the so-called ministerial exception or church autonomy doctrine. The ministerial exception functions to insulate religious organizations such as churches from claims that threaten the autonomy of the organization. More specifically, courts will trigger the exception—and thus refrain from pursuing the rights of plaintiff—in circumstances in which an investigation into the alleged legal violation (1) would interfere with the organization's right to be free from governmental intrusion with regard to its internal management or administration, or (2) would intrude in an inherently coercive manner on the organization's governance. *See* Kedroff v. St. Nicholas Cathedral (1952) (observing that religious freedom includes "an independence from secular control or manipulation, in short, power [of religious organizations] to decide for themselves, free from state interference, matters of church government as well as those of faith and doctrine").[155]

Two principal categories of matters tend to fall within the contours of the doctrine. One concerns matters regarding the employment relationship—that is to say, claims regarding hiring, firing, sexual discrimination, or other employment-related claims against religious organizations. The other category implicates sexual abuse or tort actions against religious organizations.

A recent example of the doctrine at work concerns a Methodist pastor who returned to her job following maternity leave and learned she had been dismissed. The court ruled that the termination constituted the sort of administrative action that fell within the ministerial exception (Reverend Pamela Combs v. Central Texas Annual Conference of the United Methodist Church, 5th Cir. 1999).[156] Yet another concerns a nun who instituted a sex discrimination case against her university employer, contending that the school violated Title VII in denying her tenure. The court concluded, in dismissing the claim, that *Smith II* had worked no substantial change in the doctrine (Equal Employment Opportunity Commission v. Catholic University of America, 1996).[157]

The ministerial exemption, as suggested above, receives widespread acceptance in the context of employment discrimination. Somewhat less consensus exists as to whether the exemption comes into play in connection with matters of sexual abuse and criminal violations. Some courts have held that church autonomy simply does not extend so far as to protect a member of the clergy from discovery attendant to a claim against him. In general, secular torts do apply to the secular conduct of religious leaders.[158] By contrast, some courts have concluded that subjecting a clergy member to criminal charges for sexual assault would unconstitutionally interfere with the organizational autonomy of an archdiocese. (*See, e.g.*, Ayon v. Gourley (1998),[159] and Gellington v. Christian Methodist Episcopal Church, Inc. (2000)[160] (providing a ministerial exception to a sexual harassment claim continued a long-standing tradition to the effect that religious organizations remain free from government interference into matters of governance and administration)).

Laws That Expressly Exclude the Use of Public Monies for Religious Purposes

As we have seen, an enduring theme of the constitutional law of religious freedom concerns the challenge of reconciling the respective messages of the anti-establishment and free exercise principles. Those who devote their professional lives to grappling with that challenge—in particular contemporary judges and scholars—tend to diverge sharply over how best to resolve the challenge. Some, for instance, contend that any circumstance in which tax dollars find their way to the accounts of religious organizations by virtue of a government program represents an unequivocal violation of constitutional principles. Such a perspective—perhaps the dominant one in American law up until the past two decades—could be said to elevate anti-establishment apprehensions while rendering free exercise concerns more subordinate. Others rejoin that, properly understood, nothing in the religion guarantees (or anywhere else in the Constitution) requires government to treat religion as a pariah. Such a perspective—unquestionably in the ascendancy over the past few decades—contends that religious institutions can assist in the effort to solve pressing secular problems, and for that reason (and others) no such bar should be understood to exist excluding such institutions from government largesse.

Our examination of anti-establishment law revealed that the contemporary Court remains seriously divided over the issue of whether religious institutions, consistent with *Lemon*, can be the recipients of government funds. Suppose, however, that government policymakers go out of their way to make clear that funds allocated through a particular government program may *not* be used for religious purposes. Do free exercise principles suggest that such an approach poses constitutional problems? The Supreme Court's most recent foray into free exercise law confronts this question (Locke v. Davey, 2004).[161]

In 1999, the state of Washington established a scholarship program to assist high-achieving students with the costs of college expenses. The program, dubbed the Promise Scholarship Program (PSP), permits the recipients to allocate the funds toward any education-related expense, including room and board. The legislature created a range of eligibility requirements for the scholarships. Recipients either must have graduated from a Washington high school in the top 15 percent of their class or, in the alternative, must have obtained a score of at least 1,200 on the Scholastic Aptitude Test (SAT) or at least 27 on the American College Test (ACT). The income of recipient families must be less than 135 percent of the state's median income. Recipients must enroll at least half-time in a postsecondary institution accredited by a national accrediting body. Finally, and most important for constitutional purposes, the terms of the program require that a recipient *not* pursue a degree in devotional theology.

Joshua Davey applied for, and was awarded, a Promise Scholarship. Davey, whose aspirations included to attend "a Bible college" and devote his life to the ministry as a pastor, chose to attend Northwest College, a private Christian college eligible under the PSP. Davey planned to pursue a double major in pastoral ministries and business management and administration.

At the beginning of the academic year Davey met with Northwest's director of financial aid. The director informed Davey that, in order to receive the awarded funds, Davey had to certify in writing that he would not seek to pursue a degree in pastoral ministries. Davey refused to do so. Instead, he instituted legal action, contending that the denial of funds to him represented (among other legal infringements) a violation of his free exercise rights. The Supreme Court did not agree.

Chief Justice Rehnquist, writing for seven justices, began his opinion for the Court by acknowledging the "tension" between the religion guarantees.[162] The chief justice also acknowledged that there exists "play in the joints" between the guarantees.[163] As the majority put it, "there are some . . . actions permitted by the Establishment Clause but not required by the Free Exercise Clause."[164] The circumstances surrounding the plight of Joshua Davey, the chief justice observed, implicated this "play in the joints."[165]

The majority noted that, under current anti-establishment precedent, Washington "no doubt" could have chosen to permit PSP recipients to use such funds to further religious objectives.[166] The constitutional question posed, however, did not happen to be *that* historically divisive one. Instead, the chief justice continued, the central question implicated by the facts represented a strikingly different one: Did free exercise principles render Washington's decision to *prohibit* such funds to be used for religious purposes constitutionally problematic? In answering that question in the negative, the majority found itself having to distinguish some of its recent free exercise cases from the facts before it, particularly its invalidations of the Hialeah ordinance in *Lukumi* and the Tennessee law in *McDaniel*. That effort at line-drawing can best be captured in the following important passage from the majority opinion:

> In *Lukumi*, the city of Hialeah made it a crime to engage in certain kinds of animal slaughter. We found that the law sought to suppress ritualistic animal sacrifice of the Santeria religion. . . . In the present case, the State's disfavor of religion (if it can be called that) is of a far milder kind. It imposes neither civil nor criminal sanctions on any type of religious service or rite. It does not deny to ministers the right to participate in the political affairs of the community. . . . And it does not require students to choose between their religious beliefs and receiving a governmental benefit. . . . The State has merely chosen not to fund a distinct category of instruction.[167]

In sum, the majority appeared to be saying that free exercise principles rarely will serve as an obstacle to a government decision to refrain from subsidizing a religious activity merely because government chooses to subsidize an analogous secular activity.

But the majority did not rest its conclusion exclusively on its construction of prior case law. It observed as well that important differences exist between training for religious professions and training for secular professions, that these respective endeavors "are not fungible."[168] Such differences, the chief justice explained, make it eminently reasonable for government to opt to treat differently the two categories of education—a choice, the majority contended, that simply cannot be said to signal hostility toward religion.[169]

The majority likewise summoned historical evidence to support its conclusion that a statutory ban on public monies being used for religious purposes did not clash with free exercise principles. It noted the American tradition of "popular uprisings" directed against government action that channels tax dollars to religious leaders.[170] Indeed, the chief justice noted for the majority, this very concern prompted "most" states to place into their respective constitutions explicit prohibitions against the use of tax funds to "support the ministry."[171]

Finally, the majority sought to diffuse the contention that the Washington program suffered from constitutional flaws by virtue of its allegedly hostile treatment of religion. Quite the contrary, Chief Justice Rehnquist replied that the PSP "goes a long was toward including religion in its benefits."[172] The majority pointed to two aspects of the operation of the statutory scheme to support its conclusion. One was that the PSP indeed permitted students to use their scholarships at "pervasively religious" educational institutions.[173] The second was that the program did not preclude recipients from *enrolling* in courses in devotional theology, but merely from *majoring* in such field.[174]

The Court's rejection of Joshua Davey's claim produced a characteristically fiery dissent by Justice Antonin Scalia, joined by Justice Clarence Thomas.[175] The dissent—emblematic of views increasingly voiced in American society from the conservative side of the political spectrum—leveled a vigorous bill of particulars against the majority opinion. First, it took exception to the majority's effort to square the result both with general free exercise principles and with the specific approach of *Lukumi*.[176] Second, it chastised the majority for its "misplaced" use of history.[177] Third, it mocked the majority's notion of "play in the [constitutional] joints."[178] Fourth, it maintained that Washington had at most a "*de minimus*" interest in the very prohibition it has enacted, rendering the unfairness to Joshua Davey and others like him all the more heinous.[179] Fifth, it skewered the majority for its effort to minimize the unfairness the Washington scheme exhibited vis-à-vis religion.[180] Finally, it portended some genuinely disquieting developments in constitutional law emerging out of the fruits of the majority's analysis.[181]

The dissent began by asserting that case law makes abundantly clear that a nonneutral law that burdens religious practices must withstand strict judicial scrutiny or be struck down. As the dissent put it:

> In *Church of the Lukumi Babalu* . . . the majority opinion held that "[a] law burdening religious practice that is not neutral . . . must undergo the most rigorous of scrutiny" . . . and that "the minimum requirement of neutrality is that a law not discriminate on its face." . . . These opinions are irreconcilable with today's decision, which sustains a public benefits program that facially discriminates against religion. . . .
>
> When the State makes a public benefit generally available, that benefit becomes part of the baseline against which burdens on religion are measured; and when the State withholds that benefit from some individuals solely on the basis of religion, it violates the Free Exercise Clause no less than if it had imposed a special tax. That is precisely what the State of Washington had done here. It has created a generally available public benefit, whose receipt is conditioned only on academic performance, income, and attendance at an accredited school. It has then carved out a solitary course of study for exclusion: theology. . . . Davey is not asking for a special benefit to which others are not entitled. . . . He seeks only equal treatment—the right to direct his scholarship to his chosen course of study, a right every other Promise Scholar enjoys.[182]

The dissent next turned to criticize the majority's invocation of history. According to the dissent, the public uprisings cited by the majority stemmed *not* from the fact that states had included clergy as recipients of public benefits programs such as the Washington PSP. Quite the contrary, Justice Scalia reported: the historical problem had to do with laws that *singled out* clergy for special benefits that governments had *not* extended to others. As the dissent noted, "[n]o one would seriously contend, for example, that the Framers would have barred ministers from using public roads on their way to church."[183]

Justice Scalia then confronted the majority's notion of "play in the joints" of the religion guarantees, issuing a three-part reply. First, he rejected the notion as downright silly, opining that the idea "is not so much a legal principle as a refusal to apply *any* principle when faced with competing constitutional directives."[184] Second, he noted that, assuming the notion indeed had some legitimacy, it would apply only in circumstances in which a case presented "a close call [as to] whether complying with one of the Religion Clauses would violate the other."[185] Such circumstances, the dissent contended, simply did not apply to Washington's treatment of Joshua Davey. Third, the dissent explained that Washington possessed "all the play in the joints it needs" to ameliorate any taxpayer concerns of allocating public monies to religion while nevertheless complying with the dictates of free exercise principles: the state (1) could limit the scholarships for use only at public universities; (2) could limit their use to a select course of study; or (3) could entirely abandon the PSP idea.[186]

The dissent then explained that, in its view, the people of Washington had surprisingly little *objective* reason to exclude individuals such as Joshua Davey from using their scholarships for devotional theology. After all, Scalia noted, only an exceedingly modest amount of PSP recipients are likely to pursue a degree in theology; accordingly, the state's financial stake in the matter is quite small. Even so, Justice Scalia observed, that concern evidently did not give rise to the prohibition on the use of PSP dollars for devotional theology. What produced the exclusion, the dissent explained, was the strikingly different concern "that it would violate taxpayers' freedom of conscience *not* to discriminate against candidates for the ministry."[187] Such an interest, Justice Scalia contended, simply cannot be constitutionally adequate, because if it were, the dissent mused, government could exclude religion from each and every public benefits program.

The dissent proceeded to slam the majority for seeking to soft-peddle the harm the exclusion imposed on Joshua Davey and other religiously motivated individuals like him. Justice Scalia took issue with the majority's suggestion that the burden experienced by Davey constituted a modest one, noting that the amount of the scholarship—approximately three thousand dollars a year—represents a significant price to pay for choosing to pursue a course of study reflective of one's religious principles. Apart from the financial harm, the dissent noted that "[t]he indignity of being singled out for special burdens on the basis of one's religious calling is so profound that the concrete harm produced can never be dismissed as insubstantial."[188] Moreover, the dissent lashed out at the majority's assertion that Joshua Davey should construe the harm engendered by the statute as less offensive because the harm did not emerge from any animosity toward religion. It replied that "[i]f a State deprives a citizen of trial by jury or [otherwise deprives an individual of a constitutionally protected right], we do not pause to investigate whether it was actually trying to accomplish the evil the Constitution prohibits."[189]

The dissent concluded with an ominous rhetorical flourish:

> What next? Will we deny priests and nuns their prescription-drug benefits on the ground that taxpayers' freedom of conscience forbids medicating the clergy at public expense? This may seem fanciful, but recall that France has proposed banning religious attire from schools, invoking interests in secularism no less benign than those the Court embraces today. . . . When the public's freedom of conscience is invoked to justify denial of equal treatment, benevolent motives shade into indifference and ultimately into repression.[190]

CONCLUSION

Despite the efforts of some contemporary justices to deny the fact, the constitutional law of free exercise underwent dramatic change in the final decade of the twentieth century. *Smith II* made clear that individuals who found their religious practices burdened by government action would find the legal system decidedly less sympathetic to their pleas for relief than had been the case in the three previous decades.

The ripples of *Smith II* continue to make their way through the political system, constitutional law, and the Court itself. In particular, the full impact of this dramatic change for the law of free exercise cannot yet be assessed. One aspect of the impact nevertheless can be gleaned with unmistakable clarity: The justices themselves remain strikingly divided over the most fundamental issues of free exercise law. This fact alone has produced a palpable instability in the law, as judges throughout the nation have sought to adjudicate free exercise challenges in a way that comports with the mixed signals delivered by the nine justices who work out of Washington, D.C.

As a result, the new century promises to be a time of substantial uncertainty for the ever-growing constitutional law of free exercise. New justices appointed by new presidents likely will harbor their own distinctive views about the proper understanding of this guarantee in a nation in which religious diversity becomes an increasingly conspicuous cultural fact. In this world of uncertainty, perhaps we can be sure of little other than the fact that our nation's highest court will continue to play a central role in giving meaning to this cherished American liberty.

NOTES

1. Reynolds v. United States, 98 U.S. 145 (1878).
2. *Id.* at 161.
3. *Id.* at 150–51.
4. *Id.* at 164.
5. *Id.*
6. *Id.* at 166–67.

7. *Id.* at 167.
8. *See* Kathleen Sullivan & Gerald Gunther, *Constitutional Law* 1521–22 (15th ed. 2004).
9. *Reynolds*, 98 U.S. at 164.
10. Cantwell v. Connecticut, 310 U.S. 296 (1940).
11. *Id.* at 303–04.
12. *Id.* at 304.
13. Braunfeld v. Brown, 366 U.S. 599 (1961).
14. *Id.* at 603.
15. *Id.*
16. *Id.* at 605.
17. *Id.* at 606.
18. *Id.* at 607.
19. *Id.*
20. *Id.* at 611 (Brennan, J., dissenting).
21. *Id.* at 616 (Stewart, J., dissenting).
22. Md. Const. art. XXXVII of Declaration of Rights.
23. Torcaso v. Watkins, 367 U.S. 488, 495 (1961).
24. *Id.*
25. *Id.* at 495–96.
26. McDaniel v. Paty, 435 U.S. 618 (1978).
27. *Id.* at 643 (Stewart, J., dissenting).
28. *Id.* at 633 (Brennan, J., concurring).
29. *Id.* at 626–27.
30. *Id.* at 626.
31. *Id.* at 628–29.
32. *Id.* at 629.
33. Sherbert v. Verner, 374 U.S. 398 (1963).
34. *Id.* at 404.
35. *Id.*
36. *Id.*
37. *Id.* at 406.
38. *Id.* at 409–10.
39. *Id.* at 418 (Stewart, J., concurring).
40. *Id.* at 414.
41. *Id.* at 420 (Harlan, J., joined by White, J., dissenting).
42. State v. Yoder, 49 Wis.2d 430, 82 N.W. 2d 539 (Wis. 1971).
43. Wisconsin v. Yoder, 406 U.S. 205 (1972).
44. *Id.* at 220.
45. *Id.* at 219.
46. *Id.* at 219–20.
47. *Id.* at 220.
48. *Id.* at 221.
49. *Id.* at 215.
50. *Id.* at 235–36.
51. *Id.* at 222.
52. *Id.* at 224.

53. *Id.* at 242–43 (Douglas, J., dissenting).
54. *Id.* at 247.
55. *Id.*
56. Thomas v. Review Board of Indiana Employment Securities Division, 450 U.S. 707 (1981).
57. *Id.* at 717.
58. *Id.* at 718.
59. *Id.*
60. *Id.* at 722 (Rehnquist, J., dissenting).
61. *Id.* at 722–23 (Rehnquist, J., dissenting).
62. Hobbie v. Unemployment Appeals Commission of Florida, 480 U.S. 136 (1987).
63. *Id.* at 146.
64. Frazee v. Illinois Department of Employment Securities, 489 U.S. 829 (1981).
65. *Id.* at 832–33.
66. United States v. Lee, 455 U.S. 252 (1982).
67. *Id.* at 259.
68. *Id.* at 260.
69. Bob Jones University v. United States, 461 U.S. 574 (1983).
70. *Id.* at 603–04.
71. *Id.* at 604.
72. Jimmy Swaggart Ministries v. Board of Equalization of California, 493 U.S. 378 (1990).
73. *Id.* at 392.
74. Goldman v. Weinberger, 475 U.S. 503 (1986).
75. *Id.* at 506.
76. *Id.* at 506–07.
77. *Id.* at 510.
78. *Id.* at 515 (Brennan, J., joined by Marshall, J., dissenting).
79. *Id.* at 524.
80. *Id.*
81. *Id.* at 527–28 (Blackmun, J., dissenting).
82. *Id.* at 530 (O'Connor, J., joined by Marshall, J., dissenting).
83. O'Lone v. Shabazz, 482 U.S. 342 (1987).
84. *Id.* at 349.
85. *Id.* at 354–68.
86. *Id.* at 358.
87. Bowen v. Roy, 476 U.S. 693 (1986).
88. *Id.* at 700.
89. Lyng v. Northwest Indian Cemetary Protective Association, 485 U.S. 439 (1988).
90. *Id.* at 442.
91. *Id.* at 449.
92. *Id.*
93. *Id.* at 452.
94. *Id.* at 458.
95. *Id.* at 470–72.
96. Employment Division v. Smith, 494 U.S. 872 (1990).
97. *Id.* at 874.

98. Employment Division v. Smith, 485 U.S. 660 (1988).
99. *Id.* at 672.
100. Smith v. Employment Division, 763 P.2d 146 (Or. 1988).
101. *Smith*, 494 U.S. at 879.
102. *Id.* at 880–82.
103. *Id.* at 882.
104. *Id.* at 872.
105. *Id.* at 885–89.
106. *Id.* at 888.
107. *Id.* at 886.
108. *Id.* at 888–89.
109. *Id.* at 891 (O'Connor, J., joined by Brennan, Marshall, and Blackmun, J., dissenting).
110. *Id.* at 892.
111. *Id.* at 908.
112. *Id.* at 909.
113. *Id.* at 890.
114. *Id.* at 902.
115. 42 U.S.C.A § 2000bb (1993).
116. *Id.*
117. City of Boerne v. Flores, 521 U.S. 507 (1997).
118. *Id.* at 544–45 (O'Connor, J., joined by Breyer, J., dissenting).
119. *Id.* at 544.
120. *Id.* at 549.
121. *Id.* at 564.
122. *Id.* at 565 (Souter, J., dissenting).
123. *Id.* at 566 (Souter, J., dissenting).
124. *Id.* at 537 (Scalia, J., joined by Stevens, J., concurring).
125. *Id.* at 541.
126. *Id.* at 542.
127. Yang v. Sturner, 750 F. Supp. 558 (D.R.I. 1990).
128. *Id.* at 558.
129. *Id.* at 559.
130. *Id.* at 759–60 (quoting Employment Division v. Smith, 494 U.S. 872, 908–09 (1990) (Blackmun, J., dissenting)).
131. Swanson v. Guthrie Independent School District, 135 F.3d 694 (10th Cir. 1998).
132. *Id.* at 697–98.
133. *Id.* at 698–99.
134. Catholic Charities of Sacramento, Inc. v. Superior Court of Sacramento County, 85 P.3d 67 (Cal. 2004).
135. *Id.* at 75.
136. East Bay Asian Local Development Corp. v. California, 13 P.3d 1122 (Cal. 2000).
137. Horen v. Commonwealth, 479 S.E.2d 553 (Va. Ct. App. 1997).
138. *Id.* at 557.
139. *Id.* at 559–60.
140. Fraternal Order of Police of Newark Lodge No. 12 v. City of Newark, 170 F.3d 359 (3rd Cir. 1999).

141. *Id.* at 367.

142. Keeler v. Mayor & City Council of Cumberland, 940 F. Supp. 879 (D. Md. 1996).

143. *Id.* at 882.

144. *Id.* at 886.

145. *Id.*

146. Church of the Lukumi Babalu Aye v. Hialeah, 508 U.S. 520 (1993).

147. *Id.* at 527.

148. *Id.* at 531–32.

149. *Id.* at 540.

150. *Id.* at 545–46.

151. Tenafly Eruv Association v. Borough of Tenafly, 309 F.3d 144 (3d Cir. 2002).

152. *Id.* at 178.

153. *Smith*, 494 U.S. at 880–82.

154. Ventura County Christian High School v. City of San Buenaventura, 233 F. Supp. 2d (C.D. Cal. 2002).

155. Kedroff v. St. Nicholas Cathedral of Russian Orthodox Church in North America, 344 U.S. 94 (1952).

156. Reverend Pamela Combs v. Central Texas Annual Conference of the United Methodist Church, 173 F.3d 343 (5th Cir. 1999).

157. Equal Employment Opportunity Commission v. Catholic University of America, 83 F.3d 455 (D.C. Cir. 1996).

158. Rosada v. Bridgeport Roman Catholic Diocesan Corp., 45 Conn. Supp. 397 (Conn. Super. Ct. 1998) and Society of Jesus of New England v. Talbot, 441 Mass. 662 (Mass. 2004).

159. Ayon v. Gourley, 47 F. Supp. 2d 1246 (D. Col. 1998).

160. Gellington v. Christian Methodist Episcopal Church, Inc., 203 F.3d 1299 (11th Cir. 2000).

161. Locke v. Davey, 124 S. Ct. 1307 (2004).

162. *Id.* at 1311.

163. *Id.*

164. *Id.*

165. *Id.*

166. *Id.* at 1311–12.

167. *Id.* at 1312–13.

168. *Id.* at 1313.

169. *Id.*

170. *Id.*

171. *Id.* at 1314.

172. *Id.*

173. *Id.* at 1315.

174. *Id.*

175. *Id.* at 1315–21 (Scalia, J., joined by Thomas, J., dissenting).

176. *Id.* at 1315–16 (Scalia, J., dissenting).

177. *Id.* at 1316 (Scalia, J., dissenting).

178. *Id.* at 1317 (Scalia, J., dissenting).

179. *Id.* at 1317–18 (Scalia, J., dissenting).

180. *Id.* at 1320 (Scalia, J., dissenting).

181. *Id.* at 1315–16 (Scalia, J., dissenting).
182. *Id.* at 1316 (Scalia, J., dissenting).
183. *Id.* at 1316–17 (Scalia, J., dissenting).
184. *Id.* at 1317 (Scalia, J., dissenting).
185. *Id.* (Scalia, J., dissenting).
186. *Id.* (Scalia, J., dissenting).
187. *Id.* at 1318 (Scalia, J., dissenting).
188. *Id.* at 1318–19 (Scalia, J., dissenting).
189. *Id.* at 1319 (Scalia, J., dissenting).
190. *Id.* at 1320 (Scalia, J., dissenting).

Bibliographic Essay

This bibliographical essay seeks to refer readers to much-cited sources central to the constitutional questions implicated by the religion clauses. The essay begins by discussing sources germane to the history of the religion clauses, sources that probe the context and circumstances that led to the drafting and creation of the anti-establishment and free exercise portions of the First Amendment. With that as foundation, the essay discusses materials relating to the struggle to craft a workable constitutional definition of religion. It then addresses works influential in connection with a variety of particular issues arising under the interpretation of the anti-establishment and free exercise guarantees. The essay closes with mention of some works that endeavor to reconcile the tension between the clauses as well as those that criticize the prevailing jurisprudence and offer suggestions for ways to improve on that jurisprudence.

HISTORICAL OVERVIEWS

Not surprisingly, an understanding of the First Amendment's religion clauses begins with the historical context that prompted their creation.

Michael Malbin seeks to fill what he perceives to be a conspicuous gap in the historical scholarship devoted to the religion clauses: the absence of a resource explaining "the complexities of the establishment issue or the relationship between establishment and free exercise." Accordingly, Malbin sets out to fill the gap by endeavoring to divine the intentions of the First Congress by examining its debates "on a speech-by-speech basis." Malbin concludes that the First Congress never intended the anti-establishment guarantee to mandate strict governmental neutrality between religion and irreligion. Indeed, Malbin—by contending that the original purposes of the anti-establishment guarantee would not have foreclosed governmental assistance to private religious schools—delivers a prescient expression of the outcome of the contemporary constitutional battle over school choice, at least for now. Malbin finds the meaning of the free exercise guarantee a bit more difficult to ascertain, suggesting that the congressional debates leading to the formulation of the guarantee are inadequate to convey a clear message. He nevertheless surmises that, at bottom, the meaning of the free exercise guarantee concerns "the relationship between conscientious belief and its expression." Michael Malbin, Religion and Politics: The Intentions of the Authors of the First Amendment (1978).

The Report to the Attorney General: Religious Liberty Under the Free Exercise Clause is a 1986 Justice Department publication discussing the constitutional foundations of American religious liberty. Its principal purpose is to "to remind that the Free Exercise Clause . . . is a substantive restriction on the activities of the government; that the religion clauses are expressed as a disability on the government, commanding not merely restraint or accommodation but abstention." Its self-professed secondary purpose "is to analyze carefully the text of the Free Exercise Clause, to harmonize the language with its history" in order to point out deficiencies in court interpretations of the guarantee. The report offers some provocative conclusions. First, it maintains that the religion clauses forbid government to enact a law preventing "an individual or institution from expressing or acting upon sincerely-held religious beliefs." Thus, by contrast to Malbin, the report concludes that the free exercise guarantee requires government "neutrality toward religion." Government should refrain from interfering with the exercise of religious liberty, the report contends, except under limited, compelling conditions, such as to "prevent manifest danger to the existence of the state." And, under those limited circumstances, the report argues, government may infringe on free exercise only by "the least restrictive means necessary" to prevent government's compelling justification.

Arlin Adams and Charles Emmerich take a less partisan view of the history surrounding the religion clauses. They begin by examining the historical events that culminated in the adoption of the First Amendment's guarantees for religious freedom, and in so doing readily acknowledge the impact of the Reformation on the colonists. According to Adams and Emmerich, "the Founders learned that state control of religion corrupted faith and [that] coercion of conscience destroyed true piety." Such views, Adams and Emmerich maintain, prompted the Founders to resist "planting true religion" in the new nation. The Founders worked hard, Adams and Emmerich note, to uproot established churches and cultivate an environment of religious toleration.

This examination of the historical roots of American religious liberty prompts the authors to conclude that, insofar as religion was concerned, (1) our nation's founders resided in three distinctive ideological camps, and (2) the struggle for religious liberty was rooted in four "animating principles."

"Enlightenment separationists," "political centrists," and "pietistic separationists" represented the three distinctive approaches to the appropriate relationship between religion and government. Each group championed religious liberty, Adams and Emmerich contend, but "they approached the issue from different perspectives." Enlightenment separationists, such as Thomas Jefferson, took their cues from the Enlightenment. The risk that institutional religion would dominate and ultimately corrupt government represented the central concern of these thinkers and actors. The "wall of separation" metaphor—coined by Roger Williams and popularized by Jefferson—emerged from this perspective, the authors observe. By contrast, political centrists such as George Washington, John Adams, and John Marshall "looked favorably on organized religion as necessary for social cohesion." This group, Adams and Emmerich argue, repeatedly acknowledged the importance of religion in public life. Finally, the pietistic separationists harbored precisely the converse apprehension of that motivating Enlightenment separationists: this group sought to protect *religion* from the corrupting influences of *government*.

Adams and Emmerich move from the history that gave rise to the religion guarantees to the ways in which the modern Court has applied that history to the cases it has adjudicated. The authors pause to note a conspicuous truth: Prior to 1940 the Supreme Court decided few religion-based claims. Two phenomena, they claim, account for this fact. One is that government tended to refrain from legislating in the area. The other is that not until after the enactment of the Fourteenth Amendment and the "incorporation" of the Bill of Rights did the religion guarantees begin to be used to limit the action of state and local governments.

The authors advise that contemporary courts would do well to heed the following four animating principles that inspired the language of anti-establishment and free exercise: federalism, institutional separation, accommodation, and benevolent neutrality. These principles, they contend, counsel "the judiciary to exercise restraint in formulating the role of religion in society." The principles likewise reinforce the notion that "mediating institutions are essential to the preservation of civil and religious freedom" and "permit government to foster a society committed to voluntary religious belief and practice." Arlin M. Adams & Charles Emmerich, A Nation Dedicated to Religious Liberty (1991).

Robert Alley has authored two works of note, The Supreme Court on Church and State (1988) and The Constitution and Religion (1999).

The former packs seminal free exercise and anti-establishment cases into a single volume. Alley takes note of the fact that the high court's insistence in declaring unconstitutional a range of religious observances unfolding in the nation's public schools has invited substantial criticism and exposed the justices to the charge that they have helped usher in a religion of secularism. This criticism, Alley observes, comes principally from those who belong to the "nonpreferentialist" school and contend that the anti-establishment guarantee "merely forbids any single religion from being established and in no way denies the right to create a general or plural establishment." Weighing in on the debate, Alley takes the position that a proper understanding of the events surrounding the origins of the religion clauses undercuts the nonpreferentialist argument. Indeed, he opines that "the Court's twentieth-century understanding of the term 'wall of separation' is supported by the historical record."

Alley's other noteworthy volume—arriving eleven years after the work just discussed—likewise includes essential anti-establishment and free exercise cases. But it also accounts for what the author dubs "a score of new cases demand[ing] recognition." Alley introduces the cases with a perceptive discussion of the origins of the First Amendment. He points out that the events culminating in "freedom for all religious and philosophical traditions" produced two important byproducts. First, this freedom afforded religious leaders the opportunity to "exercise voluntarily a voice of conscience on matters of justice, peace, and freedom." Second, this freedom likewise encouraged politicians "to seek rational justifications for policies, rather than retreat into pious pronouncements and national messianism." Expressing admiration for the work of the individuals whose labors produced religious liberty in a secular republic, Alley nevertheless pauses to put forward an accompanying caveat. He observes that the Framers "should not be canonized as heroes who created ideological models." Instead, Alley urges that "whatever respect is paid to such persons is dependent upon their espousal of principles considered in our current structures to be essential to representative democracy."

Leonard Levy allies himself with Alley, likewise maintaining that the historical materials surrounding the ratification of the anti-establishment guarantee undermine the nonpreferentialist stance. Levy contends that the nonpreferentialist holds a "narrow" view of the anti-establishment guarantee in an attempt to ensure that the guarantee remain subordinate to free exercise principles. According to Levy, however, history supports a broader understanding of anti-establishment principles, an understanding that government assistance to religious institutions tends to clash with anti-establishment principles. Notwithstanding what he dubs the "historically groundless" claims of nonpreferentialism, Levy acknowledges that some types of government assistance to religion remain constitutionally permissible, such as the tax-exempt status of churches. Leonard W. Levy, The Establishment Clause: Religion and the First Amendment (2d ed., rev. 1994).

By contrast to Alley and Levy, Robert Cord contends that historical events vindicate the nonpreferentialist position. Cord asserts that the Supreme Court erred at the outset of its anti-establishment jurisprudence by rhetorically erecting a "'high and impregnable' wall between Church and State." Cord argues that the Founding generation did not intend such a wall. Rather, according to Cord, history "conclusively" reveals that the Framers' purpose was to prevent the national government from instituting a national religion and from placing any particular religion in a "legally preferred position." Cord concludes that "the facts show that [the Framers] all used, in one way or another, what they viewed as nonpreferential sectarian means to reach secular government ends." Robert L. Cord, Separation of Church and State: Historical Fact and Current Fiction (1982).

Chester Antieau, Arthur Downey, and Edward Roberts likewise offer a historical account of religious freedom, striving to uncover precisely what motivated the Founders to conceive and enact the First Amendment. The authors contend that, even for the Founding generation, the effort to understand the relationship between government and religion represented a struggle. The trio candidly acknowledges that no single event or piece of historical evidence conclusively captures the meaning of the religion clauses. For that reason, they urge readers to consider "the struggles, the opposed evils, the practices, the utterances, and the aspirations of the generation that gave us for perpetuity the religion clauses of the First Amendment."

Antieau, Downey, and Roberts nevertheless purport to stand somewhat outside the debate over the historical materials. The authors identify, first, the objective harbored by the Founders to "disestablish" those churches obstructing religious freedom. For example, the authors instruct that the Founders sought to render public office accessible irrespective of religious affiliation and to ban taxes levied on individuals to support denominations to which they did not subscribe. The authors then turn to highlight forms of accommodation the Founders deemed permissible, noting that, as an example, the Founders deemed it perfectly acceptable to render public land available for use by religiously oriented educational institutions. The authors seek to probe further the meaning of "establishment" during the First Congress, concluding that the prohibition ultimately formulated essentially equated to "no preference." Their collective effort seeks to encourage others to summon history in the course of interpreting the religion clauses. It likewise affirms "the legitimacy and the imperative necessity of understanding the First Amendment in . . . light of" the Founders' practices. Chester James Antieau, Arthur T. Downey, & Edward C. Roberts, Freedom from Federal Establishment: Formation and Early History of the First Amendment Religion Clauses (1964).

Thomas Curry continues in a similar vein, probing the circumstances of colonial and revolutionary America in an effort to cull the intentions of those who crafted the religion clauses. He characterizes his efforts as an attempt to "elucidate the [Framers'] intentions underlying the First Amendment's religion clauses." Curry nevertheless widens his historical lens a bit to snap an even more expansive picture of the relevant history. Instead of limiting his examination to events surrounding ratification, Curry takes us all the way back to the reign of Henry VIII in order to "trac[e] the ideas on Church and State." Insofar as the free exercise of religion is concerned, Curry maintains that the guarantee at the very least sought to ensure an individual the freedom to live according to the dictates of her religion so long as those dictates did not manifest themselves in "overt acts against peace and order." With regard to the anti-establishment guarantee, Curry examines the evolving views animating the different state legislatures and maintains that the Founding generation viewed government efforts to organize and regulate religious support as inconsistent with the promise of the Constitution. Thomas J. Curry, The First Freedoms: Church and State in America to the Passage of the First Amendment (1986).

Philip Kurland likewise emphasizes that any attempt to understand the religion clauses requires scrutiny of the problems that the Founders confronted and sought to remedy. Undertaking his own examination, Kurland asserts that individual freedom—and a concerted effort to limit the exercise of government power over that freedom—represented the driving force behind the First Amendment, "that the objectives were to establish an equality among persons, so that each individual could choose without interference how to commune with his god, and to avoid the havoc that religious conflicts had imposed on mankind throughout history." Philip B. Kurland, *The Origins of the Religion Clauses of the Constitution*, 27 Wm. & Mary L. Rev. 839 (1986).

John Semonche has produced a volume that mixes historical documents germane to the origins of the religion clauses with landmark cases devoted to the application and interpretation of those clauses. Religion and Constitutional Government in the United States (1985). Semonche begins with a discussion that seeks to link the history out of which the religion clauses emerged with the status of religion in late twentieth-century America, when he published his work. In so doing, he seeks to disabuse readers of the notion that religious unity characterized the colonies any more than it characterizes contemporary America. Semonche reports that colonial America featured substantial religious diversity, and that such diversity both "gave rise to a pluralistic society" and "ensured religious liberty in the new nation."

Semonche acknowledges that, by the late twentieth century, the appropriate relationship between the institutions of government and religion had become a source of controversy. One side to the controversy, Semonche reports, seeks to "reintroduce the Judeo-Christian heritage into the public school classroom and rescue it from the rule of secular humanism." Opponents, by contrast, deny that "any such alternate religion" has emerged and seek to "free the educational process from any governmental support of religion." Semonche laments the chasm separating the sides of the contemporary church-state debate, expressing "hope that as persons from both sides encounter the complexities of the country's history they may find a way to begin a long-overdue dialogue."

Michael Ariens and Robert Destro have put together a textbook targeted to students of church-state relations. Their volume is substantially richer and more valuable than the typical casebook. In particular, Ariens and Destro do an outstanding job sketching the status of religion and religious freedom in the various American colonies in the period leading up to the victory in their war for independence. They trumpet their work as the "first comprehensive overview of the ongoing legal struggle" to protect religious freedom. Ariens and Destro note, as many scholars before them have noted, the scarcity of constitutional cases concerning religious freedom in the nineteenth and early twentieth century. Unlike others, however, Ariens and Destro identify the early cases as emerging out of disputes between Protestants and Catholics concerning the appropriate relationship between religion and government, as well as infighting among Protestant sects dividing "those proclaiming themselves religious and those proclaiming themselves secular." Michael S. Ariens & Robert A. Destro, Religious Liberty in a Pluralistic Society (1996).

Neil Cogan's The Complete Bill of Rights (1997) appears to reflect the work of a skilled but exasperated lawyer. Finding his quest for pertinent sources for the Bill of Rights time-consuming and circuitous—principally, it seems, because there existed no single "complete, accurate, and accessible text"—Cogan compiled such sources into this single volume. It includes every draft, proposal, and congressional discussion of each of the initial ten amendments along with other supporting documents.

DEFINING RELIGION

Throughout the history of American constitutional law, one thorny aspect of religion clause jurisprudence has been the conspicuous absence of a constitutional definition of religion. A much-cited student note undertakes the search for criteria narrow enough to serve as a workable definition yet inclusive enough to be faithful to the free exercise guarantee. The search leads the author to propose a bifurcated definition of religion, one for each of the religion guarantees. For free exercise purposes, the author suggests a functional definition that emphasizes the role belief plays within an individual's life. Religion exists, the author contends, when an individual harbors an ultimate concern, one that does not allow for subordination or compromise and, for the individual, is not vulnerable to the constraints of government action. With regard to the anti-establishment guarantee, however, the author recommends a more circumscribed notion that centers on "operational" criteria that include organization, theology, and attitudinal conformity. The author contends that this "bifurcated definition of religion fairly accommodates the individual's liberty of belief within the confines of the affirmative secular state." Note, *Toward a Constitutional Definition of Religion*, 91 Harv. L. Rev. 1056 (1978).

Stanley Ingber takes a markedly different approach to the definitional issue by exploring the differences between religion and ideology. Ingber concludes that religion can be distinguished from ideology by virtue of "the role that a sacred or transcendental reality plays in imposing obligations upon the religious faithful." He asserts that no such reality exists with regard to ideology. According to Ingber, therefore, religious beliefs (so defined) merit protection under the free exercise guarantee while ideological beliefs—which, he contends, result from human judgment—merit no such protection. Insofar as the anti-establishment provision is concerned, Ingber maintains that government support of *both* irreligious ideologies—that is to say, ideologies "opposed or hostile to religion"—*and* religion itself is forbidden. He nevertheless argues that government may promote nonreligious ideologies "for which the existence or nonexistence of religion is irrelevant" so long as there is no clash with other First Amendment restrictions. In short, by seeking to distinguish religion from ideology Ingber endeavors to offer assistance to courts in formulating a standard by which to determine conduct protected by, or excluded from protection by, the religion clauses. Stanley Ingber, *Religion or Ideology: A Needed Clarification of the Religion Clauses*, 41 Stan. L. Rev. 233 (1989).

Kent Greenawalt suggests that, for purposes of both free exercise and anti-establishment, courts should determine whether particular beliefs, practices, and organizations constitute religion by making comparisons with the "indisputably religious," such as Roman Catholicism, Orthodox Judaism, and Lutheranism. Greenawalt asserts that the analogical approach he proposes is preferable to other approaches for three reasons: (1) because the analogical approach can be made to apply in virtually every constitutional case that implicates this threshold question of religion; (2) because the approach closely approximates everyday notions of religion; and (3) because such an approach "does not dictate that the factors that count as religious for one constitutional issue will necessarily count as religious for every other." Kent Greenawalt, *Religion as a Concept in Constitutional Law*, 72 Cal. L. Rev. 753 (1984).

THE ANTI-ESTABLISHMENT GUARANTEE

Much of the scholarship devoted to the anti-establishment guarantee seeks to ascertain precisely what the clause was intended to mean or ought to be construed to mean. Some commentators contend that the guarantee means little more than that government must refrain from preferring one religious sect over another. For others, the guarantee means that government must remain neutral toward religion, neither favoring nor disfavoring it.

A significant debate in anti-establishment jurisprudence turns on whether the Constitution permits so-called "nonpreferential" government aid to religion, that is to say, aid that treats the host of religious denominations relatively equally. Weighing in on the debate, Leonard Levy, as noted above, maintains that the historical materials surrounding the establishment guarantee undermine the nonpreferentialist argument. Levy nevertheless tempers his historical interpretation with the observation that "[w]e are not bound by the wisdom of the [F]ramers; we are bound only to consider whether the purposes they had in mind still merit political respect and constitutional obedience. History can be only a guide, not a controlling factor." He urges those who advocate the strict separation of government and religion to acknowledge that the Constitution does not foreclose all forms of government aid to, or accommodations of, religion, contending that "[t]rying to ensure that the wall of separation is really impregnable might be futile and dangerously counterproductive." Leonard W. Levy, The Establishment Clause: Religion and the First Amendment (2d ed., rev. 1994).

Douglas Laycock also endeavors to disprove the claim that the Framers intended to permit nonpreferential aid to religion. Examining the debates in both states and the First Congress, Laycock concludes that substantial evidence exists to support the conclusion that the Framers and others of the revolutionary generation believed nonpreferential aid in turn would lead to an establishment of religion. In reaching this conclusion, Laycock traces the anti-establishment guarantee back to its drafting and reports that, despite the sparse historical record, the First Congress *rejected* early drafts of a clause that endorsed nonpreferential aid. Douglas Laycock, *"Nonpreferential" Aid to Religion: A False Claim about Original Intent*, 27 Wm. & Mary L. Rev. 875 (1986).

By contrast to Levy and Laycock, Robert Cord seeks to buttress the historical argument in favor of nonpreferentialism. Cord agrees that the Framers, much like early presidents and congresses, understood the anti-establishment guarantee to forbid the national government to institute a national religion or to favor one religion to another. According to Cord, however, the Framers did not view nonpreferential aid to religion as problematic. Instead, Cord argues, the Framers used "nonpreferential sectarian means to reach secular government ends," such as presidential Thanksgiving Day proclamations or Jefferson's treaty with the Kaskaskia tribe "to provide money to build a church and for other religious needs." According to Cord, the Framers choice of the anti-establishment guarantee did not represent their endorsement of a secularized society; rather, the guarantee reflected a limit on the authority of the national government. Cord concludes from this historical account that not all government associations with religion clash with the anti-establishment principle and that the relationship between government and religion remains to a considerable extent a public policy decision rather than a matter of judicial review. Robert L. Cord, Separation of Church and State: Historical Fact and Current Fiction (1982).

With regard to government neutrality toward religion, Douglas Laycock argues that government must be absolutely neutral toward religion in its own speech and in its treatment of private speech. Laycock examines, among other recent developments, the Equal Access Act, which allows student religious groups that seek to use school property for their meetings to do so. According to Laycock, the Act comports with the Constitution's demands that religious speech receive access equal to that granted private speech. Laycock likewise concludes that moment-of-silence laws—though, in his view, neither required nor generally "a good idea"—do not violate the First Amendment if drafted and implemented with care. He suggests, for example, that a state provide teachers with a prepared speech, such as the following, to be read prior to the first moment of silence and at regular intervals thereafter:

> The legislature has asked you to have this moment of silence. One reason for the moment of silence is that some students want a chance to pray. But no one is required to pray during the moment of silence. Whether you pray, and how you pray, and when you pray are entirely up to you and your parents.
>
> We have religious freedom in our country. That means that every family gets to choose its own religion or no religion at all. Some people want to pray at school. Others want to pray only at home or in their church or synagogue. Others don't want to pray at all. All of these choices are fine with the school. Students who make a different choice than the one you make can still be good students and good Americans.

Explaining the moment of silence in such a fashion, Laycock asserts, will make it clear that government is not endorsing prayer. Douglas Laycock, *Equal Access and Moments of Silence: The Equal Status of Religious Speech by Private Speakers*, 81 Nw. U. L. Rev. 1 (1986).

Michael McConnell agrees with Douglas Laycock that neutrality usually will prove an effective means of guaranteeing religious liberty. Nevertheless, McConnell contends that circumstances arise in which departures from religious neutrality are either permissible or constitutionally required. McConnell opines that, in particular, three contexts justify such departures in the name of religious liberty: (1) when facially neutral governmental action conflicts with religious practices; (2) when regulating religious institutions in the same manner as secular institutions impedes the ability of a religious institution to structure its internal affairs in accord with its doctrine; and (3) when government influence is so pervasive that, in the absence of affirmative accommodation, religious exercise ultimately becomes infeasible. Michael W. McConnell, *Neutrality under the Religion Clauses*, 81 Nw. U. L. Rev. 146 (1986).

The question that arises, of course, has to do with where to draw the line between a permissible accommodation and a prohibited establishment. According to McConnell, the fact that religious liberty represented the driving force behind the religion clauses too often gets overlooked. In *Accommodation of Religion*, 1985 Sup. Ct. Rev. 1, McConnell argues that an emphasis on religious liberty will produce principles by which to distinguish legitimate accommodations from unconstitutional establishments. Pluralism and liberty should serve as guideposts for church-state relations, McConnell contends, not secularism and separation.

In a follow-up article, *Accommodation of Religion: An Update and a Response to the Critics*, 60 Geo. Wash. L. Rev. 685 (1992), McConnell reiterates that accommodations are sometimes required and always permitted. This conclusion, he contends, emerges harmoniously from the underlying principles of the religion clauses. He thus opposes the Court's prevailing free exercise interpretation enunciated in *Smith II*—an interpretation grounded in the notion that the First Amendment generally does *not* require such accommodations—while supporting the anti-establishment jurisprudence that permits such accommodations. McConnell vigorously defends his position against the principal critics of accommodation.

Ira Lupu is one such critic of accommodation. Lupu marshals a host of arguments against government accommodation of religion. He contends that accommodation lacks a sound principle of equality insofar as religious liberty is concerned. He cites political and social concerns related to government accommodation of religion. In the aftermath of *Smith II*, Lupu contends that special treatment of religion is no longer a constitutional right but a matter of political discretion. To avoid discrimination among religions, Lupu argues that the judiciary—not the legislature—should be left to determine whether a religion is deserving of special treatment. Ira C. Lupu, *Reconstructing the Establishment*

Clause: The Case against Discretionary Accommodation of Religion, 140 U. Pa. L. Rev. 555 (1991).

Steven Smith asserts that the "no endorsement" test crafted and propounded by Justice O'Connor will not resolve the inconsistencies and defects of anti-establishment analysis. According to Smith, the fact that the test is laden with unmanageable and ambiguous concepts will exacerbate rather than ameliorate the already troublesome doctrine. Smith urges scholars and justices to stop focusing on the "no endorsement" test's symbolic effects and the perception of neutrality that it creates. He concludes that "the idea of neutrality is important" but that "analytical, interpretive, [and] historical work still needs to be done." Steven D. Smith, *Symbols, Perceptions, and Doctrinal Illusions: Establishment Neutrality and the "No Endorsement" Test*, 86 Mich. L. Rev. 266 (1987).

William Marshall, acknowledging the subjectivity attending the determination of whether an unconstitutional establishment has occurred, suggests ways to reduce that subjectivity. First, Marshall contends that anti-establishment inquiries should be differentiated depending on whether they arise in the context of public schools, parochial schools, or government practices and regulations. Second, Marshall invites the Court to adopt an overarching perspective to guide it with regard to anti-establishment challenges arising in each of the three contexts. Finally, Marshall recommends a reinvigorated commitment to stare decisis on the part of the Court. William P. Marshall, *"We Know It When We See It": The Supreme Court and Establishment*, 59 S. Cal. L. Rev. 495 (1986).

One subset of anti-establishment challenges pertains to financial support of religious educational institutions. Paul Freund has argued that such support should be deemed constitutionally permissible in only three contexts: (1) general welfare services for children; (2) prizes and awards in general academic competitions; and (3) shared time instruction programs in public schools by which children attending religious schools participate and are treated as part-time public school children. According to Freund, limiting government aid to religious educational institutions will best serve the interests of church and state. Paul A. Freund, Comment, *Public Aid to Parochial Schools*, 82 Harv. L. Rev. 1680 (1969).

THE FREE EXERCISE GUARANTEE

A useful starting point in free exercise analysis is Michael McConnell's article, The *Origins and Historical Understanding of Free Exercise of Religion*, 103 Harv. L. Rev. 1409 (1990). McConnell discusses the history of the free exercise guarantee and asserts that an interpretation of the clause that mandates religious exemptions from generally applicable laws not only was contemplated by the Framers but was consistent with the views of religious liberty and limited government that pervaded at that time. He concludes that the purposes of the free exercise guarantee were to protect religious minorities from the dictates of mainstream society and to encourage religious pluralism. Accordingly, McConnell contends that the Court should protect those religious groups unable to win accommodation in the political process.

Traditional free exercise analysis has required that religious exemptions be granted only after a finding that a particular religious belief or practice has been burdened. Ira Lupu maintains that judicial determinations of what constitutes a burden on the free exercise of religion can result in disparate treatment for, and thus harm to, nonmainstream religions. To remedy the problem, Lupu suggests that courts apply something of a common-law test: "a government policy is burdensome if an analogous act committed by a private individual would violate generally accepted common law norms." In short, Lupu contends that courts may be better equipped to reconcile religion with other social concerns if courts relied more on general principles of law. Ira C. Lupu, *Where Rights Begin: The Problem of Burdens on the Free Exercise of Religion*, 102 Harv. L. Rev. 933 (1989).

According to Douglas Laycock, most requests for religious exemptions should be granted. Laycock asserts that judicial review should protect religion from "hostile or indifferent consequences of the political process." After discussing a pair of free exercise cases—Jimmy Swaggart Ministries v. Board of Equalization and *Smith II*—Laycock criticizes the Court for not doing its part in protecting religion from majoritarian beliefs. Douglas Laycock, *The Remnants of Free Exercise*, 1990 Sup. Ct. Rev. 1.

On the issue of protection for religious *beliefs*, Christopher Eisgruber and Lawrence Sager maintain that the notion that religious *practices* are entitled to constitutional protection because of their unique *value* should be rejected. Instead, they argue, it is the "distinct vulnerability to discrimination" of such practices that makes them eligible for protection. By replacing value with vulnerability and the privilege view of religious exemptions with a protection view, Eisgruber and Sager assert that religious accommodation jurisprudence can be restored, and its "scattered precedent" can be better understood. Christopher L. Eisgruber & Lawrence G. Sager, *The Vulnerability of Conscience: The Constitutional Basis for Protecting Religious Conduct*, 61 U. Chi. L. Rev. 1245 (1994).

Michael McConnell has contributed an important review of the controversial landmark case of Employment Division v. Smith. In *Smith II*, the Court rejected the claims of two members of the Native American Church whose use of the drug peyote resulted in their being dismissed from their jobs and subsequently denied state unemployment benefits. McConnell asserts that the Court's cursory examination of the free exercise constitutional text, its failure to review the clause's history, and its "troubling" use of free exercise precedent combined to produce a decision inconsistent with the logic of the First Amendment. McConnell proceeds to dissect the *Smith* Court's argument that the disadvantages suffered by minority religions as a result of its decision are unavoidable. According to Mc-

Connell, the free exercise guarantee was inserted into the Constitution to protect both majority and minority religions from government interference. After *Smith II*, however, accommodation of those who participate in nonmainstream religions falls principally to the whims of the political process. Michael W. McConnell, *Free Exercise Revisionism and the* Smith *Decision*, 57 U. Chi. L. Rev. 1109 (1990).

William Marshall, while not exactly defending the *Smith II* Court's decision, nevertheless supports the Court's rejection of the notion of constitutionally compelled exemptions to free exercise. Marshall contends that free exercise analysis "undermines the constitutional values it purports to protect, is inherently arbitrary, forces courts to engage in a balancing process that systematically underestimates the state interest, and threatens other constitutional values." In the course of justifying his position, Marshall criticizes the McConnell position that construes the free exercise guarantee to mandate such exemptions. William P. Marshall, *In Defense of* Smith *and Free Exercise Revisionism*, 58 U. Chi. L. Rev. 308 (1991).

In the aftermath of *Smith*, Congress enacted the Religious Freedom Restoration Act (RFRA) in order to provide a cause of action for religious practices burdened by government. Christopher Eisgruber and Lawrence Sager predicted the act's demise, offering three central reasons to support their finding that it was unconstitutional: "it violates principles of religious freedom, exceeds the bounds of legitimate federal authority, and conscripts the judiciary in a constitutional charade." Eisgruber and Sager maintain that they do not oppose legislative efforts to accommodate religion. They argue, instead, that RFRA was not the appropriate means for Congress to achieve its goals. Christopher L. Eisgruber & Lawrence G. Sager, *Why the Religious Freedom Restoration Act is Unconstitutional*, 69 N.Y.U.L. Rev. 437 (1994).

Under RFRA, free exercise exemptions were permitted so long as there was no compelling government interest to the contrary. Douglas Laycock and Oliver Thomas offer an interpretation of the act by exploring the statutory text, legislative history, and the problems the law was designed to remedy. They argue, by contrast to Eisgruber and Sager, that the act's overwhelming approval in each house of Congress reflects the importance of accommodating religious exercise. Laycock and Thomas assert that instead of focusing on *the individual* seeking to practice his or her faith, RFRA should prompt courts to focus on *the government's* attempt to prevent individuals from doing so. Douglas Laycock & Oliver S. Thomas, *Interpreting the Religious Freedom Restoration Act*, 73 Tex. L. Rev. 210 (1994).

VOUCHERS AND SCHOOL CHOICE

School choice—a shorthand phrase used to capture circumstances in which government expands the educational options available to families with children attending kindergarten through twelfth grade—exploded onto the American political landscape in the last few decades of the twentieth century. With the inclusion of religious schools in the range of options available to parents, the issue not surprisingly found its way onto the state and national constitutional landscape. In *Zelman*, a divided Supreme Court held that voucher programs offering families the choice to send their children to religiously affiliated schools at government expense did not clash with anti-establishment principles. The commentary both before and after *Zelman* reveals a scholarly community likewise divided over the constitutional status of such voucher programs.

Andrew Adams argues that voucher programs that include religiously affiliated schools comport with constitutional norms because such programs rest on notions of government neutrality toward religion. Adams further contends that the fact that private decision makers—that is to say, families—ultimately determine the flow of government monies enhances the claim that such programs do not clash with anti-establishment principles. Viewing the Cleveland program examined in *Zelman* against these premises, Adams concludes—as five members of the Court would later find—that the program withstands constitutional scrutiny. Andrew A. Adams, *Cleveland School Choice, and "Laws Respecting an Establishment of Religion,"* 2 Tex. Rev. L. Pol. 165 (1997).

Milwaukee's choice program, amended to allow religious schools to participate, preceded that of Cleveland. A divided Wisconsin Supreme Court rejected a challenge to the program, concluding that the program satisfied each of *Lemon*'s three prongs. A student article examining the Milwaukee program expresses disagreement with the conclusion of the Wisconsin justices, contending that the Milwaukee program should have been invalidated because the program "as a whole" benefited religious schools. *Establishment Clause—School Vouchers—Wisconsin Supreme Court Upholds Milwaukee Parental Choice Programs*, 112 Harv. L. Rev. 737 (1999).

Michael Taylor disagrees, contending that the Wisconsin choice program meshes with the central lessons of the high court's financial assistance cases from *Everson* through *Agostini*. Accordingly, Taylor finds the Wisconsin court's rejection of the anti-establishment challenge "sound and proper." Michael Taylor, *Neutral or Non-Neutral, Is That the Question? School Vouchers and the Establishment Clause*, 16 T.M. Cooley L. Rev. 289 (1999).

A thoughtful student note likewise examines the constitutional status of including religious schools in interdistrict choice and voucher programs. The author concludes that, to withstand constitutional scrutiny, interdistrict programs *must* include religious schools, seeking to justify this conclusion through the argument that such programs tend to be need-based and the finite nature of educational resources would produce unconstitutional inequities absent the inclusion of religious schools. By contrast, she contends that voucher programs generally need not include religiously affiliated schools because the children offered participation in such a program retain the opportunity to attend other public schools. Ellen M. Wasilausky, *See Jane Read the Bible: Does the Establishment Clause*

Allow School Choice Programs to Include Sectarian Schools after Agostini v. Felton, 56 Wash & Lee L. Rev. 721 (1999).

Another essay probes the jurisprudence of Justice O'Connor against the backdrop of school choice, seeking to discern how that jurisprudence plays out in connection with the constitutional status of voucher programs. The author expresses hope that Justice O'Connor's approach to the anti-establishment guarantee would prompt the justice to be skeptical about the constitutionality of voucher programs that include religious schools. In particular, the author extracts from the O'Connor concurrence in *Mitchell* the justice's insistence that, to survive constitutional scrutiny, government monies must flow to religious institutions only as a result of a private choice that is truly private, independent, and meaningful—leading the author to suggest that a voucher program that "offers a limited universe of options and creates incentives for religious use" could meet with disapproval from Justice O'Connor. Steven K. Green, *The Constitutionality of Vouchers after* Mitchell v. Helms, 57 N.Y.U. Ann. Surv. Am. L. 57 (2000).

Nicole Stelle Garnett and Richard Garnett contend that voucher programs both satisfy constitutional principles and represent socially just exercises of government power. Their article takes a searching look at the Milwaukee and Cleveland programs, arguing that such programs, empowering private citizens to make choices about educational options, simply do not clash with anti-establishment principles. In addition, the authors endorse the public policy undergirding such programs, taking the position that "[s]chool choice is merely the educational policy of the 'Golden Rule.'" Nicole Stelle Garnett & Richard W. Garnett, *School Choice, the First Amendment, and Social Justice*, 4 Tex. Rev. L. & Pol. 301 (2000).

Ira Lupu and Robert Tuttle also analyze the Court's recent decision in *Zelman*. They argue, on the one hand, that the decision should help short-circuit some litigation concerning educational choice by resolving the federal constitutional issue in a way unlikely to be revisited anytime soon. They nevertheless take the view that, on the merits, the approach of the *Zelman* majority lacks reason and justification. Moreover, they criticize the majority for failing to adequately confront Justice O'Connor's concerns about choice and neutrality. But the authors likewise find fault with the dissenting justices, accusing them of mimicking the arguments of voucher opponents. Ira C. Lupu & Robert W. Tuttle, *Zelman's Future: Vouchers, Sectarian Providers, and the Next Round of Constitutional Battles*, 78 Notre Dame L. Rev. 917 (2003).

RECONCILING THE RELIGION CLAUSES

The anti-establishment and free exercise guarantees each seek to promote distinctive aspects of religious freedom. Not surprisingly, therefore, courts sometimes treat the guarantees as being rooted in dramatically different purposes—the anti-establishment guarantee, on the one hand, reflecting concern over issues related to government support of religion, and free exercise, on the other, being directed principally at ensuring that government not inhibit the performance of religious practices. Experts continue to offer competing approaches for resolving this supposed tension.

Jesse Choper, for example, has formulated a principle that, in his view, can and should be deployed to reconcile the conflict between the clauses. Choper expresses the principle as follows: "[T]he Establishment Clause should forbid only government action whose purpose is solely religious and that is likely to impair religious freedom by coercing, compromising, or influencing religious beliefs." According to Choper, this principle—though not explicitly referring to those situations in which the free exercise guarantee mandates religious exemptions—can assist in reconciling the tension between the guarantees by identifying in free exercise challenges the governmental interest that should be weighed against the religious burden imposed by the challenged law. For Choper, in short, the governmental interest at stake in a free exercise challenge depends on whether the anti-establishment guarantee permits or forbids the particular religious exemption claimed by the challenger. In other words, according to Choper, in circumstances in which anti-establishment principles *permit* a religious exemption—as will usually be the case—a court should balance the free exercise claim against government's interest in "maintaining its program without religious exemptions." By contrast, Choper contends that when anti-establishment principles *prohibit* such an exemption, a court should balance the free exercise claim against the government interest in "preserving its entire program, because only by abandoning it [the program] altogether could the free exercise claim be satisfied." Jesse H. Choper, *The Religion Clauses of the First Amendment: Reconciling the Conflict*, 41 U. Pitt. L. Rev. 673 (1980).

Michael McConnell contends that the religion guarantees should not be understood to require a secular public sphere. Instead, according to McConnell, the guarantees can best be construed as protecting religious beliefs and practices from unnecessary government interference. The proper way to conceive of the collective central purpose of the anti-establishment and free exercise protections in McConnell's view is to view the purpose as embracing religious pluralism rather than majoritarianism or secularism. Because of this, McConnell contends, the Constitution requires that exceptions be made to generally applicable laws that threaten religious beliefs or practices. In addition, McConnell observes that government must steadfastly refrain from demonstrating *both* preference in favor of mainstream religions *and* preference toward a secularized society. Michael W. McConnell, *Religious Freedom at a Crossroads*, 59 U. Chi. L. Rev. 115 (1992).

By contrast, Philip Kurland maintains that fidelity to the religion guarantees means that "government cannot utilize religion as a standard for action or inaction because these clauses, read together as they should be, prohibit classification in terms of religion either to confer a benefit or to impose a burden." Kurland argues that the neutral principle he proposes will direct legislatures and courts in their efforts to adhere to the constitutional dictates of the religion clauses. Philip B. Kurland, *Of Church and State and the Supreme Court*, 29 U. Chi. L. Rev. 1 (1961).

Offering a slightly different take on the issue of neutrality, Douglas Laycock provides an approach he calls "substantive neutrality." His premise is that "the religion clauses require government to minimize the extent to which it either encourages or discourages religious belief or disbelief, practice or nonpractice, observance or nonobservance." According to Laycock, his theory of "substantive neutrality is more consistent with religious liberty than is formal neutrality." Douglas Laycock, *Formal, Substantive, and Disaggregated Neutrality toward Religion*, 39 DePaul L. Rev. 993 (1990).

In his article *The Political Balance of the Religion Clauses*, 102 Yale L.J. 1611 (1993), Abner Greene asserts that the Court in *Smith II* relied on a theory of democratic politics that led it to conclude that so long as everyone is allowed to participate in the political process, one cannot claim a constitutional right to avoid adhering to an otherwise valid law simply because one's values were defeated. This conclusion, Greene asserts, is based on the flawed assumption that religious beliefs can compete with secular beliefs in the political process. Greene contends that, while the anti-establishment guarantee should be construed to forbid the enactment of legislation for the express purpose of advancing religious values, the free exercise guarantee should be construed to require recognition of religious faith as a ground for exemption from a legal obligation. Thus, he asserts, "[t]he Free Exercise Clause works as a counterweight to the Establishment Clause; it gives back what the Establishment Clause takes away."

CRITICISMS & SUGGESTIONS

There is no shortage of criticism when it comes to religion clause jurisprudence, and the following works represent only a small sample. Steven Smith argues that modern religion clause discourse is flawed in its most basic assumptions. He asserts that the efforts of judges and legal scholars to contrive a principle or theory of religious freedom are misguided because such a principle or theory is an unrealistic goal given the "complex and fluctuating relations among the often incommensurable concerns of governments, churches, and the individual conscience." It is obsession with judicial review, according to Smith, that has driven scholars to focus on questions that "were foreordained to produce oversimplification and confusion rather than understanding and fruitful discussion." Steven D. Smith, Foreordained Failure: The Quest for a Constitutional Principle of Religious Freedom (1995).

Phillip Johnson asserts that First Amendment religion doctrine is indeterminate in three key ways: (1) it can often be characterized in two or more different ways, for example, as an anti-establishment issue and a free exercise issue; (2) the Court utilizes subjective tests to determine whether the practice in dispute is forbidden, permitted, or required; and (3) there is no accepted definition of religion. He goes on to examine the ideological considerations that lead judges to one solution instead of another, and he concludes that "[w]hat we need to fear is not ideology but ideological blindness, including the blindness that takes the form of imagining that one's own views are derived logically from premises acknowledged by all reasonable persons." Phillip E. Johnson, *Concepts and Compromise in First Amendment Religious Doctrine*, 72 Cal. L. Rev. 817 (1984).

Mark Tushnet boldly asserts that "[c]ontemporary constitutional law just does not know how to handle problems of religion." He contends that the disarray results from society's failure to offer the support needed to sustain a concept of politics that encompasses religion. Mark V. Tushnet, *The Constitution of Religion*, 18 Conn. L. Rev. 701 (1986).

In Securing Religious Liberty: Principles for Judicial Interpretation of the Religion Clauses (1995), Jesse Choper proposes a set of principles designed to aid judges in their efforts to determine the constitutionality of government action under the religion clauses. The four principles Choper suggests include: (1) the "deliberate disadvantage" principle, whereby government actions that intentionally cause hardships for people on the basis of their religious beliefs will almost always be invalid; (2) the "burdensome effect" principle, which, in a narrow set of circumstances, requires exemptions from generally applicable laws that adversely affect religion; (3) the "intentional advantage" principle, which allows government action that supports religion so long as it is done on a nondiscriminatory basis and does not jeopardize religious liberty; and (4) the "independent impact" principle, which prohibits government programs that support religion and lack a secular effect. He asserts that the principles will minimize the "personal predilections" that judges inadvertently bring to the decision making process. Such biases are troublesome, according to Choper, because they upset the tenets of our democratic political society and threaten the values that the First Amendment was designed to protect.

Table of Cases

A

Agostini v. Felton, 521 U.S. 203 (1997)
Aguilar v. Felton, 473 U.S. 402 (1985)
Allegheny County v. American Civil Liberties Union, Greater Pittsburgh Chapter 492 U.S. 573 (1989)
American Jewish Congress v. City of Chicago, 827 F.2d 120 (1987)
Ayon v. Gourley, 47 F. Supp. 2d 1246 (D. Col. 1998)

B

Board of Education of Central School District No. 1 v. Allen, 392 U.S. 236 (1968)
Board of Education of Kiryas Joel Village School District v. Grumet, 512 U.S. 687 (1994)
Board of Education v. Mergens, 496 U.S. 226 (1990)
Bob Jones University v. United States, 461 U.S. 574 (1983)
Bowen v. Kendrick, 487 U.S. 589 (1988)
Bowen v. Roy, 476 U.S. 693 (1986)
Braunfeld v. Brown, 366 U.S. 599 (1961)

C

Cantwell v. Connecticut, 310 U.S. 296 (1940)
Capitol Square Review & Advisory Board v. Pinette, 515 U.S. 753 (1995)
Catholic Charities of Sacramento, Inc. v. Superior Court of Sacramento County, 85 P.3d 67 (Cal. 2004)
Church of the Likumi Babalu Aye. v. City of Hialeah, 508 U.S. 520 (1993)
City of Boerne v. Flores, 521 U.S. 507 (1997)
Committee for Public Education and Religious Liberty v. Nyquist, 426 U.S. 736 (1973)
Corporation of the Presiding Bishop of the Church of Jesus Christ of Latter-day Saints v. Amos, 483 U.S. 327 (1987)

E

East Bay Asian Local Development Corporation v. California, 13 P.3d 1122 (Cal. 2000)
Edwards v. Aguillard, 482 U.S. 578 (1987)

Elk Grove Unified School District v. Newdow, 124 S. Ct. 2301 (2004)
Employment Division v. Smith, 485 U.S. 660 (1988) ("*Smith I*")
Employment Division v. Smith, 494 U.S. 872 (1990) ("*Smith II*")
Engel v. Vitale, 370 U.S. 421 (1962)
Epperson v. Arkansas, 393 U.S. 97 (1968)
Equal Employment Opportunity Commission v. Catholic University of America, 83 F.3d 455 (D.C. Cir. 1996)
Estate of Thornton v. Caldor, Inc., 472 U.S. 703 (1985)
Everson v. Board of Education of the Township of Ewing, 330 U.S. 1 (1947)

F

Fraternal Order of Police of Newark Lodge No. 12 v. City of Newark, 170 F.3d 359 (3rd Cir. 1999)
Frazee v. Illinois Department of Employment Securities, 489 U.S. 829 (1989)

G

Gellington v. Christian Methodist Episcopal Church, Inc., 203 F.3d 1299 (11th Cir. 2000)
Goldman v. Weinberger, 475 U.S. 503 (1986)
Good News Club v. Milford Central School, 533 U.S. 98 (2001)

H

Harris v. McRae, 448 U.S. 297 (1980)
Hobbie v. Unemployment Appeals Commission of Florida, 480 U.S. 136 (1987)
Horen v. Commonwealth, 479 S.E.2d 553 (Va. Ct. App. 1997)

J

Jimmy Swaggart Ministries v. Board of Equalization of California, 493 U.S. 378 (1990)

K

Kedroff v. St. Nicholas Cathedral of Russian Orthodox Church in North America, 344 U.S. 94 (1952)
Keeler v. Mayor & City Council of Cumberland, 940 F. Supp. 879 (D. Md. 1996)

L

Lamb's Chapel v. Center Moriches Union Free School District, 508 U.S. 384 (1993)
Larkin v. Grendel's Den, Inc., 459 U.S. 116 (1982)
Larson v. Valente, 456 U.S. 228 (1982)
Lee v. Weisman, 505 U.S. 577 (1992)
Lemon v. Kurtzman, 403 U.S. 602 (1971)
Locke v. Davey, 124 S. Ct. 1307 (2004)
Lynch v. Donnelly, 465 U.S. 668 (1984)
Lyng v. Northwest Indian Cemetery Protective Association, 485 U.S. 439 (1988)

M

Marsh v. Chambers, 463 U.S. 783 (1983)
McCollum v. Board of Education, 333 U.S. 203 (1948)

McDaniel v. Paty, 435 U.S. 618 (1978)
McGowan v. Maryland, 366 U.S. 420 (1961)
Meek v. Pittenger, 421 U.S. 349 (1975)
Mitchell v. Helms, 530 U.S. 793 (2000)
Mueller v. Allen, 463 U.S. 388 (1983)

N

Newdow v. United States Congress, 292 F.3d 597 (9th Cir. 2002)

O

O'Lone v. Estate of Shabazz, 482 U.S. 342 (1987)

R

Reverend Pamela Combs v. Central Texas Annual Conference of the United Methodist Church, 173 F.3d 343 (5th Cir. 1999)
Reynolds v. United States, 98 U.S. 145 (1878)
Roemer v. Board of Public Works of Maryland, 426 U.S. 736 (1976)
Rosado v. Bridgeport Roman Catholic Diocesan Corporation, 45 Conn. Supp. 397 (Conn. Super. 1998)
Rosenberger v. Rector and Visitors of the University of Virginia, 515 U.S. 819 (1995)

S

Santa Fe Independent School District v. Doe, 530 U.S. 290 (2000)
School District of Abington Township v. Schempp, 374 U.S. 203 (1963)
School District of the City of Grand Rapids v. Ball, 473 U.S. 373 (1985)
Sherbert v. Verner, 374 U.S. 398 (1963)
Smith v. Employment Division, 763 P.2d 146 (Or. 1988)
Society of Jesus of New England v. Talbot, 441 Mass. 662 (Mass. 2004)
State v. Yoder, 82 N.W. 2d 539 (Wis. 1971)
Stone v. Graham, 449 U.S. 39 (1980)
Swanson v. Guthrie Independent School District, 135 F.3d 694 (10th Cir. 1998)

T

Tenafly Eruv Association v. Borough of Tenafly, 309 F.3d 144 (3d Cir. 2002)
Texas Monthly, Inc. v. Bullock, 489 U.S. 1 (1989)
Thomas v. Review Board of Indiana Employment Securities Division, 450 U.S. 707 (1981)
Tilton v. Richardson, 403 U.S. 672 (1971)
Torcaso v. Watkins, 367 U.S. 488 (1961)

U

United States v. Lee, 455 U.S. 252 (1982)

V

Ventura County Christian High School v. City of San Buenaventura, 233 F. Supp. 1241 2d (C.D. Cal. 2002)

W

Wallace v. Jaffree, 472 U.S. 38 (1985)
Walz v. Tax Commission of the City of New York, 397 U.S. 664 (1970)
Widmar v. Vincent, 454 U.S. 263 (1981)
Wisconsin v. Yoder, 406 U.S. 205 (1972)
Witters v. Washington Department of Services for the Blind, 474 U.S. 481 (1986)

Y

Yang v. Sturner, 750 F. Supp. 558 (D.R.I. 1990)

Z

Zelman v. Simmons-Harris, 536 U.S. 639 (2002)
Zobrest v. Catalina Foothills School District, 509 U.S. 1 (1993)
Zorach v. Clauson, 343 U.S. 306 (1952)

Index

About the Author

PETER K. ROFES is Professor of Law, Associate Dean for Academic Affairs, and Director of Part-time Legal Education at Marquette University Law School. Prior to joining the faculty at Marquette in 1987, Professor Rofes served as law clerk to the Honorable Max Rosenn of the United States Court of Appeals for the Third Circuit and practiced law in Washington, D.C.